THE NEW SOLDIER IN THE AGE OF ASYMMETRIC CONFLICT

THE NEW SOLDIER IN THE AGE OF ASYMMETRIC CONFLICT

Rumu Sarkar (Ph.D.)(Cantab)

Foreword by
Lt Gen P K Singh, PVSM, AVSM (Retd)
Director, The United Service Institution of India

Vij Books India Pvt Ltd
New Delhi (India)

Published by

Vij Books India Pvt Ltd
2/19, Ansari Road, Darya Ganj
New Delhi - 110002
Phones: 91-11-47340674, 91-11- 43596460
Fax: 91-11-47340674
e-mail : vijbooks@rediffmail.com
web : www.vijbooks.com

© **2013, Rumu Sarkar**

First Published in India : 2013
Paperback edition 2015

DEDICATION

TO COLONEL ZACHARY ZEROME KINNEY

WHO ACCOMPANIED AND GUIDED ME ON THE OFTEN PERILOUS
JOURNEY THROUGH LAW SCHOOL, LAW PRACTICE AND LIFE ITSELF,

AND WHO PROVIDED UNWAVERING SUPPORT FOR THIS WORK IN ALL
OF ITS ITERATIONS

Contents

FOREWORD

Dr. Rumu Sarkar is a pioneer and a visionary. She has found, I believe, the key to getting us close to the day when Islamic-based terrorism, the most pressing problem of our age, will cease to exist. Dr. Sarkar's book, *"The New Soldier in the Age of Asymmetric Conflict,"* accomplishes three monumental things that previous books written on the subject of global terrorism have failed to capture.

Dr. Sarkar first insight is to disaggregate Islamic-based terrorists into two groups: the secessionists and the fundamentalists. Islamic-based terrorists who fall in the secessionist group are motivated by the concept of the failure of the state. These believe that the modern state has failed to address the needs of all the members of society by failing to address fundamental human needs (e.g., providing for security, secure borders, physical infrastructure such as roads, airports, seaports, hospitals and schools, and social infrastructure such as education, health and social welfare programs). In their view, this failure means that the state should be replaced.

Islamic-based terrorists who fall into the fundamentalist group, on the other hand, are motivated by the failure of ideology. Fundamentalists or jihadists see communism, socialism, authoritarianism, democracy, and capitalism as bankrupt and inadequate. They have no interest in a modern functioning state or in the ideals of modernity such as a representative democracy, education, especially for girls and women, and protecting the rights of ethnic and religious minorities. They believe that Islamic law should be used in place of these failed ideologies. Fundamentalists, according to Dr. Sarkar, cite the fall of communism, the fall of the Berlin Wall, the ills of globalization and the havoc that followed in the wake of the end of the Cold War as proof of the failure of ideology.

The violence that Islamic-based terrorists employ is designed to advance the political agendas of the aforementioned two groups. Dr. Sarkar painstakingly lays out in her monumental book "The New Soldier," how these motivating ideas explain the origin of and the reason for Islamic-based terrorism. Dr. Sarkar believes that in order to successfully address the global terrorist problem, understanding that not all terrorists are created the same is the first step in the right direction.

The esteemed author of "*The New Soldier,*" has discovered and calls for the need to include compassion, empathy, intuition and wisdom along with the guns, rifles, bombs, and explosives traditional soldiers are currently equipped with. Dr. Sarkar advocates the creation of the New Soldier who is a traditional soldier endowed with undefeatable war fighting capabilities but also one who has the qualities of empathy and compassion in order to move the conflict onto a different plane. This fresh and original approach will allow the defeat of Islamic-based terrorism by defining the conflict in a different way.

Dr. Sarkar's contribution to the field is fresh, original and profound and is extremely well-researched. This book is a timely and fresh look at the timeworn subject of how best to combat and defeat terrorism. It is plainly obvious that the contemporary ideas and policies of combating and defeating global terrorism are not working. Islamic-based terrorists are killing innocent people and engaging in violence on a global scale on a seemingly daily basis. Dr. Sarkar makes it clear that terrorism is a tactic which is used when it is effective. She proposes the creation of the New Soldier as both a strategic and tactical approach to defeat this global menace.

Dr. Sarkar also reveals a startling truth at the core of her book; she exposes the overriding problem that Islamic-based terrorists have. The simple truth that Dr. Sarkar speaks of is that these young, disgruntled and frenzied terrorists have lost themselves and the promise of hope in their lives—in fact, they do not love themselves. This discovery is profound and is central in the final analysis to understanding what motivates Islamic-based terrorists to kill innocent people and sadly, themselves. It has been said that the only way that you can love or respect someone else is when you can love and respect yourself first. This is an insight that no one who has ever written about and it deserves our respect and attention.

- Lt Gen P K Singh, PVSM, AVSM (Retd)
Director, The United Service Institution of India

PREFACE

As a preface to this work, the genesis of how this project got underway may be of interest the reader. I had been teaching a class session entitled, "The Fearful Symmetry" for about two years in the Masters of Law (LL.M.) seminar on *International Development Law* that I taught for many years at the Georgetown University Law Center, Washington, DC. This session addressed the potential linkage between failed or fragile states and harboring illegal activities such as drug and human trafficking, racketeering, smuggling, piracy, and terrorism. Of course, the link to terrorism was not an automatic assumption. For example, Haiti and the Democratic Republic of the Congo are collapsed states in the view of most observers, yet they do not harbor known terrorists or promote terrorist activities or ideologies.

In my view, this linkage, however, problematic and attenuated, should be addressed by my students in order to forge a more complete understanding of the importance of the development process. More importantly, it is critical to understand what the failure of development can mean in this context.

It was at this time that a friend of mine sent me the weblink to the writing competition announced by the Fondation St Cyr, Paris, France. I undertook the challenge of writing the essay which addressed the specific question of "Stabilisation et Reconstruction: Une même volonté pour tous les acteurs ?" or, "Stabilization and Reconstruction: How to Achieve Coherence Between All the Players?" This, in fact, addressed the same question that I had posed to my class, and afforded me the opportunity to write a well-researched, coherent answer. Imagine my surprise when I actually won the competition!

Thus, at the outset, I wish to express my deep gratitude to the Fondation Saint-Cyr for selecting my essay entitled, "A Fearful Symmetry: A New Global Balance of Power?" as the winner of the First Prize for 2007. This is a special honor since this is the first time that the prize has been created and awarded by the Fondation.

The essay was subsequently translated into French and published in Paris under the title, *Une Symétrie de la Peur : Vers un Nouvel Equilibre Mondial Des Puissances?* (Paul Wormser, trans.)(CLD Éditions, November 2008). However, I realized that the confines of the essay were too restricted to answer certain underlying questions which this writing (in English) now attempts to do. This writing offers a more refined and deeper analysis of the underlying questions than the initial essay. Further, I felt a need to "operationalize" the concept of the New Soldier, an integral part of the analysis.

The New Soldier is, in essence, a soldier endowed with qualities of compassion, empathy, intuition and wisdom. The relevance of the New Soldier in the terrain of global terrorism will be explored in the text. I have tried to apply the concept of the New Soldier in a concrete context since it is designed for immediate use by military forces, including the U.S. military. The text also explores the potential use of the New Soldier by multilateral forces such as NATO and the African Union's Standby Force. I offer this analysis as part of the continuing dialogue on how to address and conquer global terrorism, in all its forms.

Finally, everyone speaks from varied points of view informed by vastly different life experiences, educational backgrounds, and motivations. However, for me, the opportunity to write this work allows me to bring together, in a more holistic way, the three currents of my professional life, namely, development, diplomacy and defense.

I began my career in international development law as an attorney with the Office of the General Counsel, U.S. Agency for International Development (USAID). I was given a U.S. diplomatic passport and instructed to negotiate many diverse, challenging and interesting legal agreements, understandings and accords with over 40 different countries. This professional experience greatly influenced my teaching of the subject of *international development law,* an LL.M. seminar that I taught for many years at the Georgetown University Law Center, Washington, DC. *International Development Law* is also the subject of my previously published work by Oxford University Press with the same title.

I subsequently joined the Overseas Private Investment Corporation (OPIC) as an Assistant General Counsel for Administrative Affairs. OPIC provides U.S. financing for private sector growth in new and emerging overseas markets. Afterwards, I became the General Counsel of two military commissions, the Overseas Basing Commission and later, the 2005 Base Closure and Realignment (BRAC) Commission. This is where I began to merge development, diplomacy and defense.

I believe that this "merger" will provide a new perspective for addressing global terrorism, one of the most important geopolitical challenges of our day. If, by reading this work, you add my voice and perspective to the many others writing on the same subject, I shall be most grateful to you.

A Brief Summation

In sum, the basic theme of the original essay emphasized that a failure of the state in terms of providing support for basic human needs (e.g., physical and social infrastructure) has led to a number of Islamic-based separatists' movements. The failure of the state may be seen in terms of a series of systemic failures in the development process.

In contrast, the concomitant failure in ideology created, in part, the complex alchemy giving rise to global jihadists' movements. In terms of addressing the problem of global jihadists, the original essay advocated the creation of a New Soldier who exhibits the highly subjective qualities of empathy, compassion, wisdom, and heightened intuitive and perceptive abilities that enables him or her to navigate unknown cultural, linguistic and emotional terrains. Creating and cultivating a corps of the New Soldier is an extraordinarily difficult undertaking, and one that most military establishments are unwilling to commit to. The following discussion will examine the reasons militating against such a course of action, and the reasons why such a course of action should, in fact, be pursued.

Professor Michael J. Mazarr succinctly states many of the objections to adopting a U.S.-based defense policy aimed towards developing counterinsurgency campaigns and approaches, and puts them into perspective.[1] He argues that the post-9/11 shift in defense policy that target military interventions against asymmetric threats, irregular warfare and toward stabilization operations and nation-building exercises is misguided and ultimately, quite dangerous. In fact, such attempts may actually destabilize U.S. national security rather than strengthen it.

In my opinion, he correctly points out that:

> Although it is always dangerous to generalize, much of the instability described by theories of asymmetric and nontraditional warfare stems first and foremost from causes other than military aggression. Many rebellions, insurgencies, and civil wars are the symptoms of political, economic, and psychosocial factors that undermine social stability and popular commitment to public order. Once order has collapsed, leaders and groups arise determined to seize power, and the contest becomes a clash of power-seekers. Yet, the essential problem in many so-called failed states and other contexts that give rise to civil wars, insurgencies and the radicalism at large in the Muslim world is a society or a large group of individuals beset with some combination of economic stagnation, cultural resentment, historical grievance, political or national repression, and other factors. These afflictions–injustices, in the eyes of the aggrieved–are not amenable to military solutions.[2]

In other words, these military engagements are not wars at all but small, internecine, often intrastate and inter-ethnic conflicts.

The list of downstream negative consequences from shifting to a counterinsurgency-focused military approach include, for example, underfunding the research, development, and procurement of systems for war; inappropriate or inadequate training of military forces for conventional warfare by shifting the focus to dealing with unconventional warfare; underfunding nonmilitary agencies and programs better equipped to deal with the underlying causes giving rise to irregular warfare; and risking the loss of the U.S. strategic and compelling advantage in conventional warfare arenas (especially in dealing with Russia and China's potentially expansionist ambitions).[3]

Moreover, by adopting a strategy of fighting "small wars," the United States, in particular, may be positioning itself to lose. Democracies have a limited capacity to absorb the costs of "small wars" because of an overall commitment to democratic principles, and to the general repugnance to brutal military behavior often found in such conflicts.

Jeffrey Record points out that dictatorships that use violent tactics with its own people, and who are not accountable for its actions, often have a higher tolerance for small wars than democracies.[4] Thus, the often protracted warfare of irregular wars are generally not winnable by major democracies such as the United States. Arguably, this is the case historically even with England and France who were both ultimately defeated by the asymmetric nature of many of the independence struggles that took place in their colonial eras, respectively. (The examples of India and Algeria, respectively, come to mind in this context.)

Moreover, the single-minded focus on winning the kinetic warfare stage tends to make military strategists, policy-makers and perhaps the public as well feel as though the war has been won, and the world is now a better place. But it overlooks the fact that:

> Military victory is a beginning, not an end. . . . Pursuit of military victory for its own sake discourages thinking about and planning for the second and by far the most difficult half of wars for regime change: establishing a viable replacement for the destroyed regime. War's object, after all, is a better peace.[5]

Indeed, since many small wars are intrastate rather than interstate conflicts, regime change is often a significant factor at the conclusion of the actual armed conflict. However, bringing about political transformation is often beyond the ability of a military force. "Military conflict has two dimensions: winning wars and winning the peace."[6] Military forces are designed to do the first and often do it well, but are not designed to do the latter and often fare poorly. Thus, this is precisely one of the key arguments *against* engaging in irregular warfare in the first instance.

Finally, and most importantly, the use of the military in counterinsurgency operations and related engagements substitutes military operations for diplomatic efforts and development assistance. Arguably, this is a strategic misinterpretation of Carl von Clausewitz's dictum that, "war is the continuation of politics by other means."[7] War is not meant to be a substitute for politics.

Professor Mazarr further writes,

> It is thus dangerous to view the military as the lead agency to deal with very diffuse, broad-based asymmetric challenges such as radical Islamism, nation building, stability operations, and even counterinsurgency. Talk of redirecting U.S. military emphasis to asymmetric threats amounts to a form of avoidance, allowing U.S. national security planners to ignore the truly dramatic change underway in the character of the conflict. As smart, adaptable, and courageous as U.S. military officers and men and women clearly are and will be, asymmetric challenges demand asymmetric responses–political, economic, cultural, informational, and psychological tools, tactics and techniques allowed to work organically over time, not retrained military forces whose true purpose is to fight and win wars, which are vastly different enterprises. The strategic trap is obvious: Furnished with a vast, expensive, skillful military tool, policymakers will use it again and again, as they have been doing, without confronting the tougher challenge of shifting resources into nonmilitary tools of statecraft.[8]

> By dramatically expanding the budgets for foreign aid, public diplomacy, exchange programs, and related nonmilitary forms of power, the United States can do much more to address sources of instability, stagnation, and grievance that underlie the state failure, radicalists, insurgents, and terrorist groups at large in a globalizing world. Military power is not the way to defeat such threats.[9]

Incidentally, former U.S. Defense Secretary, Robert Gates, agreed with this view. He has stated that, "We can expect that asymmetric warfare will be the mainstay of the contemporary battlefield for some time. These conflicts will be fundamentally political in nature, and require the application of all elements of national power. Success will be less a matter of imposing one's will and more a function of shaping behavior–of friends, adversaries, and most importantly, the people in between. . . . But these new threats also require our government to operate as a whole differently–to act with unity, agility, and creativity. And they will require considerably more resources devoted to America's nonmilitary instruments of power. . . . [T]here is no replacement for the real thing–civilian involvement and expertise."[10]

While there seems to be a fairly broad basis of consensus that more resources should be devoted to nonmilitary approaches, agencies and policies in the context of responding to asymmetric threats, there does not seem to be the requisite political will to implement this consensus.

Indeed, it seems that the Obama Administration "is finding that it must turn to military personnel to fill hundreds of posts in Afghanistan that had been intended for civilian experts."[11] Many of these new positions for agricultural specialists, engineers, lawyers, small business managers, veterinarians, public sanitation workers and traffic control experts, will now be filled by contractors and "reservists, whose civilian jobs give them the required expertise."[12] In fact, the U.S. State Department requested the Defense Department to fill more than 350 new diplomatic positions created in Iraq.[13]

The shortfall in civilian expertise highlights the fact that the U.S. Government civilian agencies have not been adequately funded to hire and train personnel eligible to take up reconstruction tasks in post-conflict zones. Moreover, "[u]nlike the armed services, nonmilitary agencies do not have clear rules to compel rank-and-file employees to accept hardship posts."[14] Therefore, there may not be the requisite political will or the individual will to take up these difficult overseas assignments.

The lack of an adequate, available civilian corps to undertake these necessary tasks of rebuilding Afghanistan, in particular, is highly problematic. As General David Patraeus points out, "[p]ower vacuums breed insurgencies."[15] In his view, insurgencies typically emerge from civil wars or from the collapse of a state. Generally speaking, insurgencies and global terrorism stem, in large part, from the failure of the state. Indeed, the failure of the development process derives from two related aspects of governance: a failure in governing as well as in being governed.

Secondly, there has been a failure in statecraft. In other words, there has been a systemic failure to successfully bring about sustainable development (albeit for a complex menu of reasons that lie outside the scope of this limited analysis). Nonmilitary actors on both a bilateral (state-to-state) and multilateral level have not fully succeeded in ensuring concrete development results despite their best efforts to do so.

This leaves the international community with the baleful choice of ignoring these power vacuums leading to potential insurgencies, more instability and endemic corruption, or taking some course of action in response to such conditions. While it is widely recognized and acknowledged that the preferred course of action with respect to containing forces leading to the potential collapse of the state should be undertaken by nonmilitary actors, it is clear that this has not taken place successfully in many instances. The reasons for this are complex, yet the unavoidable conclusion is that neither political transformation nor economic development can take place without security.[16]

Despite (or perhaps in response to) the failure to devote additional U.S. nonmilitary resources to the effort of quelling and preventing asymmetric threats, there has been a shift in the U.S. military paradigm. The U.S. Department of Defense (DOD) issued Directive 3000.05 re: Military Support for Stability, Security, Transition and Reconstruction (SSTR) Operations on November 28, 2005. This directive firmly establishes the defense policy of supporting stability operations in order to "help establish order that advances U.S. interests and values. The immediate goal often is to provide the local populace with security, restore essential services, and meet humanitarian needs. The long-term goal is to help develop indigenous capacity for securing essential services, a viable market economy, rule of law, democratic institutions and a robust civil society."[17]

It is understandable if the tasks referred to above do not sound familiar in the context of military operations. In fact, Section 4.3 of DOD Directive 3000.05 provides that:

> Many stability operations tasks are best performed by indigenous, foreign, or U.S. civilian professionals. Nonetheless, U.S. military forces shall be prepared to perform all tasks necessary to establish and maintain order when civilians cannot do so. Successfully performing such tasks can help secure a lasting peace and facilitate the timely withdrawal of U.S. and foreign forces.[18]

Of course, there has been significant nonmilitary intervention in conflict-ridden areas over the course of the past 60 years. In fact, one commentator notes that, "Africa has been the recipient of several Marshall

Plans worth of foreign aid since World War II's end, yet it remains arguably as impoverished today as it was in 1946."[19] This stems in large part from the reluctance of bilateral and multilateral aid institutions such as the World Bank to incorporate security needs into the development equation.[20]

While it is not certain whether broader nonmilitary interventions in the securitization, stabilization and reconstruction process is forthcoming, it is clear that military forces (whether unilateral or multilateral) are the first actors in conflict and post-conflict situations. Therefore, I would argue that the need for the New Soldier whether acting for unilateral or multilateral forces is a necessary agent of stability and paradoxically, of change. I would further argue that the New Soldier is needed in order to implement the current U.S. military SSTR paradigm. However, this discussion has a much broader vision in mind that encompasses not only U.S. military forces, but any and all military forces that are faced with asymmetric threats such as France, Great Britain, Spain, the Netherlands, India, Morocco, Indonesia, the Philippines, and many more.

The corps of the New Soldier should initially reside in multilateral armed forces and peacekeeping units such as the UN, NATO, the European Union, and the African Union. In addition, within the African context, the G-8's Global Peace Operations Initiative (GPOI), a multilateral program that was committed to creating a self-sustaining peacekeeping force of 75,000, largely African soldiers, by 2010, may also be a logical place to deploy the New Soldier. The concept of the New Soldier may also be relevant to the Africa Counterinsurgency Operations Training Assistance (ACOTA) program, and many other military and paramilitary programs.

In my view, multilateral and regional peacekeeping forces are better suited to deploying the New Soldier initially since such forces are predicated on multilateral, multilingual and multicultural approaches. Indeed, a RAND study points out that multilateral peacekeeping forces have added credibility, lower operating costs, and more access to seasoned professionals who have experience in handling crises created by collapsed states.[21] Perhaps it is time to examine taking a new approach by investing in and creating new forms of militarized interventions to be undertaken by the New Soldier.

If this approach is adopted, it will mean that the underlying commitments, missions, and rules of engagement for new military interventions with much broader goals in mind may need to be negotiated. The political implications are quite far reaching and need to be part of the paradigm shift not only for the U.S. military in support of its short-term goals, but also for other militaries that are also being strained by the demands of insurgencies and global terrorism.

The interventions that the New Soldier should initially be focused on are: (1) providing humanitarian relief; (2) securitization and stabilization; and (3) conflict resolution and prevention. Ultimately, the New Soldier should create the backdrop for initiating a diplomatic dialogue to end hostilities and begin the peace and reconciliation process. For example, based on its experience with truth and reconciliation commissions, the African Union (AU) may be tasked with setting up peace-building forces in the Philippines.

Thus, the underlying articles of association of multilateral military forces such as NATO, the UN and related organizations and units, may need to be changed or overhauled to incorporate the concept of the New Soldier. This may mean broader legal authorities, for example, to intervene internationally by regional military forces, where necessary.

There is also a significant concern that changing the focus away from the kinetic aspects of warfare to "softer" skills involved in conflict prevention and reconciliation will conflict with and demoralize existing military structures–after all, established militaries are built on a different set of skills and expectations. Accordingly, the recruitment strategies to attract the New Soldier may also need to be drastically altered. Thus, a new "track" of a military career may need to be formulated and promulgated to attract the officers and other personnel who wish to develop the new skill sets necessary for the New Soldier.

Since the New Soldier has a different and expanded mission from simply engaging in conventional warfare, the underlying core curriculum of military schools will also need to change significantly. Retired military officers may wish to lead the effort in order to share their "lessons learned" perspective with new recruits. Their efforts may help shift the military paradigm to include a different kind of soldiering by creating a different kind of soldier. As Defense Secretary Gates put it, "[n]ew institutions are needed for the 21st century, [and] new organizations with a 21st century mind-set."[22]

This may be the new challenge: to create the New Soldier, not in conflict with the soldier of today, but as a new and invaluable partner for the military of tomorrow.

of subjection to but the sovereign ruler, but it has not... The primitive tribes are treated forthwith...each... had new generations with... existence from such...

This may be the new challenge to create the New Ecology; not only a better mankind of today, but is needed in dealing in a match for the mastery of tomorrow.

ACKNOWLEDGEMENTS

I have been very fortunate in having so many patient and supportive friends and colleagues to rely on for developing my analysis, seeking new research avenues, and reading drafts of earlier versions of this work.

First and foremost, I would like to thank Monsieur Alain Wormser, former President, and Monsieur Jean-Claude Hugonnard, Director-General of the Fondation St Cyr for making the 2007 Grand Prix possible, and for all their contributions to my work. I would also be remiss if I did not thank my friend, Brian Hannon, for encouraging me to participate in the writing competition sponsored by the Foundation.

I also owe a very special thanks to my sincere and loyal friend from law school, Zachary Z. Kinney, a retired U.S. Air Force Major and currently the Judge Advocate General and Colonel for the Washington District of Columbia Defence Force. He insisted that I read his manual, "The Commander and the Law," and Carl von Clausewitz's *On War,* thereby creating the necessary foundation for embarking on this journey. I am especially grateful that he has accompanied me on this journey, every step of the way.

The foreword was generously provided by Lt Gen P K Singh, PVSM, AVSM (Retd), Director, The United Service Institution of India. I am also grateful to him for permitting me to put across my thoughts to the august audience at the institute.

My professional colleagues and well-wishers who added immeasurably to my understanding of the topic include Professor David Koplow of Georgetown University Law Center; Dr. Hans Binnedijk, Vice President for Research of the National Defense University; my former colleagues at the Africa Center for Strategic Studies, National Defense University, Ft. McNair, Washington, DC; Major General (Ret.) Robert Scales; Commander

Gary Fletcher; Dr. Al Pierce and Chaplain Eric Wester; and Professor Eric Patterson; Georgetown University.

I also wish to thank Professor Hew Strachan, All Souls College, Oxford University, who was instrumental in providing me with the opportunity to present this work at the "Staying True to Their Salt" conference held at Nuffield College, Oxford University on February 5, 2010, as part of the Oxford Leverhulme Programme on the Changing Character of War. I also appreciate the opportunity to present this analysis at a seminar on "Balancing the Force—Implications for Special Operations Forces & Conventional Forces Integration," at the Joint Advanced Warfighting School, U.S. National War College (November 19, 2009).

Finally, I wish to thank Brigadier General Pradip Vij for his support of this book and the ideas contained within, and to you, my reader, for giving me the opportunity to express my views to you.

LIST OF ABBREVIATIONS AND ACRONYMS

ACBAR	Agency Coordinating Body for Afghan Relief
ACDS	African Chiefs of Defence and Security
ACOTA	Africa Counterinsurgency Operations Training Assistance
ACT	Advance Civilian Team
AMIS	African Mission in Sudan
AMISOM	African Union in Sudan
AMU	Arab Maghreb Union
ANA	Afghan National Army
ANCB	Afghan NGOs Coordination Bureau
AQIM	Al Qaeda in the Maghreb
ARMM	Autonomous Region of Muslim Mindanao
ASF	African Union Standby Force
ASG	Abu Sayyaf Group
ASEAN	Association of Southeast Asian Nations
ASI	Afghanistan Stabilization Initiative
AU	African Union
AUSA	Association of the U.S. Army
BRAC	Base Realignment and Closure Commission
C3IS	Command, Control, Communication and

Information systems

CAT-A	Civil Affairs Team (U.S. Army)
CEWS	Continental Early Warming System
CHLC	Coalition Humanitarian Liaison Cell
COIN	Counterinsurgency
CRC	Civil Reconstruction Corps
CSIS	Center for Strategic and International Studies
CSSDCA	Conference on Security, Stability, Development and Cooperation in Africa
DCI	Defense Capability Initiative
DDR	Disarmament, demobilization and reintegration
DITF	Deployed Integrated Task Force
DOD	U.S. Department of Defense
EAC	East African Community
EACDS	East African Chiefs of Dense Staff
ECOWAS	Economic Community of West African States
EASBRIG	East African Standby Brigade
ECCAS	Economic Community of Central African States Brigade
ECOBRIG	ECOWAS Standby Brigade
FATA	Federally Administered Tribal Areas
FM	[U.S. Army] Field Manual
GPOI	Global Peace Operations Initiative
IMS	Inter-agency Management System

ISAF	[NATO] International Security Assistance Force
LIC	Low-intensity conflict
MOOTW war	Military operations other than
MNLF Front	Moro National Liberation
MILF	Moro Islamic Liberation Front
NATO	North Atlantic Treaty Organization
NEPAD	New Partnership for Africa's Development
NGOs	Nongovernmental Organizations
NRF	NATO Response Force
NSPD	National Security Presidential Directive
NWFP	Northwest Frontier Province
PLANELM	Planning Element
PRT	Provincial Reconstruction Team
PSC	AU Peace & Security Council
REC	Regional Economic Communities
SADCBRIG	South African Development Community Standby Brigade
S/CRS	U.S. State Department's Office of the Coordinator for Reconstruction and Stabilization
SOEs	State Owned Enterprise
SSTR	Stability, Security, Transition and Reconstruction Operations
SWCC	Special Warfare Combatant-Craft Crewman

UNAMA	UN Assistance Mission in Afghanistan
USAID	U.S. Agency for International Development
USCENTCOM	U.S. Central Command
USSOCOM	U.S. Special Operations Command

INTRODUCTION

Using the Dialectical Method to Analyze Fundamentalist Islamic-Based Terrorism

Rather than plunging into a law-based or political theory-based description of fundamentalist Islamic-based terrorist movements, a theoretical analysis in a broader historical context may be a useful starting point. The dialectical method, although now disfavored by some scholars, offers a highly structured means of analyzing current events and putting them into historical perspective. Certain elements of this method of analysis have been selected for the reasons set forth below. The following discussion is designed to provide an analytical framework within which to view and draw conclusions about fundamentalist Islamic-based terrorism.

A New Philosophical Framework of Analysis

Western political and philosophical thought seems to oscillate between alternate forces of idealism and materialism. While materialism may be traced back to the thinking of Democritus (fifth century B.C.E.) and the ethics of Aristotle and Epicurus, the European belief in a fundamentally spiritual universe ruled by God almost completely dominated Western philosophy until the 17th century.

However, the translations of Greek texts during the Renaissance, the rise of natural sciences, and the application of the scientific method to new inquiries on the nature of the physical universe and man's relationship to God created a new context for materialist thought. Scientific reasoning was also applied to social sciences by Enlightenment scholars. A new rationalism was particularly evident in the political commentaries of Thomas Hobbes, and particularly in the works of John Locke who was pivotal in formulating man's natural rights to property.

However, the rigid empiricism, materialism, and rationalism of post-Enlightenment scholars such as David Hume were later refuted by Immanuel Kant, an 18th century German idealist. His *Critique of Pure Reason*[1] posited that while the world is composed of concrete objects, the perceptions and experiences of the individual actually structure and create order in that objective universe. He thus placed a new importance on the subjectivity of human perception, and the human reasoning that orders such perceptions in a cognizable way. Further, he elevated the process of constructing knowledge out of sense impressions and forming universal concepts into a transcendental ideal.

Georg W.F. Hegel moved beyond the empiricists and Kant's transcendental idealism by creating a highly structured philosophical system of dialectical idealism as set forth in his *The Phenomenology of the Mind*.[2] He unites reason with sensory experience by creating a sense-based perception of an object such as a book (thesis) to comparing it with other books and creating a mental concept of a book (antithesis) to creating a fuller, more idealized realization of a book (synthesis).

For Hegel, history was a dialectical process being played out on a global scale. Each stage in the dialectical process is rife with internal contradictions, and contains the seed of its own destruction (the "negation of the negation"). The dialectical process leads to a holistic, final synthesis that inexorably moves towards the attainment of the highest goal of history–to achieve universal freedom.

Frederick Engels (working in collaboration with Karl Marx) took the "idealism" out of Hegel's dialectical idealism and replaced it with dialectical materialism. Rather than adopting Hegel's approach of starting with the idea or concept of some concrete object, Engels started with the human events that preceded notions or ideas about such events. Further, the desired (and inevitable) end goal of the progression of human history did not lie in achieving universal freedom but in establishing a communist state.

Needless to say, the dialectical method as a means of analyzing history, and even the dialectical idealism of Hegel have fallen out of favor. Therefore, it may be surprising to see it revived in this context. Nevertheless, I feel that the analytical approach of the dialectical method has some intellectual merit, and I wish to capture certain intrinsic elements of it. Specifically, I wish to use the dialectical method as a limited diagnostic tool to analyze a broad-based historical problem– it is not my intent to further a discussion of dialectical materialism within its own philosophic or historical context.

The elements of the dialectical method that I find useful are, first, the disaggregation of historical events into a tripartite structure of thesis–antithesis–synthesis. This is a very useful approach to define certain sequential and interdependent stages of historical evolution. Secondly, the idea that a subsequent historical stage arises from an internal contradiction contained in the previous phase is very important. It creates a foundation for viewing progressive stages of historical growth as evolutionary in nature and organically connected to each other. This permits the observer to see historical events in a more holistic fashion which, in my opinion, is more useful than sharply and arbitrarily dividing historical events into pre-set categories. Thirdly, the fact that the use of the dialectical method permits the observer to view history not as a steady continuum but as punctuated with discrete occurrences which eventually become historical events. This helps create a framework of historically significant events rather than a blur of undistinguished occurrences.

Therefore, I request the reader's indulgence in agreeing in advance to divorce the dialectical method from its socio-historical application in the 20th century in order to further this analysis. Admittedly, the idea of history moving in a certain predetermined, unilinear way is highly problematic. However, rather than taking an "end of history" approach resulting in universal freedom, the communist state, a clash of civilizations or liberal democracy, it may be wise to avoid such apocalyptic visions. Perhaps the Hindu world view of history moving in circles is a more value-neutral approach that is better designed to analyze and interpret rather than obfuscate and polarize the issues discussed below. Hopefully, this approach will better incorporate historical, political and legal dimensions of the analysis giving the reader a wide angle view of the problems and proposed solutions.

The Cold War era locked the United States and the former USSR into a political and military stand-off based on the grim possibility of nuclear warfare leading to their mutually assured destruction. The two superpowers were polarized not only in terms of their underlying ideology and means of governance (democracy vs. communism) but also in their means of economic production (capitalist-based free market economy vs. state-led socialism).

Further, the two superpowers also insisted on polarizing the rest of the world. Like the African proverb that says that when two elephants fight, the grass gets trampled, the policies of containment, proxy wars, and creating spheres of influence took its toll on countries extraneous to the Cold War conflict. Although the political and economic approaches of the former superpowers were strikingly dissimilar, the overarching "symmetry" of the United States and the former Soviet Union, the two most powerful nation-states at the time, creates the "thesis."

The contradictions contained within socialist regimes eventually led to their collapse, but the peaceful lull that followed the fall of the Berlin Wall in 1989 was shattered on September 11, 2001. We now find ourselves in the second stage of the "antithesis" or the "asymmetry" posed by global terrorism acting through non-state actors such as Al Qaeda and related terrorist groups. In fact, the U.S. military fully recognizes the so-called "asymmetric threats" posed by such groups, and responded to these threats by establishing the Asymmetric Warfare Group within the U.S. Army in 2005.[3]

Asymmetric warfare is not a new tactic, but an ancient one where unconventional tactics are used to counter the overwhelming conventional military superiority of an adversary. The decisive technological and military superiority over the conventional military forces of virtually any conceivable adversary is met not by conventional warfare but by unconventional means which may, in the current context, include terrorist attacks, weapons of mass destruction, guerrilla warfare, cyber-attacks and information warfare. This "asymmetry" of these warfare tactics underscores the relative imbalance in size, tactical approaches and objectives of the actors. Powerful nation-states (not just the two former superpowers) are now threatened by these nebulous terrorist groups that have no organized center, armies, or formal governance structure.

The next stage or the "synthesis" that I propose that we are moving toward is the "Fearful Symmetry." The idea of the Fearful Symmetry is based on a poem by the English romantic poet, William Blake, who published *Songs of Experience* in 1789 that included the poem, *The Tyger.*

> Tyger Tyger, burning bright,
> In the forests of the night;
> What immortal hand or eye,
> Could frame thy fearful symmetry?[4]

Not only are we terrorized by the acts of terrorists (an obvious outcome since that is their aim), but I feel that many Islamic-based terrorists are also fearful (if not actually terrorized) by the perceived threat posed by Western ideals and institutions. In other words, the ideas of universal suffrage and representative government, participatory democracy, respecting the rights of women, protecting the rights of ethnic and religious minorities, and free market economic practices and institutions are deeply problematic for fundamentalist Islamic-based terrorist networks and operatives.

Indeed, "to many of our potential opponents we appear to be as asymmetric as they appear to be to us. To the al-Qaeda fighter, cowering in a cave in a remote part of Afghanistan, fuel air explosives, dropped with deadly precision from aircraft miles away and thousands of feet up, directed by laser designators wielded by highly trained and stealthy special operation forces (SOF), is as asymmetric to him as his tactics are to us."[5]

The transformation from the "antithesis" of the asymmetric threats posed by global terrorism to the "synthesis" of "A Fearful Symmetry" is being prompted by a fundamental change. There has been a palpable shift from the mere tactical level of posing asymmetric threats perpetrated by global terrorists to an overarching psychological dimension where both sides instill fear in each other. The asymmetric threat of global terrorism is no longer confined to conflict zones with specific military engagements underway, but now affects civilians in every walk of life.

In fact, ordinary life has been transformed to accommodate the impact of the asymmetric threat of global terrorism as illustrated by new protocols with regard to airline travel, heightened security in almost every dimension of everyday life, and a new fearful consciousness of the presence of implicit danger. Moreover, this stage has reached a "steady state" where neither the targets nor the effects of global terrorism are dissipating.

The previous examples merely illustrate some of the symptoms of asymmetric conflict, but the actual causes lie much deeper. William J. Olson points out that, "[t]he United States is engaged in the first post-modern conflict. It is not ready. . . . it is a struggle in which it can win all the battles and still lose the war. . . . We have moved from the era of modern war into the era of post-modern war, into an age of war without a center of gravity."[6] (The concept of a "center of gravity" for war originates with Claus von Clausewitz, and is an idea that we shall return to.) Olson, however, recognizes that "[m]odern war was not possible without the modern state."[7]

Professor Olson further states, "[p]ost-modern war is not possible without the disintegration of the modern state. If modern war was the product of the emergence of the state based on new organizing principles, post-modern war is the product of the collapse of the state and the emergence of new organizing principles."[8]

In addition, Professor Olson points out:

> The peace that ended the Thirty Years' War was more than a peace that ended a war. It ended an era and began another one. It, along with the English Civil War, set the major themes shaping the modern world: the end of wars of religion and the beginning of secular wars; the beginning of secular thought leading to the so-called Enlightenment; the consequent explosion of science that helped to fuel intellectual and industrial revolutions; with the further consequence of an emerging doctrine of individual conscience and government based on social contract rather than divine right; the establishment of the idea of the sovereign state within a system of states; the birth of nationalism, of an idea of countries based on common, shared identity rather than as the personal holdings of dynastic families. These themes unleashed powerful forces, creative and destructive, that shaped Europe in the years following, and through that medium the world, America included.[9]

These complex themes characterizing "modernity" have been questioned in fundamental ways by the asymmetric threats posed by Islamic-based global terrorism.

Thus, a discussion of the failings of the Westphalian-based nation-state is integral to an analysis of fundamentalist Islamic-based terrorism. For modern readers, it is easy to take the structure of the modern nation-state for granted, to assume that it arose *sui generis*. This viewpoint fails to take into account that, "the history of the modern state is a short one–and not a particularly happy one. . . . it was not until 1648, when the Peace of Westphalia ended the Thirty Years' War, that the modern international system of sovereign state began to develop. Even after this symbolic starting point, it took centuries of conquest and many more years of war before anything truly resembling today's state system took shape. . . . [and] even in Europe, the birthplace of the modern state, the history of the state is a history of repression and war."[10]

For the more cynical viewer, the viability of the nation-state structure may be called into question in light of the alarming rise of ungovernable territories, systemic corruption, the inability to govern (or to be governed), the inability to provide public services in support of basic human needs, and the lack of accountability, all of which have led to dismal results.

Indeed, "[o]ne of the principal lessons of the events of September 11 is that failed states matter–not just for humanitarian reasons but for national security as well. If left untended, such states can become sanctuaries for terrorist networks with a global reach, not to mention international organized crime and drug traffickers who also exploit the dysfunctional environment. As such failed states can pose a direct threat to the national security of the United States and to the security of entire regions."[11]

In fact, the globalization of organized crime in narco-wars, human trafficking, money laundering, illegal arms dealing (often involving other commodities such as diamonds), cybercrime, piracy, illegal nuclear proliferation and other illegal activities have often taken advantage of failed states. In seeking a safe harbor from local policing authorities or international law enforcement in general, criminals and criminal syndicates have acted, in some cases, almost like opportunistic viruses using failed or failing states as hosts. While the relationship of failed states to fundamentalist Islamic-based terrorism may not be automatically presumed, the complex dynamic between the two is a critical component of this analysis. Further, the relationship of international crime to global terrorism, and the ways in which both are synergized by each other, is also an important dimension of this discussion.

The discussion below will focus on the implications of global Islamic-based terrorism rather than on the law enforcement aspects of other illegal activities. Nevertheless, it is important not to lose sight of the fact that terrorists are criminals too. For purposes of this discussion, however, Islamic-based global terrorists offer an ideological spectrum in which to view their acts–whether this "ideology" is real or illusory is certainly a fair question that requires a closer examination.

Nonetheless, the suggestion of an ideological conflict offers a different and more complex dimension than simple economic-based crimes that merely seek to accumulate ill-gotten gains. The damage that such economic crimes may inflict on the body polity of the host state may be more in the nature of collateral damage. To date, there is no real evidence to suggest that a stated goal (or actual intention) of crime warlords and syndicates is to destroy the modern nation-state. This provides a sharp contrast to global jihadists who vehemently argue that the downfall of Western-based democracies is a desired outcome of their actions.

In looking back, one of the central themes of the symmetry of the Cold War was the concurrent policy of "containment" practiced by both the U.S. and the former USSR. Containment permitted both sides to wage war without actually fighting one. However, the end of the Cold War ended the era of the modern war. The era of post-modern warfare began with the attacks of September 11, 2001 acting as the first salvo. Containment is no longer possible. The genie of the Fearful Symmetry is already out of the bottle.

Asymmetric Conflicts

In returning to the issue of fighting asymmetric conflicts, it would be misleading to assert that asymmetric elements of warfare are completely unknown to modern warfare. In fact, there is a fascinating evolution of U.S. military concepts of irregular warfare, small wars, low intensity conflicts, military operations other than war (MOOTW), special operations, counterinsurgencies, guerrilla warfare, counterterrorism, covert wars, unconventional warfare, and stability operations, peacekeeping operations, and contingency operations.

One commentator remarked:

> In the specialized military literature, the concepts are not always precisely defined. As a result, "low-intensity warfare" (LIW) and "low-intensity conflict" (LIC) are generally used as synonyms. Related terms like "foreign internal defense", "counterinsurgency", "counterterrorism", "special warfare", "special operations", "revolutionary/counterrevolutionary warfare", "small wars", "limited wars" and others are not clearly explained. Sometimes they are employed as synonyms for LIC, sometimes as conceptual antitheses, sometimes as sub-categories. Almost every essay on LIC in a U.S. military journal begins with the result of furthering the terminological confusion.[12]

The U.S. Department of Defense (DOD) no longer lists low intensity conflict, military operations other than war, or small wars in its list of official definitions.[13] Nevertheless, the U.S. Marine Corps has an extensive list of "small wars" dating from the 1800s.[14] Moreover, the needs of irregular or unconventional warfare are tactically supported by U.S. special forces (e.g., U.S. Army Special Forces (Green Berets), Delta Force, Army Rangers, (75th Ranger Regiments), and the 160th Special Operations Aviation Regiment (Night Stalkers); and by the Navy SEALS, Special Warfare Combatant-Craft Crewman (SWCC), and the Helicopter Sea Combat Squadron 84 (HSC-84); by the U.S. Marine Corps Special Operations Command; and the Air Force Special Operations Forces). This seems to indicate a somewhat confused picture of overlapping doctrine, strategy and force projection.

Following the conclusion of the Vietnam War, counterinsurgency doctrine, theory and practice was left to the special operations military community. A number of humanitarian and peace operations took place throughout the 1990s including Somalia, Haiti, and the Balkans, but there was no major U.S. military thrust to developing counterinsurgency theory and practice.

Thus, when the U.S. invaded Iraq in 2003, the existing doctrine on counterinsurgencies was very limited. "In the fall of 2005, over two and a half years into the struggle to stabilize Iraq and four years into the operation in Afghanistan, General David Petraeus partnered with Marine

Corps General James Mattis to lead a year-long effort to craft a new Army and Marine Corps Counterinsurgency Field Manual (FM-3-24). This new doctrine, which was edited by counterinsurgency expert Dr. Conrad Crane, drew heavily on current operational experiences as well as historical case studies and 'best practices' of past counterinsurgencies. The final draft of the manual was published in the fall of 2006."[15]

A condensed guide was published by the U.S. State Department in 2009 in an inter-agency effort entitled, "U.S. Government Counterinsurgency Guide." This guide makes it clearer than the original Army field manual that the U.S. role in an insurgency is that of *supporting* the host government in quelling the insurgency. This role is related to the host government's role, but is not the same. Further, the U.S. role changes as the host government defeats the insurgents and builds its capacity to govern again.[16]

The dilemma posed by the Fearful Symmetry is the challenge of fighting a post-modern war under rules of engagement that do not exist for one side, and that are unclear for the other. Not only is it not clear who the enemy is from a Western point of view, but their objectives of fighting this conflict are also unclear. Is the total destruction of all modern nation-states the desired result for fundamentalist Islamic-based terrorists? Is a negotiated peace possible? If so, whom do we negotiate peace with? In light of how high the stakes are in terms of assuring the safety and well-being of millions (if not billions) of people, these are very consequential questions. Therefore, establishing a coherent framework of ideas and action with which to respond to the threat of global terrorism may be the most important geopolitical challenge of the 21st century.

Not only are we fighting a post-modern war but it is a war that is also being fought in what has been termed a "post-American world." Fareed Zakaria points out that America "remains the most open, flexible society in the world, able to absorb other people, cultures, ideas, goods, and services. The country thrives on the hunger and energy of poor immigrants. Faced with the new technologies of foreign companies, or growing markets overseas, it adapts and adjusts. When you compare this dynamism with the closed and hierarchical nations that were once superpowers, you sense that the United States is different and may not fall into the trap of becoming rich, and fat, and lazy."[17]

Despite his optimism, he also warns that:

> Americans—particularly the American government—have not really understood the rise of the rest. This is one of the most thrilling stories in history. Billions of people are escaping from abject poverty. The world will be enriched and ennobled as they become consumers, producers, inventors, thinkers, dreamers, and doers. This is all happening because of American ideas and actions. For 60 years, the United States has pushed countries to open their markets, free up their politics, and embrace trade and technology. American diplomats, businessmen, and intellectuals have urged people in distant lands to be unafraid of change, to join the advanced world, to learn the secrets of our success. Yet just as they are beginning to do so, we are losing faith in such ideas. We have become suspicious of trade, openness, immigration, and investment because now it's not Americans going abroad but foreigners coming to America. Just as the world is opening up, we are closing down.[18]

Fareed Zakaria further explains that, "[b]eing on the top for so long has its downsides. The U.S. market has been so large that Americans have assumed that the rest of the world would take the trouble to understand it and them. They have not had to reciprocate by learning foreign languages, cultures or markets. Now, that could leave the United States at a competitive disadvantage. . . . Learning from the rest is no longer a matter of morality or politics. Interestingly, it is about competitiveness."[19]

In ushering in a post-American world, he observes that, "[o]n every dimension other than military power–industrial, financial, social, cultural– the distribution of power is shifting, moving away from U.S. dominance. This does not mean that we are entering an anti-American world. But we are moving into a post-American world, one defined and directed by many places and many people. . . . The world is changing, but it is going the United States' way. . . It might be a world in which the United States takes up less space, but it is one in which American ideas and ideals are overwhelmingly dominant. The United States has a window of opportunity to shape and master the changing global landscape, but only if it first recognizes that the post-American world is reality–and embraces and celebrates that fact."[20]

In a post-American world, it is important to understand the implications of the changing roles of the nation-state and how nations interact with each other. Indeed, this new world order has been characterized as "nonpolar," where numerous centers wield meaningful power.[21] "Nonpolarity complicates diplomacy. A nonpolar world not only involves more actors but also lacks the more predictable fixed structures and relationships that tend to define worlds of unipolarity, bipolarity or multipolarity. Alliances, in particular, will lose much of their importance, if only because alliances require predictable threats, outlooks, and obligations, all of which are likely to be in short supply in a nonpolar world. Relationships will instead be more selective and situational. . . . . The United State will no longer have the luxury of a 'You're either with us or against us' foreign policy. Nonpolarity will be difficult and dangerous."[22]

The single biggest complicating factor in confronting global terrorism is that the structure of the nation-state has been badly compromised in some instances, and it is this critical failure that forms the basis of our examination into the rise of fundamentalist Islamic-based extremism.

The challenge now is to understand how to prosecute and win a post-modern war where none of the former rules apply. But more importantly, it is important to understand why this conflict came into being, and how it may be successfully concluded, not just for ourselves but also for the enemies that we face. Perhaps it seems counterintuitive that a "win-win" scenario may be contemplated in these circumstances. But since the world is engaged in a conflict of ideas as much as in an armed conflict, the ascendency of certain ideas may signal the transformation of ideals, governance, and a new view of history for everyone, friend and foe alike.

PART I

Global Fundamentalist Islamic-Based Terrorism:

One Size Does Not Fit All

1

Radical Islamic-Based Separatist Movements

At the outset, it is important to make a very basic distinction between Islamic-based separatist (or secessionist) movements that employ terrorist means, and the so-called global fundamentalist Islamic-based terrorist movement. The reason for doing so is that the nature of Islamic-based terrorism determines, in part, the international response to it.

A. Separatist vs. Terrorist Movements

The primary example of an Islamic-based separatist movement is, of course, Palestine. It has engaged in a decades-long struggle for autonomy, self-determination and establishing its own statehood, the causes and implications of which will not be addressed here. In light of the fact that Hamas was designated by the U.S. State Department to be a Foreign Terrorist Organization,[1] Hamas surprised U.S. and other policy-makers by winning the Palestinian Authority's (PA) general legislative elections in January 2006. Hamas defeated Fatah, the party of the PA's president, Mahmoud Abbas, thereby setting the stage for a prolonged and continuing power struggle.

While Hamas uses terrorist tactics of suicide bombings along with launching short-range rockets and mortars in order to achieve its political goals, it also provides basic human services such as educational, sports, health and religious facilities to its constituents. The fact that Hamas has been responsive to the basic needs of Palestinians and allegedly has a reputation for honesty in contrast to the corruption that Fatah officials often stand accused of, may explain, in part, its political victory. In essence, Hamas combines Palestinian nationalism with Islamic fundamentalism.[2]

Another example of an Islamic-based secessionist movement is the Muslim uprising in Mindanao staged by secessionist groups that include the Moro National Liberation Front (MNLF), the Moro Islamic Liberation Front (MILF), and the Abu Sayyaf Group (ASG) which has known ties to the Al-Qaeda network of Osama bin Laden.[3] Despite signing a 1996 peace accord with the Philippine government establishing the Autonomous Region of Muslim Mindanao (ARMM) for five provinces, the MNLF staged a revolt in November 2001, thus continuing to destabilize the country.[4] Filipino President Benigno Acquino, announced a peace plan on October 7, 2012 that gives up the MNLF's right to an independent homeland in return for an autonomous new area called Bangsamoro.[5] Moreover, the jihadist-based secessionist movements in the Philippines are actively supported by other terrorist groups in Indonesia, Malaysia, Iran and Libya.[6]

Kashmir provides another example of a localized, territory-specific fundamentalist Islamic-based secessionist movement that long predates 9/11. This is a somewhat problematic example since the insurgencies in Kashmir are not truly indigenous but are instigated by outside actors.[7] Like the previous example of the Philippines, however, there is credible evidence that Al Qaeda has developed closer ties to Kashmiri terrorist groups, such as Lashkar-e-Taiba and Jaish-e-Muhammad.[8] Yet despite the decades of war and insurrection, there is reason to feel hopeful about Kashmir since businesses are now open again, roads are being repaired and offices are being rebuilt.[9] However, the Indian Government will need to decide whether transitional justice for the region will be a national priority.

Thus, the Philippine and Kashmiri separatist movements (along with Hamas in Palestine and Hezbollah in Lebanon)[10] are localized "terror-based" movements that perhaps may be narrowly viewed in the same light as the former Basque separatists in Spain, the Irish Republic Army, the Tamil Tigers in Sri Lanka or the Chiapas rebels in Mexico, to cite a few examples of "terrorist" groups who also used to have discrete political objectives and goals.[11] In contrast, other fundamentalist global jihadist movements are more closely aligned in principles and tactics to the Red Brigade in Italy that had a more diffuse political agenda of revolutionary change to be achieved through violent means.

The examples of the Philippines and Kashmir also highlight a disturbing convergence of separatist political objectives with the global intifadah promulgated by Al Qaeda. These recent examples may represent the next evolutionary step beyond the more strictly defined goals related to establishing statehood and political legitimacy that is being pursued by Hamas in Palestine and, to a lesser extent, by Hezbollah in Lebanon. In fact, the clear danger posed by these examples is that they will lose their separatist character altogether and simply merge with the global fundamentalist Islamic-based terrorist network.

This "convergence" theory has been addressed by one commentator to highlight circumstances where:

> Terrorist groups . . . become so engaged with their involvement in criminal activities . . . that they merely maintain their political rhetoric as a façade for perpetrating criminal activities on a wider scale. . . . No longer driven by a political agenda, but by the proceeds of crime, these formerly traditional terrorist groups continue to engage in the use of terror tactics for two primary reasons. First, to keep the government and law enforcement authorities focused on political issues and problems, as opposed to initiating criminal investigations. Second, terror tactics continue to be used as a tool for these groups to assert themselves amongst rival criminal groups. . . .

> Groups that are illustrative of a terrorist entity evolving into a group primarily engaged in criminal activities include Abu Sayyaf, the Islamic Movement of Uzbekistan, and the Revolutionary Armed Forces of Colombia (FARC). . . . It has been estimated that in 2000 alone, kidnapping deals garnered Abu Sayyaf $20 million. In light of Abu Sayyaf's operations, which are focused on criminal activities, there is little indication that the groups remains driven by its original political aim, which was to establish an independent Islamic republic in territory currently comprising Mindanao, surrounding islands, and the Sulu Archipelago. (Citations omitted.)[12]

In conclusion:

> Growing reliance on cross-border criminal activities–facilitated by open borders, weak states, immigration flows, financial technology, and a highly intricate and accessible global transportation infrastructure–

and an associated interest in establishing political control in order to consolidate and secure future operations, have all contributed to the rise of the crime–terror nexus. As a result, non-state actors in the guise of transnational organized crime and terrorism are directly challenging the security of the state–arguably for the first time in history. The realization that economic and political power enhance one another, suggest that more and more groups will become hybrid organizations by nature. This is enhanced by the fact that criminal and terrorist groups appear to be learning from one another, and adapting to each other's successes and failures. (Citations omitted.)[13]

Indeed, there is now evidence that Hamas may be shifting its political tactics by abandoning the use of rockets and initiating cultural initiatives and public relations as a means of winning support both at home and abroad.[14] Hamas has duly noted that the international condemnation of Israel over allegations of its use of disproportionate force may have worked in Hamas's favor. Rather than resisting Israeli occupation and military tactics by force, Hamas is initiating a "culture of resistance" that may ultimately lead it to a tactical victory over Israel in the end.

There are other examples of Islamic-based separatist movements that may be cited here, but rather than belaboring the point, it may be useful to consider whether there is an historical relationship (however tenuous) between post-colonial movements that established new nation-states, and the examples cited above. Revolutionary forces in former colonies generally did not have access to organized armies or arms, and often resorted to using unconventional means to achieve their revolutionary goals. Most notably, Mahatma Gandhi eschewed violence in order to gain India's independence, truly an unconventional war tactic! This approach was later successfully replicated in the civil rights movement of the United States and in the anti-apartheid movement in South Africa, where Gandhi first began his journey.

While Palestine is not emerging from a colonial past *per se*, it has not yet managed to successfully achieve its own statehood. The fact that this and other separatist movements are now being energized by the global terrorism espoused by Al Qaeda is a profound departure from the past practice of using international law principles of self-determination to create internationally recognized statehood. In fact, the Israeli-Palestine conflict is no longer catalytic to global terrorism, but is being overshadowed and surpassed in importance by the global jihadist terrorist movements in the view of the jihadists themselves.[15]

A significant underlying theme that unites the examples of Islamic-based separatist movements discussed above is the failure of the state as an institution of governance that creates an ordered society. A second failure that can no longer be ignored is the failure to hold state leaders accountable by their own people. Thus, the failure of the state may be viewed as being two-fold: both in terms of governing and in being governed.

However, definitions of what constitutes a "failed state" can be highly polemical, political, and problematic. In a collaboration between *Foreign Policy* and the Fund for Peace, the 2011 Failed States Index lists the following 12 nations as "failed states," namely, Somalia, Chad, Sudan, the Democratic Republic of the Congo, Haiti, Zimbabwe, Afghanistan, the Central African Republic, Iraq, Côte d'Ivoire, Guinea and finally, and perhaps most notably, Pakistan.[16] It is indeed a dubious honor to be included in this "dirty dozen."

This chapter will explore the dynamics of failed states and whether a failed state may attract global terrorism. If so, why and how? We start with three very important failing or failed states: Pakistan, Somalia and Yemen. A discussion of Mali has also been included in this context since there are a number of downstream implications flowing from the conflict there. We will then broaden the discussion to an overall analysis of how failed states, in some instances, create a cauldron of discontent where terrorism may be sheltered, indoctrinated, trained and launched in violent, cowardly and desperate attacks on innocent civilians.

B. Case Examples of Failing or Failed States

1.   *Pakistan: A Difficult Dilemma*

The widely-touted claim that Pakistan is facing an "existential threat" from violent extremists, and that Pakistan is in the process of being "Talibanized" has been met with stiff resistance in certain quarters. One commentator notes sharply that, "Pakistan is neither Somalia nor Sudan, nor even Iraq or Afghanistan. It is a thoroughly modern state with vast infrastructure, a fiercely critical and diverse media, an active global economy and strong ties with regional powers such as China and Iran. It is not a 'failed state'. . . The monotonous drone of 'failure' implies that its fragile democracy is not worth preserving. It encourages the marginalization of the civilian government and boosts the claims of both the military and the militants."[17]

This somewhat sanguine, overly reductionist view is difficult to support in light of current events which may indicate far deeper trends. On April 15, 2012, members of the Pakistan Taliban stormed the prison located near Bannu, Pakistan, freeing nearly 400 prisoners, including Adnan Rashid, a junior air force officer who had been sentenced to death for his part in attempting to assassinate former president General Pervez Musharraf on December 14, 2003.[18] Bannu adjoins North Waziristan, a largely lawless region in Pakistan that is widely believed to harbor militants and terrorists from Al Qaeda and the Haqqani Taliban network, among others. This area has been a consistent target for U.S. drone strikes as a result.[19]

This jailbreak was the largest in Pakistan's history and highlighted the breakdown in the response of Pakistani security forces. Militants blockaded all roads to the prison and Pakistan security forces were only able to reach after two hours by which time all the militants and escapees had fled. Indeed, the prison guards offered "little resistance to the Pakistan Taliban," according to news reports.[20] Thus, the fact that Pakistan Taliban militants are able to act so brazenly and without an effective military or security response by the Pakistan Government is alarming. While this may not be a definitive example of the "Talibanization" of the Pakistan Government, it offers very cold comfort.

In fact, as early as 2010, General David Patraeus, then the U.S. military commander in Afghanistan, recommended to President Obama that the Haqqani network be placed on the U.S. State Department's list of terrorists in large part because of the network's stronghold in North Waziristan.[21] Although the designation of the entire Haqqani network (as opposed to individuals operating within it) would help interdict fund-raising activities the network conducts in Saudi Arabia and the United Arab Emirates, the Obama Administration continues to be worried about its impact on its relations with Pakistan, peace talks with the Taliban and negotiations for the release of Sgt. Bowe Bergdahl, a U.S. soldier held in captivity by the Haqqani network since 2009.[22]

Since 2008, however, the Haqqani network's suicide bombers in Kabul have attacked the Indian Embassy, hotels and restaurants, the NATO-led International Security Assistance Force (ISAF), and the U.S. Embassy.[23] The network is also suspected of controlling attacks on Kabul, Afghanistan and against Bagram Air Base outside of Kabul, then controlled by U.S. military forces. In fact, the U.S. Treasury Department added two Taliban and two Haqqani network affiliated individuals to its list of designated terrorists on June 21, 2010.[24]

"But the group's real power may lie in its deep connections to Pakistan's spy agency, the Inter-Services Intelligence [ISI] Directorate, which analysts say sees the Haqqani network as a way to exercise its own leverage in Afghanistan."[25] Although the Haqqani network alleged pledges its loyalty to the Afghan Taliban, it is financially autonomous based on a crime empire centered in Waziristan, Pakistan, that relies on extortion kidnapping and smuggling. Moreover, the suspicion is the ISI allows Haqqani operatives to run legitimate businesses in Pakistan, facilitate travel to the Gulf States, and receive donations for their operations.[26] Infact, Admiral Mike Mullen directly accused the ISI of launching an attack on the U.S. Embassy in Kabul, Afghanistan on September 13, 2011.[27]

Indeed, when the Taliban advanced to Buner, 60 miles away from the capital of Islamabad in 2009, "Pakistani authorities sent only several hundred poorly equipped and underpaid constabulary forces."[28] President Asif Ali Zardari was in Washington, DC at the time. More disturbingly, however, the Pakistan Government's recent political actions give rise to grave concerns. Pakistan's political and military leaders have endorsed a peace agreement known as the Malakand Accord that allows for the imposition of *shari'a*, or Islamic law in a large portion of the Northwest Frontier Province, and ends the Pakistan Government's military operation in Swat. The past peace agreements, which began under former President Pervez Musharraf's regime in 2004, have served to give the Taliban the time it needed to regroup from fighting with the Pakistani military, and reorganize its forces.[29]

In fact, the Malakand Accord has granted the Taliban nearly complete control over a region that encompasses more than 1/3 of the Northwest Front Province, thereby doubling the Taliban's recruiting base along with its taxation base. Moreover, there is evidence the Taliban is beginning to branch out beyond the Northwest Frontier Province. The Taliban began attacking the Punjab districts of Dera Ghazi Khan and Mianwali during the spring of 2009, thus forcing the Punjab provincial government to consider closing down its borders with the two provinces.[30]

Fareed Zakaria denounced the Malakand accord in no uncertain terms: "This was not a peace deal: it was surrender."[31] Examining the deeper implications of this struggle, he notes that, "the real core of this struggle has to be fought by the Pakistani army. They would need to fight a civil war against these militants to protect their own country, something they are loath to do. They have preferred the 'phantom' war against India, a simple old-fashioned deployment that they understand. Insurgencies are tough, and they are trying to avoid dealing with it. But they need to understand, this is the existential threat to their country. India is not trying to capture Punjab, the Taliban is."[32]

This raises the specter of Pakistan as a potentially failing state, the downstream implications of which are dramatic. A failed state lacks the ability to exert full territorial control of the state, a test which Pakistan may be failing at this point.

Robert Rotberg remarks that, "[i]n contrast to strong states, failed states cannot control their borders. They lose authority over chunks of territory. Often, the expression of official power is limited to the capital city and one or more ethnically specific zones. Indeed, one measure of the extent of a state's failure is how much of the state's geographical expanse a government genuinely controls."[33] If this standard of review is accepted, then Pakistan's course of action in entering the Malakand accord with the Taliban is chilling indeed.

Of course, the lack of political will to confront and control the Taliban in Pakistan has increased worries in Washington, DC about controlling Pakistan's nuclear arsenal consisting of about 60-100 nuclear weapons. "The Pakistanis, not surprisingly, dismiss those fears as American and Indian paranoia, intended to dissuade them from nuclear modernization. But the government's credibility is still colored by the fact that it used equal vehemence to denounce as fabrications the reports that Dr. Abdul Qadeer Khan, one of the architects of Pakistan's race for the nuclear bomb, had sold nuclear technology on the black market. In the end, those reports turned out to be true."[34]

The number and severity of the flashpoints between the United States and Pakistan are too numerous and complicated to recite here, and the infractions perceived by both sides continue to grow.[35] As of this writing, talks between the United States and Pakistan failed in April 2012 in the aftermath of very hard feelings resulting from the U.S. airstrikes in November 2011 that left 24 Pakistani soldiers dead; a 2011 shooting involving a CIA employee, and of course, the killing of Osama bin Laden, widely viewed in Pakistan on all levels as a "stunning breach in Pakistan's sovereignty."[36]

In the meantime, the Pakistan government has refused to reopen NATO supply routes to Afghanistan closed since November 2011, and the United States has refused to release between $1.8 and $3 million in military aid to Pakistan. The two countries cannot seem to come to terms on four vital issues: counterterrorism, including drone strikes in Pakistan by the U.S. military; NATO supply lines to Afghanistan; military aid to Pakistan; and, the Taliban peace process.[37] This leaves the two nations locked in an uncomfortable embrace for the foreseeable future with no endgame in sight.

Moreover, there is an additional concern since there is now tangible evidence reported in June 2009 that Al Qaeda and other militants are leaving Pakistan's tribal areas and moving to Somalia and Yemen.[38] As a report by the U.S. Senate Committee on Foreign Relations points out, "[a]s Al Qaeda members continue to resist U.S. and Pakistani forces along the Afghanistan-Pakistan border, some of their comrades appear to be moving to Yemen and Somalia, where the political climate allows them to seek safe haven, recruit new members, and train for future operations."[39]

For the present, Ayman al-Zawahri, Al Qaeda's nominal leader following the death of Osama bin Laden, continues his sphere of influence. But with the death of his deputy leader, Abu Yahya al-Libi in June 2012, there may be a shift in Power from Pakistan to autonomous franchises in Yemen, Somalia and the Maghreb in North Africa, extending even into Nigeria where an Islamist movement in the north, Boko Haram, may be acting in concert with other Qaeda branches.[40] Terrorist cells, if seen as opportunistic viruses, are already metastasizing far beyond the rugged terrain of the Afghanistan-Pakistan border.

2.   *Somalia*

Somalia is a failed state that bears an eerie resemblance to Afghanistan before the September 11, 2001 attacks were launched. General Mohamed Farrah Hassan Aideed, popularly known as a warlord, seized power and defied the presence of the United Nations and the U.S. in Somalia in 1992. Former U.S. President Bill Clinton ordered Special Forces in the so-called Battle of Mogadishu to capture General Aideed, but the mission failed as popularized in the film, "Black Hawk Down."[41] The U.S. withdrew its forces shortly thereafter, and the UN withdrew in 1995. Although General Aideed proclaimed himself President in June 1995, he was not accorded international recognition. He was wounded in a subsequent battle and died of his wounds or a fatal heart attack on August 1, 1996.[42]

Somalia has been without an effective government since 1991.[43] Although Hassan Sheik Mohamud, chairman of the Peace and Development Party, has been elected President by Somalia's Parliament in September 2012, he faces incredible challenges.[44] The election itself was held in a highly fortified police academy. His administration replaces the internationally-backed transitional government formerly led by President Sheik Sharif Sheik Ahmed who was able to control very little territory outside of his presidential palace.[45] Even that little control is backed by the presence of AU peacekeeping troops.[46] Newly elected President Mohamud is expected to name a Prime Minister soon who will form a council of ministers to run the country.[47]

Notwithstanding the election of a new president, the collapse of Somalia's federal government in 1991 left a tremendous power vacuum. As the following discussion will demonstrate, the lack of a central government or any effective governance structure for the past two decades has led to a Hobbesian universe where the lives of everyday Somalis have indeed become "solitary, poor, nasty, brutish, and short."[48]

The Somali radical Islamist-based group, Al Shabab, originally emerged as a wing of militant youths within the Islamic Courts Union (ICU), a group that controlled much of Somalia prior to its occupation by Ethiopian forces in December 2006.[49] The ICU was in a struggle for power with the Somalian Transitional Federal Government who invited the cooperation of the Ethiopian Government.

The ICU eventually dissolved, but the presence of foreign troops in Somalia triggered a complex insurgency effort[50] during the course of which Al Shabab and their allies seized control of Mogadishu, the capital. Eventually, Al Shabab imposed a tyrannical form of radical Islam on the occupants of the city, and elsewhere. The Shabab are using their jihadist ambitions to attract foreign radical militants from around the globe, including Pakistan.[51] Although there is evidence that Al Shabab has withdrawn its presence from Mogadishu, retreating to the port town of Kismayu, the end result of this power struggle is as yet undetermined.[52]

However, on a more hopeful note, on September 28, 2012, the Kenyan Defense Forces have now claimed to have captured Kismayu, the last stronghold of Al Shabab.[53] The port city was used as a staging ground to launch piracy attacks on oceangoing vessels, import weapons, and impose fees on imported goods. While victory is being claimed by the Kenyan army under "Operation Sledge Hammer," Al Shabab has vowed to go underground and use insurgent tactics to reclaim Kismayu and wider territory. Again, this is a story that is still unfolding.

Indeed, there is sobering evidence that there is now a "boomerang" effect underway whereby Somalia immigrants to the United States, settling principally in an enclave in Minneapolis, Minnesota, for example, are now being recruited by Al Shabab agents, and returning to Somalia to engage in terrorist activities. As of July 13, 2009, a federal grand jury indicted two Minnesota men in connection with the recruitment of Somali immigrants to fight with Islamic insurgents in their home country. Both were charged with one count each of providing material support to terrorists and conspiracy to kill, kidnap, maim or injure people overseas.[54] The recruiting effort took place between September 2007 and December 2008, and the FBI has been investigating what appears to be a "massive recruiting effort by the al Qaeda-linked Somali insurgent group Al Shabab in immigrant communities in the United States."[55]

In terms of what caused more than a dozen young men of Somali descent to disappear from the Minneapolis area in recent years and return to Somalia was, in part, a response to the Ethiopian invasion of Somalia to push the Islamists out of Mogadishu in December 2006, as discussed above. The Ethiopian presence in Somalia was an outrage to most Somalis, and became a rallying cry for Al Shabab. Although Ethiopian troops left Somalia in 2009, Somalia's weak transitional government has not been successful in battling the insurgents. In fact, Ethiopia has rejected the request by the Somali transitional government to return to fight the insurgents stating that such an intervention would need an international mandate. [56]

While some of the Somalian-American recruits came from impoverished circumstances and were struggling in school, others left the United States not for a lack of opportunity, but because they were "driven by unfulfilled ambition."[57] This has forced U.S. federal agents and antiterrorism experts to rethink their assumptions concerning the successful assimilation of foreign-born Muslims into the fabric of American life. Losing the struggle again barriers of race, class, religion and language, such immigrants may be returning to their homeland to become terrorists.

The same fear is now stemming from Sweden which accepts more than 1,000 Somali refugees per month. There is reason to believe that pro-Al Shabab militants heavily recruit from this population, encouraging them to return to Somalia for training and indoctrination.[58] Moreover, there are increasing linkages in recruitment and funding between the notorious Somali pirates and Al Shabab. Indeed, the President of the semi-autonomous Somali state of Puntland, Abdirahman Mohamud Farole, believes the two groups have active links.[59]

Adding another layer of complexity, the African Union Mission in Somalia (AMISOM) was created by the African Union's Peace and Security Council on January 19, 2007, as a peacekeeping mission.[60] It is operated by the African Union with the approval of the United Nations. On February 20, 2007, the UN Security Council authorized it to deploy a six-month peacekeeping mission, and after four years on August 5, 2011, AMISOM finally seized control of Mogadishu.[61] Its nearly 12,000 troops were recruited mainly from Burundi and Uganda, although its commander, Major-General Fred Muguisha, estimated that 20,000 troops will be needed if the military gains are to be secured.[62]

It should be noted that Al Shabab mercilessly killed 74 Ugandan civilians in Uganda watching the World Cup finals in 2010,[63] perhaps in an attempt to make Uganda pull out its troops. While this may serve the short-term goals of Al Shabab, it deeply affected the desperate Somalis seeking refuge in Uganda. Their access to a safe haven may now be soon cut off.[64]

Senior leaders of Al Shabab have also vowed to send their militant fighters to Yemen, or wherever jihad beckons. Al Shabab has now strengthened its ties to Al Qaeda and is prepared to unite with another militant group, Hizbul Islam, and engage in militant struggles in Somalia and beyond.[65]

3.   *Mali*

One of the unintended consequences of deposing Colonel Qaddafi in Libya in October 2011 was that fighters and weapons easily moved across Algeria into Mali. While Mali lacks Libya's strategic importance since it does not have oil or other resources, it bears a striking resemblance to Afghanistan when the Taliban assumed power in the late 1980s. Mali's insurgent population is mainly composed of Tuaregs, a nomadic Berber people, whose uprising in the Spring of 2012 wrested control of the northern half of Mali which they renamed Azawad.[66] The weak response of the central government led to a military coup in the capital of Bamako. The coup d'état effectively replaced the civilian government with a military junta that vowed to defeat the rebels, but the northern part of the country has been, in effect, abandoned.[67]

The insurgent elements of the Tuareg rebellion also included a radical Islamist group known as Ansar Dine which is affiliated with Al Qaeda in the Islamic Maghreb. Ansar Dine's fighters have seized various Malian cities and imposed a Taliban-styled rule that includes vandalizing and demolishing sacred tombs and monuments, administering repeated whippings and other punishments in the street for ostensibly violating Islamic law, thus provoking the outrage of the international community.[68] Although the military junta has ostensibly ceded political control to a civilian government, the Malian Army is seen as being in total disarray. Thousands are fleeing Mali which is now being regarded as a magnet for Islamic extremists.[69] This is a particularly incendiary situation since francophone West Africa, including

Togo, Côte d'Ivoire and Gabon, are all in a state of siege, complete with mass demonstrations, assaults against police.[70] This is precisely the powder keg that leads itself to infiltration by extremist elements.

The Economic Community of West African States (ECOWAS), at the formal request of Mali's interim leader, Dioncounda Traore, is ready to deploy a standby force of some 3,000 troops to northern Mali, where Islamist rebels are trying to impose a harsh form of Shari'a, or Islamic law. In the words of ECOWAS's communications director, "For every day that there is a delay, the situation deteriorates and now we can see the evidence of this deterioration, which makes it more compelling for us to act in unity and for us to act as expeditiously as possible in resolving the situation."[71] The situation is unfolding, and we can only hope for a speedy, peaceful and civil society-based resolution in Mali.

4.   Yemen

It is difficult to determine whether Yemen is a failing state, but there is reason to feel hopeful that it is not. Yemen was part of the remarkable so-called Arab Spring of 2011 that will be discussed in further detail in Chapter 3. President Ali Abdullah Saleh was ousted after a 33-year rule following massive street protests for over a year where hundreds were killed. In February 2012, Yemeni voters took part in presidential elections as part of a power transfer deal voting in Mr. Saleh's former deputy, Abdu Rabbu Mansour Hadi, as President. Nevertheless, former president Saleh's relatives still maintained control of the army.

President Hadi announced that he was replacing or reassigning 20 military officers and governors of four provinces, thus purging several of Mr. Saleh's loyalists. President Hadi has left the former president's son in charge of the powerful Republican Guard. However, Mr. Saleh's half-brother, Mohammed Saleh al-Ahmar, commands the air force, and has refused to leave.[72] In response to the continued control of the armed forces by Saleh's cronies, Yemeni protesters have not moved from Change Square as the protest site in front of Sana'a University in the capital city of Sana'a is known. "We will stay here until they restructure the army; then we will consider our revolution a success," said a youth activist.[73]

Moreover, there are additional problems in bringing about true regime change. Although north and South Yemen unified in 1990, the south has been ignored economically and politically, and fractions and secessionist movements have arisen in the midst of this discontent.[74] Separatists are not a monolithic group but are composed of Bedouin gangs and others but more importantly, Ansar al-Sharia, an affiliate of Al Qaeda. Ansar militants have killed and captured many Yemeni soldiers including those at a military post west of the Abyan Province, Zinjibar, northeast of Aden, a port city in the south of Yemen.[75]

Even more disturbingly, Ansar al-Sharia functions as a de facto government in the Abyan and Shabwa provinces of Yemen. They have taken a page out of Hamas' playbook and distribute food rations to civilians, provide police services and run strict Islamic courts, thus providing government services that the central government has failed to provide. This wins them the loyalty of locals and strengthens their political and tactical base. In the end, a Hobbesian dilemma faces the Yeminis as well since "[t]here is no central leadership. We have no economy. There is no foundation anymore for an independent country. We just end up fighting among ourselves."[76]

(a)   Yemen: Constitutional and Legal Implications for the United States

Yemen also poses a difficult challenge for the United States. Al Qaeda in the Arabian Peninsula (AQAP) provides English language videos, newsletters and a magazine called, *Inspire*, replete with bomb-making instructions.[77] The Yemini operational arm of AQAP focused on the speech-making of American-born Anwar al-Awlaki (reputedly the spiritual leader of U.S. Army Major Nidal Malik Hasan accused of 13 counts of murder in the 2011 Ft. Hood killings) and American-born Samir Khan, both of whom were killed in a U.S. drone attack in September 30, 2011, thus severely debilitating the AQAP English language franchise.[78]

Although the following discussion lies outside the scope of this particular framework of analysis, it is an important digression to make. The deaths of American-born or U.S. citizen "jihadis" raise important, complex and in some ways, intractable legal and political issues for the United States.

At the outset, it is important to keep in mind that the U.S. has spent over $326 million in security and civilian aid to Yemen since 2007, partly in response to the threat posed by AQAP.[79] This aid was halted in the wake of civilian unrest during 2011, prior to the ouster of former President Saleh. However, the Pentagon is contemplating spending upwards of $75 million in military and related aid to Yemen beginning in 2012.

In fact, in 2010, the U.S. Central Command proposed supplying Yemen with $1.2 billion in military equipment and training over a period of six years. The military aid would have included automatic weapons, coastal patrol boats, transport planes and helicopters, training of Yemeni forces, and supplying U.S. logistical advisers accompanying Yemenis troops on helicopter missions.[80]

"The Yemen operation has raised a broader question: who should be running the shadow war? White House officials are debating whether the C.I.A. should take over the Yemen campaign as a 'covert action,' which would allow the United States to carry out operations even without the approval of Yemen's government. By law, covert action programs require presidential authorization and formal notifications to the Congressional intelligence committees. No such requirements apply to the military's so-called Special Access Programs, like the Yemen strikes."[81] Blurring the line between soldiers and spies could have the downstream effect of compromising U.S. troops by denying them Geneva Convention protections, and weakening Congressional oversight over secret operations overseas.[82]

To provide a fuller background on how the U.S. Government may engage in hostilities, Article I, section 8 of the U.S. Constitution gives the U.S. Congress the power to declare war, fund troops and support the armed forces.[83] Article II gives the president the Commander in Chief role.[84] In response to the Vietnam era, the U.S. Congress enacted the War Powers Resolution of 1973[85] which checks the president's power to engage in covert armed operations by requiring him to consult with Congress "in every possible instance"[86] before committing U.S. armed forces into armed conflict. The President must report to Congress within 48 hours after he has authorized U.S. troops abroad[87] and must end hostilities within 60 days unless Congress has declared war or where an attack on the United States has rendered the removal of such troops impossible.[88]

Moreover, political assassinations abroad are prohibited by Executive Orders issued by Presidents Gerald Ford and Ronald Reagan, respectively.[89] Despite the ban, President Reagan authorized an aerial strike of Colonel Gaddafi's Libyan home in 1986, and President Clinton also ordered the capture or assassination of Osama bin Laden. However, the U.S. Justice Department in classified opinions has found that the assassination ban does not apply to military targets. Since terrorists were deemed to be legitimate military targets, the Justice Department held that the ban does not apply to them.[90] (Additionally, there is a federal statute that bans Americans killing other Americans overseas.)[91]

Following 9/11, the U.S. Congress passed the Authorization for the Use of Military Force (AUMF) giving the President the authority to use "all necessary and appropriate force" against those responsible for the 9/11 attacks.[92] This act has been used to justify military operations against Al Qaeda and other terrorist networks and operatives. Concerned that the AUMF may be used to legally justify extra-judicial killings overseas, the American Civil Liberties Union (ACLU) filed a lawsuit on behalf of Anwar al-Awlaki's father challenging the authority to kill him in Yemen using a drone strike. The federal district court judge dismissed the lawsuit as one raising a non-justiciable political question, holding that the matter should be resolved by Congress and not the courts.[93]

Specifically, the Court held in relevant part that:

> Rather, the Court only concludes that it lacks the capacity to determine whether a specific individual in hiding overseas, whom the Director of National Intelligence has stated is an 'operational member' of AQAP, . . . presents such a threat to national security that the United States may authorize the use of lethal force against him. This Court readily acknowledges that it is a 'drastic measure' for the United States to employ lethal force against one of its own citizens abroad, even if that citizen is currently playing an operational role in a 'terrorist group that has claimed responsibility for numerous attacks against Saudi, Korean, Yemeni, and U.S. targets since 2009, . . . Because decision-making in the realm of military and foreign affairs is textually committed to the political braches [of U.S. Government], and because courts are functionally ill-equipped to make the types of complex policy

judgments that would be required to adjudicate the merits of plaintiff's claims, the Court finds that the political questions doctrine bars judicial resolution of this case.[94]

However, this case raises difficult legal questions on whether U.S. citizens abroad are entitled to due process protections such as the filing of formal charges of treason or other criminal charges, the right to counsel, and the right to a jury, the right to a speedy trial, and other U.S. Constitutional protections.[95]

In elucidating the criteria used by the Executive Branch in ordering such extra-judicial killings overseas, U.S. Attorney General, Eric Holder, stated that a three-part test must be met in order to determine whether a targeted killing is justified: (1) that the U.S. citizen poses an imminent threat of violent attack against the United States; (2) capture is not feasible, and (3) the killing would be consistent with the laws of war.[96] He also denied the suggestion that this type of killing mandated that the president seek federal court permission before taking lethal action against a U.S. citizen. Moreover, the Obama Administration is still refusing to release the Justice Department legal opinion on al-Awlaki's killing through the Freedom of Information Act process.[97]

As an additional complication, the action to kill al-Awlaki was taken without the knowledge and consent of the Yemeni government on its territory. The question of whether al-Awlaki was an enemy combatant and its legal implications fall outside the scope of this examination, but these are serious and sobering legal questions that need to be addressed by the United States.[98] These are all difficult legal and constitutional questions made more difficult to resolve by the exigent circumstances of a so-called global war on terror.

Returning to our main discussion, the franchising effect of radical jihadism is being spurred on by the availability of safe havens in which to plan and launch their attacks. This effort by Al Qaeda operatives to expand their bases of operation now includes the Sahel, an ungoverned terrain between Saharan and sub-Saharan Africa. Indeed, there is evidence that Al Qaeda's affiliate in North Africa has carried out a number of killings, bombings and other lethal attacks against Westerners and African security forces recently. Counterintelligence officials claim that foreign fighters are returning from Iraq and, further, that these recent attacks in North Africa "reflect Al Qaeda's growing tentacles in the northern tier of Africa, outside the group's sanctuary in Pakistan's tribal areas."[99]

The implications of the potential territorial expansion were so alarming that the U.S. State Department began its Pan-Sahel Initiative in 2002, a counterterrorism program that partnered with local militaries in Mali, Niger, Chad and Mauritania.[100] The program expanded in 2005 in conjunction with the U.S. Agency for International Development (USAID) and the Pentagon to include Nigeria, Senegal, Morocco, Algeria and Tunisia. Succinctly stated, "Al Qaeda established sanctuaries in the Sahel, and in 2006 it acquired a North African franchise."

C.   Failed States

Moving away from the particularities of Pakistan, Somalia, Yemen and the Sahel, a broader examination into what constitutes a failure of the state is warranted here. While there may not be a universally accepted definition of a failed state, certain overarching themes have emerged. For example, the definition of a failed state used by the British Department for International Development is, "[g]overnments that cannot or will not deliver core functions to the majority of its people, including the poor. . . . The most important functions of the state for poverty reduction are territorial control, safety and security, capacity to manage public resources, delivery of basic services, and the ability to protect and support the ways in which the poorest people sustain themselves."[101]

More broadly speaking, "[n]ation-states exist to deliver political goods—security, education, health services, economic opportunity, environmental surveillance, a legal framework of order and a judicial system to administer it, and fundamental infrastructural requirements such as roads and communications facilities—to their citizens. Failed states honor these obligations in the breach. They increasingly forfeit their function as providers of political goods to warlords and other nonstate actors. In other words, a failed state is no longer able or willing to perform the job of a nation-state in the modern world."[102]

However, there is an even more dire possibility. A failed state may simply collapse or implode. "A collapsed state is an extreme version of a failed state. It has a total vacuum of authority. A collapsed state is a mere geographical expression, a black hole into which a failed polity has fallen. When a state such as Somalia collapses (or Lebanon and Afghanistan a decade ago and Sierra Leone in the late 1990s), substate actors take over. . . . Yet, within the collapsed state prevail disorder, anomic behavior, and the kinds of anarchic mentality and entrepreneurial pursuits—especially gun and drug running—that are compatible with networks of terror."[103]

Thus, there is a disconcerting spectrum of weak, fragile, failing, failed, and collapsed states. What is the internal dynamic that makes a weak state become a fragile one? Why does a failing state actually fail or even collapse? Why, for example, did Somalia collapse?[104] In contrast, why does Indonesia, a weak state continue to weather tsunamis, secessions, corruption and ethnic strife yet continue to strengthen its democracy? This complex alchemy lies outside the scope of this writing, but it forms the backdrop of what may be creating the maelstrom giving rise to fundamentalist Islamic-based terrorism.

In trying to bring some policy cohesion to this complex phenomenon, USAID,[105] for example, refers to "fragile states" as a broad range of failed, failing and recovering states. USAID defines "vulnerable states" as states that are unable or unwilling to adequately assure the provision of safety and basic services to significant portions of their populations and where the legitimacy of the government is in question. This includes states that are failing or recovering from crisis." States "in crisis" refers to states "where the central government does not exert effective control over its own territory or is unable or unwilling to assure the provision of vital services to significant parts of its territory, where the legitimacy of the government is weak or nonexistent, and where violent conflict is a reality or a great risk."[106]

USAID also proposes the "Fragility Framework" as the means for analyzing governance in fragile states, reproduced below.

It is worth keeping in mind, however, that, "[n]ot all failed states are created equal. Not all will be equally important to the United States and the international community. Each stable country must gauge its involvement in failed or failing states according to its own resources and interests. Nor can

**Table 1. Analyzing Governance in Fragile States: The Fragility
Framework**

	Effectiveness	**Legitimacy**
Security	Military and police services that secure borders and limit crime	Military and police services that are provided reasonably, equitably, and without major violation of human rights
Political	Political institutions and processes that adequately ensure response to citizen needs	Political processes, norms, and leaders that are acceptable to the citizenry
Economic	Economic and financial institutions and infrastructure that support economic growth (including jobs), adapt to economic change, and manage natural resources	Economic institutions, financial services, and income-generating opportunities that are widely accessible and reasonably transparent, particularly related to access to and governance of natural resources
Social	Provision of basic services that generally meet demand, including that of vulnerable and minority groups, is assured	Tolerance of diverse customs, cultures, and beliefs

Source: USAID, "The Fragile States Strategy," (PD-ACA-999)(January 2005)
available at http://www.usaid.gov/policy/2005_fragile_states_strategy.pdf at 4.

a 'one size fits all' approach be used to address the broad diversity of cases.
Although conceptual threads link these situations, the approach to dealing
with failed and dangerously weak states must be tailored to each case."[107]

Eight policy options have been offered in order to deal with failed
states by the Center for Strategic and International Studies (CSIS), a review
of which may be useful in this context. The first option is to do nothing,
and hope that the problem resolves itself on its own. This is a tried and true
approach of the foreign policy of most governments, but it may have its
drawbacks as the example of Afghanistan illustrates. American withdrawal

from and inattention to Afghanistan following the cessation of hostilities with the former Soviet Union in 1989 proved to be disastrous in the end. And while a wholehearted intervention following a post-conflict situation may also not be warranted, a clear and objective policy review of what may be at stake certainly is.

A second option is to quarantine a state by monitoring and intercepting potential threats such as in the case of North Korea or Somalia. However, this piecemeal approach may be costly and ineffective over time if an overall strategic approach is not developed and implemented. A third option is to "disassemble" the state in question and create smaller entities. Again, Somalia affords an example of this, but the long-term viability of Somaliland, Puntland and other provinces as independent quasi-state entities remains questionable. A fourth option is to integrate or absorb the failed state into another entity. While territorial expansion may be an attractive option to resource-starved states, absorbing a failed state is often politically and economically unviable for a host of complex reasons.

A fifth option is to establish a transitional international authority or trust arrangement to permit a transition to actual viable statehood. This was the case in East Timor and Kosovo, and requires the active participation of the international community. This may, in fact, be a viable political option in certain instances. A sixth option is to establish a regional authority as a "watchdog" as with the Association of Southeast Asian Nations (ASEAN) acting in Cambodia, and the Economic Community of West African States (ECOWAS) acting in Liberia and Sierra Leone, respectively. The utility of this type of arrangement remains open to question since the underlying sources of the conflict are not addressed in this situation. The seventh option is to support one of the sides in the conflict with the hope that it ultimately prevails–a tactic used extensively in the proxy wars of the Cold War which often led to uneven and politically unsustainable results.

A final, eighth option proposed by CSIS is encouraging the international community to develop a post-conflict reconstruction strategy to maintain regional stability, definitively end the conflict, and begin the political and economic reconstruction process.[108] I realize that the "Washington consensus" view presented here perhaps limits the utility of this analysis, but it still has a broad range of reasonable policy options to offer.

Further, CSIS urges that the term, "post-conflict reconstruction" be used in lieu of "nation-building" for several reasons. First, nation-building was associated with the post World War II U.S.-led reconstruction efforts in Japan and Germany. A salient political aim was to convert the defeated governments into "friendly" allies of the U.S. Government and its political allies. The historical associations of the term "nation-building" implies that there is an underlying political agenda that is not as quite as palatable or "politically correct" in the current context. Moreover, the international community is providing tactical assistance to encourage the post-conflict reconstruction process. In contrast, the actual task of *nation-building* falls to the host country and its citizens.

Finally, four pillars of action are proposed by CSIS, namely, (1) security; (2) justice and reconciliation; (3) social and economic well-being; and (4) governance and participation. Adopting a unified international effort using a strategic approach was strongly recommended.[109] These four pillars are reflected, in essence, by the essential tasks outlined in April 2005 by the U.S. State Department's Office of the Coordinator for Reconstruction and Stabilization (S/CRS). The S/CRS was created in July 2004 by the Department of State in response, in part, to several pieces of legislation introduced by the U.S. Congress reflecting the widespread recognition that the U.S. Government needed a strategic approach to carrying out post-conflict operations.[110]

The S/CRS document, "Essential Tasks" set forth the "requirements to support countries in transition from armed conflict or civil strife to sustaining stability."[111] This document builds on the "Joint CSIS/AUSA Post-Conflict Reconstruction (PCR) Task Framework" from *Winning the Peace: An American Strategy for Post-Conflict Reconstruction*, edited by Robert C. Orr, and published by the CSIS Press in 2004. It was the baseline S/CRS used at its inception to lead six interagency working groups through a discussion and amplification of the task matrix.

After several months of interagency discussion, the original CSIS/AUSA task framework was divided into five technical sectors: (1) security; (2) governance and participation; (3) humanitarian assistance and social well-being; (4) economic stabilization and infrastructure; and, (5) justice and reconciliation.[112] The policy considerations for strengthening weak states and preventing their failure are obvious. As the example of Afghanistan demonstrates, the process of post-conflict reconstruction is a long, time-consuming, expensive and contentious process.

Richard Rotberg observes that:

> Strengthening states prone to failure before they fail is prudent policy and contributes significantly to world order and to minimizing combat, casualties, refugees, and displaced persons. Doing so is far less expensive than reconstructing states after failure. Strengthening weak states also has the potential to eliminate the authority and power vacuums within which terror thrives. . . . Preventing state failure is imperative, difficult, and costly. Yet, doing so is profoundly in the interest not only of the inhabitants of the most deprived and ill-governed states of the world, but also of world peace.[113]

Many countries in the developing world are fragile, weakened or collapsed. While the causes for the "failure" of such states differ, and the classifications of "failed states" change constantly, there is basic agreement on the definition of a failed state: a state that has failed in its basic obligation to provide for the basic human needs of its population.[114]

Other indicia of a failed state are its inability to provide security, its flawed institutions, decaying infrastructure, endemic corruption, ineffective public health and education systems, and unparalleled economic opportunities for the privileged few.[115]

In essence, these states failed to create, implement and sustain viable infrastructure growth in four discrete respects: (1) physical infrastructure (e.g., transportation, telecommunications, and power); (2) social infrastructure (i.e., institutions supporting education, health and welfare); (3) financial infrastructure (creating viable indigenous capital markets and ensuring access to world capital and trade markets); and (4) legal infrastructure (creating and implementing a Rule of Law framework that adequately supports the internal and external economic and investment needs of the country along with courts, judicial and alternate dispute resolution processes, and a government-led regulatory framework that is both rational and transparent.)

Sudan, Afghanistan, Angola, the Democratic Republic of Congo, Liberia, and Sierra Leone are often cited as "failed states" while Colombia, Indonesia, Georgia, Kyrgyzstan and Uzbekistan are sometimes cited as being at risk for failure.[116] In fact, in the Atlantic Council's Ten-Year Framework for Afghanistan, it points out that Afghanistan is now ranked at the fourth most war-torn, fifth most corrupt, seventh most fragile, and second weakest state in the world as of April 2009.[117] In sum, not only have certain states failed in fulfilling their most basic obligations to their citizenry, the failure of the state has also been one of governance itself.

Aside from the systemic corruption that acts like a sieve in these societies, the commitment to a representative, participatory democracy has often been supplanted by autocratic rule, nepotism, military coups, and non-transparent elections and practices. Attempting to address the causes of the many political failures of states now believed to be harboring or supporting fundamentalist Islamic-based terrorists would be an impossible task. Nevertheless, ameliorating and correcting some of these state failures is key to formulating an international response to Islamic-based separatist movements.

As far as a U.S.-specific response to failed states is concerned, I would urge that the expression "winning hearts and minds" be eliminated from the military and political lexicon of the United States. "Winning over" the hearts and minds of others tends to imply that this is a propaganda-based war effort. Certainly, ideas are at the core of all struggles (whether armed or unarmed). However, "convincing" others of the soundness of certain ideas of Western liberal democracies especially through the use of armed force, where necessary, seems to perpetuate the neo-colonial imprint of these ideas. If these ideas and ideals are not understood and adopted by Iraqis, Afghans, or others of their own accord, then the persuasive value of such ideas seem highly impeachable, especially when they are being disseminated at the point of a gun.

For example, the world was spellbound watching the large-scale, dramatic protests in Iran following the Presidential election in Spring 2009. It is difficult to determine whether true democratic values, a respect for free, fair, transparent elections, and the peaceful assembly of Iranian citizens are actually their core values. However, these values were so compelling to

Iranians that they risked their own lives to express such values in defiance of their own government.[118] This was particularly significant since the demonstrations, and the underlying values that may have prompted them, were not forced on Iranians by outside powers or influences. Thus, rather than insisting on "winning over the hearts and minds" of captive audiences, it may be preferable to simply let historical events play out. There is no real need to refer to a potential clash of values as a "war to be won."

Another important inquiry to be made here is whether the voluntary adoption or the military imposition of Western ideals, methods, and institutions help in this context? Regrettably, the answer is a qualified "no" with regard to the voluntary adoption of a Rule of Law agenda that is designed in theory to support the process of development. The answer is an unqualified "no" in cases where such a prescription for overarching reform is militarily imposed from without by external forces.

Regime change should come about organically from within the society in question. Forcing it upon them by outside powers, no matter how well-intentioned, may actually stifle and delay rather than facilitate regime change. The process of self-determination, no matter how painful the human cost, may be a necessary, if bloody, birthing process into true nationhood. The importance and value of the Spring 2009 uprising in Iran will form the foundation for the discussion in Chapter 3 on the implications and downstream impact of the so-called Arab Spring of 2011 which took place two years later.

On a more optimistic note, if Islamic-based separatist movements are seeking to establish new political entities (whether nation-states or some other form of autonomous self-governed unit), then perhaps this is a hopeful sign that they have not abandoned the structure of the state altogether despite its many failings. In other words, if the creation of new political entities is being actively pursued by fundamentalist, Islamic-based non-state actors, then perhaps there is still hope of entering into a constructive dialogue with them (as attempted by the Government of the Philippines, for example).

The most notable example of creating a new political entity in this context is, of course, Palestine. Unfortunately, Palestine is such a complicated and thorny political dilemma it may not, therefore, be the best model. But it does illustrate the point that there is room for a structured peace process that will hopefully end in a state-led solution.[119] A state-centered approach is far more manageable since it is both geographically contained and it fits within the generally accepted and familiar constructs of international political relations and diplomatic dialogue. It is certainly far less threatening than the "asymmetric threats" posed by Islamic fundamentalist-based global terrorism.

While the specifics of how to structure a multi-tiered, multi-actor approach to a disciplined peace process with substantive benchmarks along the way will be discussed at length later in the text, a brief summary of that approach follows:

> Stabilize the conflict area through multilateral and/or regional military intervention (such as UN peace-keeping forces where needed) in order to end civil war, strife or unrest;

> Structure a coherent and well-developed agenda with well-known, publicized and accepted benchmarks for an internationally brokered peace process that includes, *inter alia*, a truth and reconciliation process for healing purposes; and,

> Strengthen the infrastructure of the failed or collapsed state as a commitment of the international community acting in partnership with the groups in conflict, NGOs, neighboring countries, regional and multilateral organizations, the media and other non-state actors.

Of course, this begs the following question: if the infrastructure (physical, social, financial and legal) of the conflict area has collapsed in part or in whole, despite efforts to the contrary, what will make it work now? This is a complex issue that will be addressed not from the perspective of politics, but economics.

D.   Development as a Security Concept

The failure of the state as an economic actor is particularly relevant in this context. In the decades following the independence of most developing world nations, the state was the only institutional actor large enough and sufficiently creditworthy to assume an entrepreneurial function. In other words, the state was the only actor capable of borrowing funds and providing for basic human needs, including power generation, transportation, and telecommunications.

In response to the urgent needs of its population in such sectors, many states created state-owned enterprises (SOEs), which borrowed capital to support the capital infrastructure and other nation-building needs of the state. The SOEs, however, generally engaged in inefficient borrowing practices that burdened numerous developing states with high levels of debt leading to the debt crisis and the continuing debt overhang of many countries. Over time, the collapse of SOEs, the failure to create adequate private sector growth and private capital markets, the continuing debt burden, and many other complex factors led to stagnant economic growth and, in some cases, to political instability.

Susan Willett points out that:

> The relationship between poverty and conflict is evident in recent figures supplied by the Organisation for Economic Co-operation and Development. In 1998, of the thirty-four poorest countries in the world, five were engaged in conflict (Afghanistan, Cambodia, Congo Democratic Republic, Sierra Leone, and Somalia), while sixteen (Angola, Burundi, Central African Republic, Chad, Djibouti, Eritrea, Ethiopia, Haiti, Liberia, Mali, Mozambique, Niger, Nigeria, Rwanda, Uganda and Yemen) are undergoing the fragile process of transition from conflict to peace. [Footnote omitted.]

> In the developing world, the root causes of insecurity and conflict are often due to the failure of development to take hold. [Footnote omitted.] Not only does the deficiency of development lead to conflict, but conflict itself results in missed developmental opportunities.[120]

Additionally, Willette points out that most of these conflicts are intra-state (not international) in nature, and that the militarization of security problems in developing countries aggravates the problem further. Thus, long-term sustainable development is necessary not only to alleviate poverty but also to create political and economic stability that is the key to preventing conflict. She clearly states that, "[t]he plight of the poor, the marginalized and the displaced are only taken seriously when they become a *threat* to the perceived global order."[121] (Emphasis in original.)

Willett further indicates that these failures in the development process may be attributed, in part, to the policies of international financial institutions. The emphasis on "[s]tructural adjustment via market reforms and privatization–while important–are not sufficient mechanisms to provide the necessary incentives to prevent conflict, to ensure the demilitarization and rebuild war-torn economies."[122] The reluctance of such multilateral institutions to integrate conflict prevention as part of their development mandate is another shortfall in the overall development process itself.

While supporting a Rule of Law agenda is a laudable political undertaking, it is very difficult (but not impossible) to succeed. The successes of the development agenda in Asia, Eurasia, Latin America and Africa has led to mixed and uneven results. The reasons for success are few and difficult to emulate, and the reasons for failure are numerous and very complex.[123] The idea of more fully and clearly supporting a development agenda by international actors will, however, be revisited later in this discussion.

In fact, it may be argued that by creating sustainable development in fragile or failing states, the perceived need to engage in terrorist acts by separatist Islamic-based "terrorist" movements may be ameliorated and diminish over time. As discussed above, these types of movements evolved partly in response to a failure of the state; therefore, creating a more robust state entity that provides for the basic human needs of its population may stem the tide of such terrorism. Taking this approach is quite a challenge, and depends largely on external policy changes enacted by international actors working in partnership with developing nations who themselves may need to institute systemic internal policy changes.

Nevertheless, despite the best efforts that may be taken by all concerned to encourage sustainable development in developing countries with separatist fundamentalist Islamic-based terrorism, there is no guarantee that these measures will actually prevent such terrorism in the long-run.[124] The issues may simply be too complex to be fully resolved by policies that encourage sustainable development. One can only hope that such measures will help ameliorate the terrorist manifesto over time. But regardless of whether sustainable development helps to stem the tide of separatist Islamic-based terrorism, it is still a worthwhile goal to pursue in itself insofar as it ends human suffering and misery caused by poverty, both in body and in spirit.

With respect to militarily imposing Western ideals of democratic governance, market-based economies, and the Rule of Law, the only two successful modern examples of this are post-World War II Germany and Japan. In a seminal two-volume work produced by the RAND Corporation, post-World War II nation-building over the last 60 years has been systematically examined.[125] The study points out that nation-building,[126] peace-building or stabilization operations, the defining term depending on one's perspective, has been the predominant paradigm for the use of international force in a post-Cold War era. In fact, since 1989, the frequency, scale, scope and duration of these operations has steadily increased.

The study concludes that the German and Japanese occupations set a standard for post-war reconstruction that has not been equaled since. However, the determinants for success do not depend on the level of pre-existing Western culture, the relative economic development and prosperity of the country, being surrounded by other Western-styled democracies, or even on the cultural homogeneity of the population. The true determinant for success was apparently the level of effort put forth by the international community in the transformation of these post-conflict societies. Moreover, the study points out that democracy can be transplanted in non-democratic societies, and that more importantly, nation-building is not principally about economic reconstruction but about political transformation.[127]

Thus, certain preliminary conclusions may be offered here. First, the failure of the state has led to several Islamic-based separatist movements that pose grave security challenges. Secondly, nation-building is about political rather than economic transformation that *must* be undertaken by the host country in order to be successful. Finally, state failure may or may not attract global jihadists just as conversely, the success of an individual state may not necessarily stave off terrorism—there is no formulistic, predetermined relationship between the two.

Moreover, the success expected of external militarily-imposed stabilization and reconstruction operations is limited, even under the best of circumstances, and is certainly not expected to rise to the level of the successes of the German and Japanese examples. But there is another factor that, in my view, will limit the efficacy of such military solutions and ultimately produce substantially reduced positive outcomes.

The "global intifadah" philosophy and tactics of Al Qaeda and affiliated terrorist groups and cells clearly implies that they are not interested in the political or economic stability of their host nation-states. These states (in the case of Afghanistan, or the territory of Waziristan in Pakistan, for example) are all substantively "ungovernable" at present for various complex reasons. The essential conflict is not one of stabilization, reconstruction and nation-building, thereby correcting the failures of the collapsed or failing state, but rather one of a conflict in ideology, a theme that will be explored in the next chapter.

2

Global Jihadism and Its Discontents

The previous discussion drew a clear-cut distinction between two different types of fundamentalist Islamic-based terrorism: separatist-based movements and the so-called "global terrorism" of Al Qaeda and related terrorist cells and networks. I do wish to underscore the importance of making this distinction. If Western nations were to "cover all terrorists (let alone all terrorist sympathizers) with the same blanket, [this] would be a terrible mistake. Terrorists are extremely diverse in their identities and in their objectives. . . . terrorism is not an enemy that may be vanquished. It is a violent tactic that will continue to be used for as long as it is deemed effective."[1] Thus, the last chapter outlined separatist-based movements based on a failure of the state, and this chapter will discuss global jihadist movements that are based on a failure of ideology.

The failure of ideology in the 20th century is embodied in the demise of fascism, communism, Stalinism, and Soviet-backed socialism in Africa and Asia. The dramatic fall of the Berlin Wall in 1989 heralded a new post- Cold War era where old policies of containment, proxy wars, and non alignment have now become defunct. But if these ideologies have failed, what remains in its place?

The new ascendancy of the "Rule of Law" on a global scale is certainly worth considering. In the fracas of dying and defunct ideas, a core ideal of Western thought has endured, namely, Adam Smith's elevation of the drive to acquire material wealth to a classical economic ideal. This, in combination with John Locke's demand that the state protect private property and individual liberties, sets the stage for liberal political theory. In other words, the pursuit of one's own personal happiness through the material acquisition of personal wealth as well as the state's protection of individual liberties, has been elevated to a Western classical ideal. Indeed, the terrifying force of this ideal may be its universality.

While Western societies developed legal structures over the centuries to protect private property—such as contract enforcement, mortgages, secured loans, liens, and bankruptcy proceedings—and to ensure the protection of individual liberties—for example, by passing a Bill of Rights and ensuring the due process of law, non-Western societies did not, for the most part, develop similar institutions. What began revolutionizing our world at the end of the last millennium was not the adoption of a Western classical ideal by the non Western world, but the adoption of the Western *methodology* of achieving this ideal through private property, democratic governance, and the Rule of Law. The adoption of this Western-based methodology is what has fueled, in principal part, the legal reform efforts in the developing world for the past 60 years.

However, merely adopting Western-styled institutions and approaches without understanding or accepting the underlying philosophical and ideological foundation that supports liberal democracies and market-based economies has been proven to be a fallacy. It is deceptively misleading to expect the same successes in democratic governance and economic growth without at least examining the ideological foundation of such systems.

In other words, Western-styled approaches and institutions have been adopted by many developing countries in principle, but not the underlying philosophical ideal that forms its foundation. This has led to somewhat anomalous results insofar as the "illiberal" ideologies and tactics of "terrorist" groups such as Hamas in Palestine and Hezbollah in Lebanon have now been legitimized politically. These so-called "terrorist groups" have now formed political parties, and their respective political platforms of using terrorism to achieve their political goals have been legitimized through an electoral process. Both parties are now parliamentary members of those countries, respectively. In other words, these groups (considered to be terrorists in the view of the U.S. Government)[2] have used parliamentary elections, for example, as a new, sophisticated means by which to acquire political power. Thus, "terrorist means" have been used to accomplish "political ends."

If the failure of ideology on a worldwide scale in the past century has led to the superficial ascendancy of Western-based institutions, the failure of ideology in the Arab world in the post-World War II pursuit of modernity has been perhaps even more painful, and has not led to the same result. Fareed Zakaria writes: "for the Arab world, modernity has been one failure after another. Each path followed–socialism, secularism, nationalism–has turned into a dead end. . . . .If there is one great cause of the rise of Islamic fundamentalism, it is the total failure of political institutions in the Arab world."[3]

Modernization is now viewed as Westernization, globalization or worse, Americanization but, as Zakaria points out, "[i]mporting the inner stuffings of modern society–a free market, political parties, accountability and the rule of law–is difficult and dangerous."[4] Going back to an earlier theme, the failure to demand that state leaders take a more informed and critical approach to issues of governance and economic growth by the people that they govern also constitutes part of the failure of the state.

The profound transformation of the frustration, sense of humiliation, and despair in the Arab world into an ideology of hatred involves a very complex alchemy. On the surface, it appears that Islamic-based separatists have responded to the crisis of the state in a secularized fashion using violence as a means to gain political power. Other scholars have, however, pointed to a historical genesis and a culturally specific predisposition that may be worth visiting as a backdrop to this discussion.

Eric Chaney, a Harvard University economics professor, looks the "democracy deficit" in the Arab world and posits that merely being a Muslim-majority country does not cause a lack of democracy.[5] He points to Muslim majority states such as Albania, Bangladesh, Malaysia, Indonesia and Turkey, all of whom has functioning democracies. He also looks to whether Arab culture is to blame. But the democracy deficit is also found in non-Arab states such as Chad, Iran, Azerbaijan, Tajikistan, Uzbekistan. So, if Islam as a religion or the Arab culture cannot be blamed, who is the culprit?

He looks to history and asserts that "the democracy deficit exists in lands that were conquered by Arab armies after the death in A.D. 632

of the Prophet Mohammad. Lands that the Arabs controlled in the 12th century remain economically stunted today. This correlation is not simply a coincidence. . . . Arab imperial control tended to mean centralized political authority, weak civil society, a dependent merchant class and a large role for the state in the economy."[6] This, compounded with fewer trade unions and less access to credit, meant that civil society in Arab societies remained underdeveloped.

On an optimistic note, Fareed Zakaria concludes that, "Chaney does not point to immutable factors such as culture or religion as the causes of the problem. History—and the habits it engendered—are democracy's biggest foes in the Arab world. If political structures and institutional design and its legacies are to blame, then as these change, things should improve. It is a prescription for the very long term, but at least it is a prescription."

An emotional prism has been used as well to explain this strange alchemy. Dominique Moïsi explores how fear, humiliation and hope are reshaping the post-modern world in dramatic ways. Why fear, hope and humiliation instead of anger, despair, hatred, resentment, love, courage, honor or other emotions? He asserts that these three emotions "are closely linked with the notion of *confidence,* which is the defining factor in how nations and people address the challenges they face as well as how they relate to one another." (Emphasis in original)[7]

He explains:

> Fear is the absence of confidence. If your life is dominated by fear, you are apprehensive about the present and expect the future to be more dangerous. Hope, by contrast, is an expression of confidence; is based on the conviction that today is better than yesterday and that tomorrow will be better than today. And humiliation is the injured confidence of those who have lost hope in the future; your lack of hope is the fault of others, who have treated you badly in the past. When the contrast between your idealized and glorious past and your frustrating present is too great, humiliation prevails. . . . These three emotions express the level of trust you have in yourself. Confidence is as vital for nations and civilizations as for individuals, because confidence allows you to project yourself into the future, to fulfill your capabilities, and even

to transcend them.[8]

Interestingly enough, there seems to be a superficial convergence between the two lines of thinking between Moïsi and Chaney. Moïsi identifies the primary cause of humiliation in Arab societies is a sense of historical decline which he traces back to the end of the 17th century. "If in the seventh century Arabs were able to create a world into which other peoples were drawn, in the nineteenth and twentieth centuries they themselves were drawn into a new world created by Western Europe."[9]

So, it may be argued that the decline of the flowering of Arab conquest (not the actual conquest itself) led to a sense of decline, defeat and humiliation. Interestingly, a different response could have resulted. Instead of feeling the pain of humiliation, young Arabs could look to the reasons for the decline of Arab domination and the reasons for the ascendancy of Western values, institutions and law. Rather than modeling themselves on Western democracies, the Arab world could have looked to other non-Arab Muslim nations such as Turkey, Malaysia and Indonesia for a sense of how to reconcile Islamic values and practices in a post-modern world.

Instead however, "[f]or most Arabs and Muslims living in Western countries, the sense of humiliation and frustration that they feel is as much cultural as it is socioeconomic in nature. What leads them to despair is their deep feeling of alienation from most of the modern world, a frustration that is all the more painful because of the scars from a not so distant colonial past. Where the colonial history has a particular resonance, the sense of alienation is particularly profound."[10]

Thus, it appears that in response to the failure of modernity and its accompanying ideological foundation, Al Qaeda has developed a more profoundly religiously-influenced "new ideology of hate."[11] This ideology empowers its adherents through hatred and the single-minded pursuit of disruption, terrorism, and the destabilization of Western-styled economies. Its actions are largely of symbolic value that feed off the despair, disempowerment and disenfranchisement of frenzied young Muslims. Rather than holding Arab leaders accountable for their actions, this distrust has metastasized into an uncompromising hatred of Western ideals, values, institutions, symbols and peoples.

This new generation of terrorists has no interest in undertaking the hard work of nation-building. In fact, this brand of terrorism is not based on the failure of the state–the state has already imploded as in the failed state of Afghanistan, or is in the process of gradual decline and potential collapse in Pakistan unless its political and, at times, armed conflict with Taliban forces ends. This type of terrorism is not only based on a failure of Western-based ideology supporting "liberal democracy," but, more disturbingly, is also based on the ascendancy of a new ideology of hatred.

For a more informed view of the ideological motivations of global jihadists, I turn to Ekaterina Stepanova, who writes:

> According to the modern interpretations, holy war [jihad] may take several forms. The principal distinction is between internal (or greater) jihad–religious and spiritual self-perfection and self-purification–and external (or lesser) jihad–armed struggle against aggressors and tyrants. In these interpretations, external jihad is not necessarily the most important, is defensive in nature and is a means of last resort. In contrast, the ideologues of violent Islamism believe armed jihad to be the main weapon in countering the multiple threats and challenges to 'the rule of God' on earth. . . . This extremist view is supported by the belief in both historical and more recent injustices, ranging from political suppression and direct occupation of Muslim lands to the socio-economic marginalization of Muslims by the West. The strongest dissatisfaction is expressed with regard to the policies of the USA, the United Kingdom and Israel. Extremists also build on the lack of legitimacy of the ruling elites and governments in their own countries and have a record of undermining secular nationalist regimes (e.g., in many Arab states).[12]

Apart from the internal/external jihad distinction, there are three other subdivisions applicable to external jihadism: liberation, anti-apostate, and global jihad. Liberation jihad is an armed struggle to forcibly remove "occupiers" or "non-believers" from Muslim territories such as Afghanistan, Kashmir, Mindanao or Palestine. Liberation jihad defines the separatist movements discussed in Chapter 1, and conforms to the basic contours of nationalist or ethno-separatist insurgency movements. In contrast, the anti-apostate movements target "impious" Muslim regimes such as those in Egypt and elsewhere, and are not relevant to this particular analysis, but will be addressed in the next chapter.

Finally, global jihad is "a transnational (or more precisely, supranational) movement founded by [Osama] bin laden and al-Qaeda with an ultimate goal of establishing Islamic rule worldwide. . . the use of terrorist means in global jihad qualifies as superterrorism. This categorization is dictated by the unlimited, universalist nature of its ultimate goals and agenda. Thus, if the categorization of jihad into liberation, internal and global is to be accepted, global jihad is the most radical and poses the greatest challenge to international security."[13]

In the view of the U.S. Government, Al Qaeda's ultimate goal is to establish a Caliphate (a Muslim empire) to wage war with the United States and its allies beginning with the expulsion of U.S. forces from Iraq.[14] This point of view, also held by academics, military strategists and others, tends to superimpose order on highly disordered asymmetric threats.[15] While establishing a caliphate may be the declared objective of global jihadists, [16] it is unclear whether there is an actual overall strategic approach in place by them that will ultimately establish a caliphate.

One commentator writes, "[t]oday, in contrast, we face a foe who rejects the (Western) Westphalian model, an enemy who is not interested in a war of self-determination in the classic sense of postcolonial independence. Instead, he fights for a worldwide religious supremacy, and this is why there is so much talk of al Qaeda and Associated Movements (AQAM) as representing the first global insurgency, and now we must counter with a global counterinsurgency. [Footnote omitted.] His idea of self-determination is not tied to the nation-state, but to a global theocracy, the Caliphate, within which all shall be subject to the will of Allah, and not the will of the people."[17]

Indeed, even if Al Qaeda's actions are designed to impose political change from within as witnessed in the regime change in Spain following the train bombings in Madrid in 2004, the downstream political impact stemming from these bombings seem to be more accidental than deliberately planned by the terrorists.[18] While lacking a discernable overall strategic vision or mission, two themes implicit in jihadism seem to be relatively clear:

(1) to free the Muslim world from Western political, economic and cultural influences and, to a lesser extent, (2) to impose Shari'ah-based Islamic law, free from the confines of a Western "rule of law" regime.

Perhaps more broadly speaking, "[t]he Islamic terrorist agenda is more inflexible than most of us imagine, and its ends are defined, not in terms of the transient political parameters of the discourse of international relations, but by a perspective rooted in religious absolutisms that will endure long after the reverberations of the crises in transition in Afghanistan or in Iraq have come to an end."[19]

If, however, Taliban rule in Afghanistan heralds the new form of fundamentalist Islamic-based governance, it still leaves in place two glaring problems: poverty and political repression. Economic backwardness, political repression, systemic violations of the rights of women and ethnic and religious minorities, and the lack of international legitimacy marginalizes such a regime. While it may be following the strictures of Islamic law (and even that may be open to question),[20] it cannot achieve its own political integrity or economic progress.

In fact, there is new thinking on the relationship of violence to poverty. The authors of a 2011 World Bank report argue that violence is not just one cause among many in creating poverty: it is the primary cause.[21] The trap nowadays may be the violence trap rather than the poverty trap. If true, this has truly profound consequences for poor countries affected by internal strife and for the advanced countries trying to help them. Indeed, the symbiotic nature of violence and its relation to poverty often poses the circular question of whether countries are violent because they are poor, or poor because they are violent?[22]

The World Bank report points out that the legitimacy of government matters as well.[23] The report counsels that more attention needs to be given to the prevention of violence and quickly restoring the peoples' faith in government. Also, the report urged that outside actors stop treating these conflicts as civil wars with clearly defined roles for diplomats, soldiers, humanitarian and aid workers. People need to act together regardless of how an aid worker may feel about working in tandem with soldiers or police officers. (This is a question that will be revisited in Chapter 7.) Finally, much more patience is needed by all actors, albeit a difficult pathway to take for all concerned.[24]

The creators and the adherents of Al Qaeda's new ideology of hatred are educated, wealthy, privileged and successful by Western standards, as are their new recruits who are Western-educated engineers, physicians, and other affluent professionals. This ideology is not one that advances the economic or political stability of a nation-state in order to create stable, viable state-oriented structures of governance and economic production–this is not at all the goal of "global terrorists." In fact, it may be argued that global terrorists emerging from the European context demonstrate that living in stable political economies does not deter them from adopting the ideology of hatred. Nor does it deter them from engaging in acts of terrorism–quite the contrary, in fact.

One study points out that terrorists have traditionally been well-educated individuals. In fact, well-educated counter-elites have formed the leadership cadre for violent extremist movements throughout time, beginning with the late-19th century Russian anarchists and Marxists.[25] Other studies have revealed that the members and supporters of Hezbollah in Lebanon and Hamas in Palestine tend to have a higher educational and socio-economic profile than their fellow citizens.[26]

The genesis of the ascent of radical Islamic-based global jihadist movements began with the formation of Israel in 1948, with the tipping point being the 1967 war. The sociological profile that is emerging from more recent global jihadist movements seems to indicate that the "old guard" of the 1980s came from predominantly upper and middle class backgrounds. The second wave of the 1990s were predominantly middle class, and were less well-educated. The third wave of new jihadists who joined following the invasion of Iraq in 2003 tend to be poorer, less educated, and more socially marginalized than their predecessors. Many are only marginally literate and have not finished high school.[27]

It may be unclear as to what these "waves" may suggest. Perhaps this latest wave of jihadists reflect both the recruitment practices and the appeal of the jihadist message to individuals with a lower socio-economic profile and less privileged life experiences. Perhaps their motivations for becoming violent extremists may be based less on ideology and intellectual thought and more on emotional values and responses. The underlying emotional motivations may lie in a deep-rooted desire to be accepted and belong to a larger group or cause. Indeed, there may also be an economic motivation insofar as suicide bombers may regard pay-offs to their family as a means of income generation even if it is earned at the cost of their own lives.

Two aspects of global jihadism are important to highlight in this context. First, the relationship of poverty to global terrorism forms a necessary component of this analysis. Secondly, the relationship of civil liberties and democratic governance is also a key determinant of fundamentalist Islamic-based terrorism.

While definitive statements that "poverty has little to do with terrorism,"[28] have been offered, this conclusion may overlook the context that poverty plays in driving individuals toward violent extremism. Poverty impedes a state's capacity to stem the flow of corruption, protect its borders effectively, ensure equitable development for all of its citizens, provide physical and social infrastructure to support the basic needs of its population, and provide equitable participation in its governance through free and fair elections. Thus, these factors lead to a downtrodden and depressed state of its citizenry where educational, economic and entrepreneurial opportunities may be limited to the elite or privileged classes, or simply be non-existent.

In fact, there is evidence that the Taliban in Pakistan has taken advantage of the underlying class rifts coupled with a lack of governance and a failure to provide fair, speedy and equitable justice. Following its independence in 1947, Pakistan maintained a privileged class of landowning elites while the workers on their land remained poor, uneducated and economically downtrodden. The Pakistani Government failed to provide even the rudiments of proper health care, educational facilities and land reform.[29] Landless tenants often were trapped in a corrupt and inordinately time-consuming justice system where their claims were not effectively heard or resolved.

The Taliban exploited this environment of systemic corruption, and the lack of effective access to education, health and justice systems. The Taliban operating in the Swat Valley of Pakistan gradually put pressure on the locals to pay the Taliban their rent money rather than to absentee landlords. Propertied landlords were persuaded to withdraw their sons from English medium schools and enroll them in madrassas and also permit one or more of them to train as Taliban fighters.[30] The *shari'a* law and traditional Islamic means of conflict resolution gradually started to replace secular, state-run law courts. Thus, the absence of adequate systems of education, health, land entitlement, and justice were all elements of an impoverished society that provided fertile ground for the Taliban to establish a stronghold.

When former President Musharraf tried to regulate the growing madrasas by offering cash to teach more general subjects, the money was accepted, but the educational practices did not change. Even in the view of the Pakistani Government, the "madrasa reform project failed."[31] Indeed, recent reports also confirm that wealthy landlords are not returning to the Swat Valley. In fact, the "reluctance of the landlords to return is a significant blow to the Pakistani military's campaign to restore Swat as a stable, prosperous part of Pakistan, and it presents a continuing opportunity for the Taliban to reshape the valley to their advantage."[32]

The removal of landlords from the Swat region may also have repercussions in the neighboring Punjab province where the militants are gaining power. This may have the effect of a "property redistribution" where support for the Taliban is tied to the absence of landlords. In fact, the local landlords have fled, in large part, due to the failure of the Pakistani army to protect their families and their lands.

However, the local Pakistani population may be losing their attraction to Taliban-enforced norms. Pakistanis living under Taliban rule are becoming disillusioned since the underlying causes that allowed the Taliban to exert their influence in the first instance—poverty, a non-functioning local government, the lack of economic opportunity—remain in place. Once the Taliban took power, it only "seemed interested in amassing more."[33] Thus, the cycle may be completing its circle.

The Pakistani Government is scrambling to recruit new judges and has assigned 3,000 new police officers to the Swat region.[34] These government actions may give rise to the hope that a functioning secular modern state will be reimposed in a more effective and sustainable way in this region.

However, this story is still unfolding and the outcome is uncertain.

In fact, the Pakistani Government may need to take note of the observation that, "the Afghanistan-Pakistan Frontier example shows the classic instance of an accidental guerrilla syndrome, with heavy-handed government intervention in a highly traditional and xenophobic society producing a major backlash with extremely far-reaching implications for regional security."[35]

David Kilcullen outlines a four-part cycle that forms what he terms the "accidental guerrilla syndrome" whereby Al Qaeda (or an affiliate) establishes a presence within a remote, ungoverned or conflict-affected area during the *infection* stage.[36] During this stage, the terrorist operatives establish cells, logistical support systems and information-gathering mechanisms.

While this presence may initially be resisted or disapproved by the locals, the next stage is the *contagion* phase where the extremist group's influence spreads while still operating below the radar screen.[37] The third phase of *intervention* is where external authorities begin to take action against the extremists–this action may be taken by local government authorities, regional powers or by the international community. In fact, the intervention may be in the form of delivering humanitarian aid, a gesture that it often violently rejected by the extremists.[38]

The final phase of *rejection* is where accidental guerrillas are created. In other words, local people become accidental guerillas fighting along side the terrorist forces not because they necessarily support their extremist ideology but because they oppose outside interference with their internal affairs, or because they are simply alienated by the heavy-handed actions of the intervening forces.[39] Thus, while the Pakistani Government is now trying to assert the trappings of a functioning modern, secular state, it may be too little, too late after decades of profoundly neglecting these regions and these peoples. In fact, their intervention may inadvertently spark the accidental guerrilla syndrome–only time will tell.

In fact, this conflict in Pakistan signals a far deeper and more threatening possibility: the looming danger of Pashtun separatism. The conflict has implicit ethnic tensions as well since the Pakistani Army is mainly Punjabi and the Taliban is entirely Pashtun.[40]

Historically, the Pashtuns were politically unified across Afghanistan and Pakistan before the British Raj. (In fact, there is no discernible ethnic difference between Pakistani and Afghani Pashtuns.) The British defeated the Pashtuns in 1847, and later gave the defeated tribes a semi-autonomous status by establishing the Federally Administered Tribal Areas (FATA). During the partition of India, the British gave these conquered areas to the newly formed Pakistani Government in 1947.[41]

The political domination by Pakistan was never accepted by the Pashtuns who lobbied for an autonomous state or "Pashtunistan" to be created within Pakistan. The fear of this possibility led Pakistan to support jihadists (*mujahidin*) operating during the Afghan resistance during the Soviet occupation of Afghanistan in the 1980s. Later, Pakistan was instrumental in supporting the Taliban which took power in Afghanistan following the Soviet withdrawal.[42]

In fact, the "post-1979 joint struggle that Pakistan waged with the U.S.-led international coalition against Soviet occupation . . . famously relied on Islamic fighters to eject the Russians from Afghanistan. This war of unintended consequences bequeathed to Pakistan a witches' brew of problems that continue to plague the nation today, weakening the traditional fabric of society in its western provinces. The explosive legacy of the Afghan jihad included militancy and violent extremism, millions of Afghan refugees, and the exponential growth of madrasas, narcotics, and proliferation of arms. The most dangerous aspect of this legacy was that some 40,000 Islamic radicals were imported from across the Arab world to fight along side the Afghan mujahideen. They later became the core of al Qaeda."[43]

With this as a backdrop, there may be anecdotal evidence that the accidental guerrilla syndrome may already be in effect in this area. Using the accidental guerrilla analysis, it is clear that the infection, and contagion stages have already occurred. Moreover, former President Bush insisted that former President Musharraf send troops into the FATA in 2002, thereby displacing 50,000 people. This, along with other Pakistani Government actions, may be called the intervention stage. "By arousing a Pashtun sense of victimization at the hands of outside forces, the conduct of the 'war on terror' in FATA, where al-Qaeda is based, has strengthened the jihadist groups that the U.S. seeks to defeat."[44] This may lead to the rejection phase, and the subsequent creation of accidental guerillas.

The Pashtuns now wish to merge the FATA with the Pashtun Northwest Frontier Province (NWFP) to form a unified "Pashtunkhwa" that operates autonomously from Pakistan and its constitution. If there is a merger between the Taliban and Pashtun nationalism, there may be an effective "Talibanization" of Pashtunkhwa which would be disastrous in the view of the Pakistani Government. In the words of Pakistan's Maj. Gen. Mahmud Ali Durrani, "I hope that the Taliban and Paushtun nationalism do not merge. If that happens, we've had it and we're on the verge of that."[45]

One commentator admonishes, however, that, "[f]or its part, Pakistan has to more purposefully meet the challenge of good governance and manage its economic and security issues with greater energy and competence, while building public consensus and support for its goals of economic and political stability. This requires something from the politicians that they have shown little of in the past year, consumed and distracted as they have been in power plays and political confrontation: leadership."[46]

While it may be somewhat misleading or confusing to discuss the Taliban in the context of global jihadism, the above discussion illustrates that the relationship between separatists' movements and global jihadism is not easily disentangled. The Taliban may be exhibiting "nationalist" sentiment is trying to unify territories, and change the method of governance from secular, democratic principles to Islamic-based education, conflict resolution and other matters. This pattern of conduct illustrates that the Taliban is reacting to decades (if not centuries) of poor governance and neglect with an Islamic-influenced and energized agenda to seize and expand their territory of control and political power base.

Indeed, the Afghans have been fighting for their national identity for over a century, first again the British, then the former Soviet Union, and now the United States, Pakistan and even against themselves. The withdrawal of the former Soviet Union from Afghanistan in 1989 was followed by a 23-year civil war in Afghanistan. By late 2001, Afghanistan was a "failed state" whose "economy, educational establishment, and governmental institutions had almost ceased to function."⁴⁷

However, at the outset, it is important to redefine the contours of this conflict. What the international community tends to see as a rugged, unforgiving terrain, the Pashtuns see this land as their own country, a reflection of themselves. Their love of this land is so profound that it has fueled a struggle that has lasted for over a century, and one that has been fought by throwing stones that only later were replaced with bullets.

Very little has been said in the international press about this conflict being a struggle for self-determination, independence and the unification of the same (or similar) ethnic peoples in a self-governed autonomous state or territory. "Self-determination" formed the rallying cry for independence movements of former colonies during the latter part of the 20ᵗʰ century, and has recognized legitimacy under international law principles. However, the self-determination of the Pashtuns poses a quandary for the international community. The nature of the Pashtuns' desire to form a self-governed unit is highly problematic for two reasons, one internal and the other external.

First, a clear distinction should be drawn with other independence struggles of the 20ᵗʰ century–scores of Asian and African nations wished to form a modern nation-state governed (at least in principle) by the accepted principles of modernity: a representative government, the Rule of Law, and a respect for human rights. Whether these ideals have actually been implemented or achieved is, of course, another question.

However, the Pashtuns under the leadership of the Taliban have displayed no interest in modernity whatsoever, however modernity may be defined. Thus, in terms of what kind of a state they may wish to form, it is a pre-feudal, warlord-dominated society that does not resemble the accepted form of modern nation-states.

Moreover, it is clear that a respect for human rights, representative government or the other trappings of the modern state are not part of the vision for their rulership. This is a problem for the international community which has an obligation to safeguard certain common ideals regarding the sanctity of life, the respect of human rights generally, among other matters. Thus, from within, the type of governance practiced by the Taliban is highly problematic.

Secondly, supporting a failed state that is an acknowledged supporter, if not an actual state-sponsor of international terrorism, is not an inviting prospect for the international community. The presence and influence of Al Qaeda in Afghanistan and Pakistan is another serious complicating factor. The Taliban's complex relationship with Al Qaeda also requires an immediate response from the international community since the danger that Al Qaeda and its operatives pose is so real and tangible.

In addition, the fact that the opium trade is so prevalent in Afghanistan, and the fact that the profits generated by this illegal trade are used to financially support terrorist activities, are highly problematic factors.[48] Thus, for both internal reasons related to the style of governance of the Taliban, and for external reasons related to its implicit support of global terrorism and illegal drug trafficking, it may be very difficult for the international community to support the goal of Taliban-led self-governance or self-determination.

It appears that the Taliban is engaged in a power struggle where power is best gained and preserved by denying empowerment to others. Whether this is accomplished by denying education, free elections or entrepreneurial opportunities to the members of its society, the end goal is political rather than religious–to obtain and retain political power. In other words, religious means are being used to create a political end.

The systemic denial of basic freedoms as the basis for governance has resulted in a form of political oppression rather than a sustainable model for governance in the long-run. This, combined with the fact that there is so much violence implicit in the Taliban's governance[49] tends to make its long-term viability highly fraught with legal and practical problems from an international perspective.

As a rather dismal footnote to this discussion, Pakistan's struggles with nationalist sentiments within its borders may not be confined to the Pashtun any longer. Now, there is evidence that Baluch nationalists are launching an insurgency. While this one is not on the same scale as the Taliban insurgency in the northwest, it is nevertheless, steadily gaining ground. Moreover, the "Baluch conflict holds the potential to break the country apart–Baluchistan makes up a third of Pakistan's territory–unless the government urgently deals with years of pent up grievances and stays the hand of the military and security services. . . . those abuses have continued under President Asif Ali Zardari, despite promises to heal tensions."[50] Again, reverting to the failed states analysis, Pakistan's status as a nation-state seems very much weakened, making it a fragile, if not a failing state.

In fact, U.S. Congressman Dana Rohrabacher introduced a resolution on the floor of the U.S. House of Representatives urging Pakistan to recognize the Baluch right to self-determination.[51] Claiming that Baluchs are divided among Iran, Afghanistan and Pakistan, he believes that they are entitled to the right to self-determination and their own sovereign country.[52] Although this resolution was subsequently tabled, it set off a firestorm of vehement condemnation by the Pakistan Government calling it a violation of international law and a blatant interference with Pakistan's domestic affairs.[53]

Thus, while the issues of poverty may be more directly related to separatists' sentiments and political agenda, it is not completely disconnected with global jihadism. The relationship between the two is not direct or necessarily transparent, but very few of the issues discussed herein are. In sum, the synergism between separatist sentiments and global jihadism is a serious and sobering reality.

In addition, the relationship of democratic freedoms as a deterrent to global jihadism is also a critical inquiry to be made in this context. One commentator has concluded that, "there is no relationship between the incidence of terrorism in a given country and the degree of freedom enjoyed by its citizens. [The statistics] certainly do not indicate that democracies are substantially less susceptible to terrorism than are other forms of government. . . . . Terrorism stems from sources other than the form of government of a state. There is no reason to believe that a more democratic Arab world will, simply by virtue of being more democratic generate fewer terrorists."[54]

This may not actually be the case. In a masterful study of the drivers of violent Islamic-based extremism prepared for USAID, several layers of analysis revealed interrelated causal and other factors pertinent to this discussion. The study examines the root causes breeding terrorist mindsets, socio-economic factors, and political drivers of violent extremism.

The overall conclusion was somewhat surprising: "Terrorists and other violent extremists do not exhibit common psychological attributes. They do not have a shared psychopathology. Analyses of the personal backgrounds of even those who have engaged in the most gruesome form of terrorism–suicide bombing–typically reveal strikingly normal lives, and no prior evidence of psychological dysfunctions. The readiness to kill for the sake of a particular political and/or agenda–and sometimes sacrifice oneself in the process–cannot be predicted through potential insights into the psychology or personal history of whose who commit these acts."[55] Thus, creating a terrorist "profile" does not seem feasible under these circumstances.

The study did identify, however, eight political "drivers" of violent extremism. The first is the denial of basic political rights and civil liberties; the second is harsh, brutal and repressive rule that includes gross violations of human rights. The third factor is systemic corruption and widespread impunity for the elites of the society. The fourth is the existence of ungoverned or poorly governed areas or territories; the fifth is the presence of long, protracted local conflicts; and the sixth is the governance by illegitimate, bankrupt and repressive political regimes. The seventh factor may be specific to Pakistan since it involves the loss of control of insurgents, mercenaries or other violent political operatives.[56]

In drawing with a very broad brush, conditions of poverty do seem more related to separatist Islamic-based movements. The lack of civil liberties and effective political representation seems more relevant to global jihadist movements. In fact, global terrorists emerging from Europe may illustrate this relationship.

"European governments have typically not engaged in heavy-handed intervention in immigrant [Muslim] communities, but where such intervention has occurred, those communities have tended to close ranks and adopt a siege mentality which created further opportunity for extremist penetration and manipulation. Thus, while not a full-blown accidental guerrilla syndrome, the evidence from Europe tends to suggest that the same dynamics that occur in remote traditional societies can also occur within more developed societies, or within certain sections of the populations in those societies."⁵⁷ Thus, it is clear that living a life without the means to acquire educational and economic opportunities, and where certain basic human dignities are not guaranteed, creates a sense of hopelessness and desperation. All these disparate elements form the incendiary caldron that incubates violent extremism.

However, "what distinguishes violent extremists from the rest are to a significant extent at least, the values they embrace, the quest for an intense and exacting form of spirituality that often animates them, as well as the broader worldviews and convictions that they have in common, and which typically portray violence as a logical and acceptable form of retribution for the deprivation they feel they are made to endure."⁵⁸

What then are the "deprivations" that are so deeply felt by extreme global jihadists?

"One manifestation of the role of ideas and beliefs [that have] shaped so profoundly the outlook of extremist movements. . . .is the perception of *collective victimization and personal humiliation*. [Emphasis supplied.] Where it can be detected, such a perception typically reflects colonial histories, as well as other forms of repeated foreign interference, manipulation and oppression. . . . The wars in Afghanistan and Iraq are viewed as only the most recent manifestations of such longstanding schemes. Many Muslims feel very strongly not only that the West never made serious amends for the past suffering and oppression it inflicted on them, but that it is currently engaged in a renewed effort to victimize and oppress them, as well as to denigrate and demonize their most cherished values and beliefs. Against this background, violence is seen not only as a form of retribution for past wrongs, but as a necessary defense by individuals who feel that they are fighting for the very survival of a culture under siege."⁵⁹

Indeed, as Franz Fanon pointed out in his seminal analysis of the psychological dimensions of those victimized by colonization, violence is often cathartic in this context. "At the level of the individual, violence is a cleansing force. It frees the native from his inferiority complex and from his despair and inaction; it makes him fearless and restores his self-respect."⁶⁰

Moreover, as a Pakistani friend of mine pointed out, the systematic repression and denial of any positive and constructive avenues of self-expression through music, art, dance, or creativity of any kind leaves only one avenue through which one may express emotion: violence. He notes that there is a general lack of public spaces or entertainment, cafes, restaurants or means of social interaction in many of the Islamic countries breeding or supporting global jihadists.

Indeed, in Pakistan's case itself, Pakistan has consistently chosen violence: the violence of poverty, the violence of corruption, and the violence of terrorism. At first, Pakistan's policies of supporting terrorist cells such as Lashkar-e-Taiba were directed outward toward India (e.g., Kashmir, Mumbai)[61] and then in the form of the mujahideen, toward the Soviets in Afghanistan.[62] But now, these home-grown terrorists are attacking the state of Pakistan and endangering its future viability, as described in more depth in Chapter 1.

Ultimately, the denial of one's individuality, creativity, humanity and dignity may all lead to a malaise of frustration and resentment. Moreover, witnessing a constant pattern where ethnic or religious minorities are treated unfairly or reduced to a lesser political, socio-economic or religious status all help to create an environment that is fraught with implicit tension. This environment may become one, in short order, where fundamental human rights are not acknowledged, at best, or viciously repressed, at worst.

Indeed, it is tempting to conclude that orthodox or reactionary forms of Islam such as the form practiced by the Taliban tend to encourage violence. If, in fact, the doctrinaire views of Muslim clergy support violence, whether in the context of global jihad generally or against women specifically, this seems to further block avenues for creative non-violence. Violence becomes a sanctioned form of activity with which to express a wide range of emotions, all of which seem (from an outsider's point of view, in any case) to be lamentably negative and hostile in nature.

This environment combined with a narrative of victimization, collective humiliation, a violation of one's own personal honor and integrity may give rise, in certain circumstances, to "a pervasive sense of loneliness, isolation, utter despair and hopelessness. . . [promoting a sense] of total rejection, abandonment and betrayal–by the state, by political and economic elites more generally, and even by the rest of society."[63]

The promise of nationhood has already been betrayed to global terrorists somehow, and their alienation is now so complete and so virulent that they have no interest in nation-building on any discernable level. Indeed, the sense of betrayal may lie far deeper than just one emanating from the systemic failures of the state. The true betrayal may not simply lie with Western-based geopolitics and its negative consequences, but instead with the betrayal of the promise of hope to themselves. Rather than pursuing an illusion of power through destruction and the wanton disregard for the sanctity of human life (including their own), the adherents of this virulent form of Islamic-based global terrorism should give serious consideration to redeeming this hope. Otherwise, there may not be much to be gained from a discussion of this sort.

Interestingly, one may be tempted "to assume that an inability to reap the benefits of globalization and modernity represents a primary motivating force behind the resort to terrorism. In reality, however, in the past three decades a disproportionate number of violent extremist organizations have rejected modernity altogether. They have done so explicitly and unconditionally, pointing to, for instance, what they view as modernity's lack of spiritual content and its ethical poverty. The violence in which they have engaged has been intended, in part, to display, in an intentionally spectacular and dramatic fashion, their contempt for, and complete repudiation of post-enlightenment values and secular humanism. They have portrayed these values as an unacceptable quest for a Godless universe. They have also blamed modernity for the ascent of unbridled individualism and hedonism, and for the triumph of materialism and moral relativism.

"In those circumstances, [violent extremism] should *not* be viewed as the enraged response of individuals who feel betrayed at having been promised the benefits of modernity–only to be subsequently denied them. [Emphasis supplied.] The resort to violence, instead, should be understood as an effort to roll back modernity by fighting its symbols and manifestations. To many violent extremists, modernity is *not* something to be aspired to; it is a threat around which a wall must be built or a looming danger that must be confronted head-on. [Emphasis supplied.] Religious extremists, in particular, tend to view modernity as encroaching on sacred values; they regard it as an all-powerful force that, if left to its own devices, inevitably and irremediably will destroy the integrity of their societies and cultures."[64]

Thus, the power of religion helps to organize and otherwise animate this struggle against modernity, foreign oppression, and a fundamentally unjust and ungodly world order that threatens to destroy the intrinsic values of Islam. Religion not only supplies the necessary intellectual framework (and accompanying moral justification) for violence, but provides the means to acquire political power. This is especially evident in Palestine where former and present Hamas "terrorists" have assumed parliamentary power and represent actual political constituencies.

What then is the essential nature of this ideological conflict? Is it a global war that is couched in the religious terms of a jihad (struggle) or intifadah (uprising)? Is it a new kind of political coup to gain political power along with access to resources and autocratic decision-making through terrorist means? Is it an ideological conflict between post-modern nation-states and a revivalist form of an Islamic-based type of pre-feudalism?

Although there are differing points of view on this matter, it appears as though the conflict is ideological in nature rather than religious.[65] In other words, the conflict does not seem to be an Islamic-based "crusade" to convert non-believers into believers in Islam: the struggle is political in nature. Although establishing a Muslim Caliphate is regarded by some observers as the end goal of global Islamic-based terrorism, this viewpoint–even if taken at face value–establishes a political (not religious) objective.

Indeed, I find it somewhat ironic that while establishing a so-called caliphate may be a touted ideal of extremists, the four actual caliphates established after the death of Mohammed governed non-Muslim populations without the kind of religious, cultural and political oppression contemplated by modern extremists.[66] Indeed, the Umayyad Caliphate of Córdoba (929-1031) in Spain experienced a flowering of culture, art, philosophy, astronomy, mathematics in a diverse population of non-Muslims, including Jews.

The goal of the "global intifadah" appears to be winning political power, and using terrorist means to accomplish that goal. Thus, if the essential conflict is viewed as being ideological in nature in order to achieve political goals, what should the response of the international community be?

At the outset, it does not appear that fundamentalist Islamic-based global terrorism is sustainable in the long-run since it contains the seeds of its own destruction. This type of Islamic-based terrorism will, over time, be destroyed from within since it leaves in place and deeply exacerbates existing structural problems of political governance and economic growth.

If permitted to govern (following the Taliban model), the imposition of pre-feudalistic, tribalistic structures does not help alleviate poverty nor does it provide for effective political governance. In fact, this is a recipe for continued marginalization and failure. It is foreseeable that the deepening human misery caused by the failure to address the basic human needs of its population will lead to a further collapse of the societies where fundamentalist Islamic-based global terrorists establish a foothold.

On a deeper level, the ideology of hatred fundamentally misunderstands man's acquisitive nature. From an outsider's point of view, much of their furious hatred of global jihadists seems to be based on their envy and deep mistrust of Western economic successes, political dominance, and cultural hegemony—its luxury goods, in fact. However, the ultimate luxury good is the freedom of choice. The freedom to choose and to take risks to support those choices is the ultimate freedom.

Deliberately choosing (and imposing on others) the "unfreedom"[67] of having no or few choices that are dictated by religious leaders or tribal warlords does not constitute real empowerment. Indeed, far from disempowering other nation-states, global terrorism acts to disempower its own adherents by cultivating despair and a lack of hope in the future— or simply the belief that tomorrow will be better than today. While this ideology claims to be faith-based, it mocks faith-based values that are universal in nature.

If, on the other hand, Islamic-based global terrorists have not fundamentally misinterpreted man's nature and are willing to kill for it and, more importantly, to die for this state of "unfreedom," then we are all lost. They have, in effect, created a new kind of human being that is impervious to the values of human civilization not the least of which is the regard for the sanctity of human life. In fact, the systematic indoctrination of a creed of violence, and the uncompromising repression of human creativity affecting all spheres of life may create a new terrifying sensibility that implicitly encourages a wanton disregard for human life. There truly is no real response to someone who is willing to die, when we clearly are not.

However, waiting for the dialectic method to run its historical course of "negating" Islamic-based fundamentalist terrorism is an unattractive course of non-action. The role that international actors must assume now is a complex matrix of military, political and diplomatic, economic, and cultural initiatives, as discussed below.

3

Implications of the Arab Spring: Where Do We Go From Here?

The following discussion on the Arab Spring explores the theoretical foundation of the so-called "ideology of hate" employed by global jihadists. This ideology is both ebbing and flowing with the current tide of events. While the strength of this ideology may be waning (very slowly), there is room to believe, however, that this jihadist ideology is struggling to maintain its relevance. Regime change of so-called "apostolic regimes" was always one of the key planks of revolutionary change that would usher in an orthodox shar'ia law-based Caliphate. However, the remarkable events highlighted below demonstrate that the rest of the Arab world has moved past this pipe dream. Arab nations are quickly moving toward the initiation of democratic and electoral reforms by starting to put the building blocks of a true democracy in place.

These concrete and visible changes are in the nature of creating the infrastructure of democracy (e.g., parliamentary and constitutional reforms, strengthening the judiciary, electoral reforms). Nevertheless, the latest wave of violence in September 2012, calls into question whether such democratic reforms are sustainable over time since they are not rooted in true and deep traditions of civil society and religious tolerance. Civil society traditions of a free press, organized political parties, open and free elections and political discussions, respecting the rights of women, ethnic and religious minorities have all been suppressed for decades. It is now unclear whether there is sufficient internal support to keep these newly reforming Arab countries from disintegrating from within despite the best of intentions from within and without these societies. Further, there is a chilling and sobering possibility that jihadist elements may usurp the democratization process underway in these countries by introducing chaos and orchestrated violence designed to disrupt and confuse fragile governments.

On a more positive note, to the outside observer, it appeared that the so-called "Arab Spring" completely rejected the jihadist-endorsed means of violence in favor of peaceful mass demonstrations followed by free and fair elections, democratic reform, and steps to end corruption. In contrast, the protesters have endured the violence visited upon them, and have not sought revenge; instead they are working towards a common future with well-defined goals. The end is different as well: no one is speaking of a Caliphate but of a true modern nation-state with all of its strengths and weaknesses. Other than Libya, there has not been a violent overthrow of the government followed by a killing of the incumbent rulers. (At this writing, Syria is in still in the throes of a violent civil war or conflict that is still unresolved.)[1]

The "Arab Spring" is generally seen as beginning on December 19, 2010, when a 25-year old Tunisian vegetable seller, Mohamed Bouazizi, was reportedly slapped and publicly humiliated by a policewoman for selling vegetables without a license. In response to his clash with police on that fateful morning, he set himself on fire.[2] Although he was rushed to the hospital, he later died of his wounds and, by so doing, set the entire Arab world on fire. In less than a month, the 23-year rule of Tunisian president, Zine el-Abidine Ben Ali, ended when he was forced out of power following massive protests that left over 200 people dead. He fled to Saudi Arabia on January 14, 2011, after his security forces refused to fire on civilians.[3] Within hours, protesters took to the streets of Cairo, Egypt in Tahrir Square, and within weeks, Egyptian President, Hosni Mubarak, had also been forced from power after nearly 30 years of autocratic rule.

The results of Tunisia's so-called "Jasmine Revolution" of January 2011 are still filtering in, '[b]ut for travelers, a visit to Tunisia right now offers a chance not only to witness this pivotal moment in the country's history, but also to get a sense of the struggles and stakes of the Arab Spring in general. As dictators around the region fall or are challenged, Tunisia, while far from untroubled, offers a reassuring example of what might emerge

from the wreckage. Elections in October 2011 produced results that would
have been unimaginable during the Ben Ali years, when Islamist groups and
dissent were smothered: a prime minister from a moderate Muslim party
and a president with a résumé as a human rights campaigner."[4]

Indeed, the mood in Tunisia after the uprisings was hopeful. In May
2011, G-8 countries promised over $20 billion in loans and grants to Tunisia
and Egypt to support their economic growth, respectively. "Tunisia could
be an amazing place," says Jalloul Ayed, the finance minister, a former
Citibank banker and composer of classical symphonies. "We have a bright,
highly educated population. We're close to Europe's markets. We have the
right to dream of Tunisia as the Singapore of the Mediterranean. We could
achieve it in five to seven years—with a few adjustments."[5]

Those "adjustments" may actually be quite difficult to achieve in light
of the complex challenges facing Arab states. These challenges include
forging a new relationship between Islam and the modern nation-state,
including ethnic and religious minorities as well as women in the national
political discourse, and instituting wide-scale legal and institutional reforms
aimed at transforming decades of corruption, a lack of transparency and
accountability, dysfunctional bureaucracies and courts, and subsidies and
rent-taking in virtually every aspect of everyday life.

Nevertheless, in examining these and other remarkable events of 2011,
a common theme of civil unrest, civil disobedience, mass protests and rallies
all seeking regime change of corrupt and moribund governments seems to
prevail. While much of history does seem to come into being *sui generis*,
in the case of the Arab Spring, I would actually backdate it to another time
and country: Iran in June 2009.

Massive protests in support of Iran's main political opposition leader,
Mir Hosein Mousavi, following disputed election results in mid-June 2009
led to several deaths.[6] This initiated the so-called Green Movement, green
being the color of the opposition, which I see as a precursor to the Arab
Spring. While President Mahmoud Ahmadinejad remained and remains
in power, it was an uneasy victory in light of the fact that, "[t]he fight
in the political corridors of Iran [was] one between rival factions of the
same regime. Mr. Ahmadinejad represents conservatives, backed by Mr.

Khamenei. Mr. Mousavi stands for a more pragmatic group and is backed by reformists who believe that he has a decent chance of unseating Mr. Ahmadinejad. But he is a stalwart of the revolution, committed to the ideal of the Islamic republic. What he calls for is a more democratic version, one that is more competent and pragmatic."[7]

Not only did the Iranian protests set the tone and tenor of such protests, it was a template that was very closely followed by other countries in the region. First, it was a protest that disputed election results and was aimed at fairness, transparency and most of all, regime change. Secondly and perhaps more interestingly, the method for the protest changed dramatically—it was social media driven. So much so, the U.S. State Department in an unprecedented request, approached *twitter.com* to delay its network upgrade to 1:30 am Tehran time to better enable protesters to coordinate their efforts via internet media.[8]

"So what exactly makes Twitter the medium of the moment? It's free, highly mobile, very personal and very quick. It's also built to spread, and fast. . . and can be received and read on practically anything with a screen and a network connection."[9] Although connections were made quickly to share information, it was the hands-on sifting through hundreds of "tweets" by desk reporters at traditional media outlets such as newspapers and cable television that provided the necessary analytical framework from an avalanche of disconnected bits of information. Thus, the merger of traditional news media and social media was effectively forged.[10] (We will return to this issue later in this chapter.)

The following discussion will examine the cascade of events that followed the self-immolation of Mohamed Bouazizi in Tunisia. The domino effect will be grouped into three categories for the sake of clarity: first, the countries of Egypt, Yemen and Bahrain; second, the monarchies of Morocco, Saudi Arabia and Jordan; and, third, Libya (discussed in full in Chapter 8) will be contrasted with Syria. Finally, the phenomenon of social media to invoke regime change will be re-examined with the examples of Russia, the UK and the United States as the backdrop.

A.   Regime Change and Political Upheaval in the Arab World

1.   Egypt

While the following discussion is not intended to give a descriptive account of all the significant events that transpired during the tumultuous year of 2011, it will attempt to highlight certain important developments that may hold a particular significance in this context. On February 11, 2011, President Hosni Mubarak resigned from the presidency after 29 years in power, following 18 days of popular demonstrations in Egypt. The 83-year old former president was admitted to a military hospital and was tried for corruption and related charges. Although he faced the death penalty, he was given a life sentence by the trial judge who issued his verdict on June 2, 2012, after reviewing the testimony of 2,000 witnesses and over 40,000 pages of documents.[11]

Presiding over a three-judge panel, Judge Ahmed Rafaat found that Mubarak was an "accessory to murder" by failing to stop the killings of 240 unarmed protesters in demonstrations in January 2011 that ended his 30-year rule.[12] The judge also sentenced Egypt's Interior Minister, Habib el-Adly to a life sentence for the same reason. However, the panel dismissed the corruption charges against Mubarak's two sons on grounds that the statute of limitations for the charges had expired. Thousands protested in Tahrir Square and in Alexandria, Suez and other cities to protest what they considered to be a miscarriage of justice.[13]

After Mubarak's departure from power, the Supreme Council of the Armed Forces (SCAF), composed of military officers in leadership positions in the Mubarak regime, assumed power. Under an interim cabinet led by Prime Minister Essam Sharaf, the SCAF oversaw a March 2011 referendum. This popular referendum approved amendments to Egypt's constitution, and issued new laws on the formation of political parties and the conduct of upcoming parliamentary elections. The amended constitution also laid out a transitional framework in which the elected People's Assembly and Shura Council will, in conjunction with the SCAF, select members for a 100-person constituent assembly to draft a new constitution subject to a referendum in 2012 or 2013.[14]

A graphic overview of Egypt's political transition appears below in Table 1.

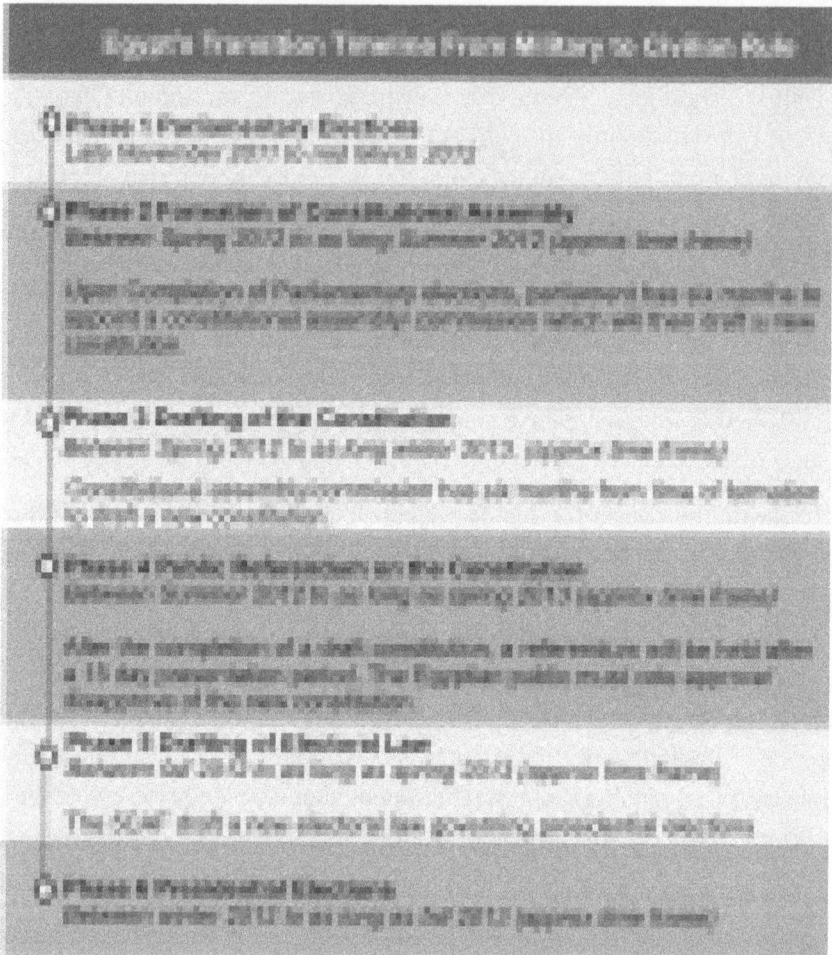

Source: Amber Hope Wilhelm, Publishing and Editorial Resources Section, Congressional Research Service. Based on the Supreme Council of the Armed Forces Constitutional Declaration and other SCAF announcements.[15]

"For observers, it is clearly evident that two forces have become the main political players in Egypt—the military (Supreme Council of the Egyptian Armed Forces or SCAF) and the Muslim Brotherhood (MB)."[16] The clash was evident in demonstrations held in Tahrir Square to celebrate the first anniversary of Egypt's revolution. Liberal activists, demonstrators and Islamists were torn between celebrating the forced ouster of Hosni Mubarak and agitating against the continued rule of military generals in

Egypt.[17] The Muslim Brotherhood was previously outlawed under the Mubarak regime, but is now Egypt's most powerful political force. In parliamentary elections held between November 2011 and January 2012, the Muslim Brotherhood's political arm, the Freedom and Justice Party, won over 40 percent of the seats in Egypt's parliament.[18] The Muslim Brotherhood party's elected officials have endorsed a timetable for the military's handover of power to an elected president by the end of June 2012.[19]

The election campaign for President was a hotly contested one, and full of unexpected surprises. For example, Egyptian election authorities of the High Election Commission disqualified a total of 10 electoral candidates, including three very significant ones. A leading strategist for the Muslim Brotherhood, Mubarak's former vice-president and intelligence chief, and an ultra conservative Islamist were disqualified by the Commission.[20]

The Commission was composed of five senior judges who were appointed by former President Mubarak. The Commissioners have already proved their independence of judgment since it eliminated a Mubarak insider and a leading Islamist, thus infuriating his followers. The judges used narrow technical legal grounds such as past criminal convictions and submitting notarized signatures that did not meet geographic distribution requirements.[21] This may herald a new respect for the Rule of Law.

One of the former candidates, Hazem Salah Abu Ismail, an ultraconservative Islamist known as a Salafi, was disqualified on grounds that his mother had been a U.S. citizen, therefore making him ineligible to run for President under Egyptian law. In response to this decision, protesters staged a sit-in near the Ministry of Defense which resulted in severe clashes where at least five people died as a result of gunshot wounds to the head. Five presidential candidates suspended their election campaigns, some indefinitely.

Mohammed el-Morsi, leader of the Muslim Brotherhood's political party, and now president of Egypt, "warned the ruling military council against using the violence as an excuse to delay the elections, reflecting a widespread fear that the council is looking for a pretense to retain power. But his comments also reflected an intensifying power struggle between the

Muslim Brotherhood and the military as the presidential vote approaches."[22] The presidential election was scheduled for May 23-24, with a run-off in June, if necessary.[23] On June 24, 2012, Mohammed Morsi was declared the winner of the presidential race with 51 percent of the vote, and the new president of Egypt.[24]

The struggle between Egypt's military and the new president have been ongoing. On July 9, 2012, Egypt's highest court and its most senior generals dismissed President Morsi's order to restore the dissolved Parliament.[25] The court and the generals called on President Morsi to respect legal precedent whereas the President urged them to respect the will of the people. This raises serious separation of power questions that are beyond the scope of this discussion, but it is clear that executive and judicial and legislative branches of Egyptian government are in conflict with unelected, but powerful, officials in the military.

President Morsi has moved powerfully to reclaim his power by announcing the retirements of his powerful defense minister, the army chief of staff and other senior generals. The former defense minister, Field Marshal Mohammed Hussein Tantawi, was a critical ally of former President Mubarak. His forced retirement following his recent reappointment to his position by President Morsi, was viewed as deeply embarrassing and signaled a sea change in relations between the presidency and the military. President Morsi named the former head of military intelligence, General Abdul Fattah el-Sisi, as the new defense minister.

Moreover, President Morsi nullified a constitutional declaration, issued by the Egyptian military on June 30, 2012, before he assumed office, which took away critical powers of his office. He replaced it with his own executive declaration that gives him broad-based legislative and executive powers, and a decisive role in drafting Egypt's new constitution.[26]

Although the violent clashes between the military and the Muslim Brotherhood and other parties and peaceful demonstrators is unfortunate, it may be the crucible through which a legitimate civil society is taking shape and perhaps being restored to Egypt. Regrettably, there is a high price to pay for democracy. There is also demonstrable yet fragile evidence of a newfound respect for Rule of Law principles, and perhaps for women's rights as well. Although Egyptian women were in the forefront of the protests leading to the overthrowing former President Mubarak's government, few have had significant roles in the revolution's aftermath and almost none have won parliamentary seats.

This changed in December 2011, where several hundred thousand women marched through downtown Cairo to protest military rule and to express their anger over the images of soldiers beating, kicking and stripping women demonstrators in Tahrir Square.[27] It is too early to tell what the downstream implications of this movement for the full participation of Egyptian women in political life and civil society may mean, but it is a refreshing breath of Arab Spring air.

One other note related to the ascendancy of the Muslim Brotherhood may have far-reaching consequences. Officials of Egypt's Muslim Brotherhood have approached its militant offshoot, Palestine's Hamas which controls Gaza, to begin making compromises with Fatah, the Western-backed Palestinian leadership that controls the West Bank. Fatah is trying to forge peaceful solutions with Israel.[28] Although the Muslim Brotherhood previously condemned Fatah for collaborating with Israel, it is now trying to persuade Hamas to work with Fatah in order to bargain with Israel to create a new state of Palestine.

This shift, while subtle, has far-reaching consequences. It is a marked movement away from former Egyptian President Mubarak's policy of exclusively supporting Fatah and its commitment to the peace process with Israel.[29] Israel has affirmed that it will not negotiate with a Palestinian government that includes Hamas (also recognized as a terrorist organization by the United States).[30] Nevertheless, a unified Palestinian front may cause Israel to re-examine this policy.

Hamas is now apparently willing to recognize President Mahmoud Abbas of Fatah as the leader of Palestine, a position that is unprecedented. Hamas has also indicated its support for a return to the 1967 borders with Israel, a position that is also supported by President Obama.[31] A Muslim Brotherhood initiative to unite both factions of the political leadership of the Palestinians could be the first real step towards negotiating a final peace solution to the Israel-Palestine question that has been festering since 1948.

2.   *Bahrain*

Moving onto Bahrain, its Sunni-ruled monarchy has been struggling with popular protests from its Shiite majority subjects for more than a year. The United States Navy's Fifth Fleet has a major naval base in Bahrain and patrols the Persian Gulf, and this presence is generally regarded by the U.S. as a bulwark against Iran's influence.

A complicating factor stems from the use of U.S.-made tear gas shells by Bahrainian government forces to repress and quell the insurrection.[32] Tear gas is the generic term for at least 15 riot-control chemicals that disable persons by irritating their lungs, skin and eyes.[33] The Physicians for Human Rights has issued a report, "Weaponizing Tear Gas," that criticizes the Bahraini monarchy's use of tear gas by its police officers who, according to its report routinely fire tear gas upon the Shiite majority at point blank range. Tear gas is dispersed into crowds, homes and vehicles. This has led, over the past 18 months, to an alarming increase in miscarriages, respiratory and other ailments.[34] The empty canisters of tear gas found in the street suggest that they are imported from the U.S., France and Brazil; however, as the United States has withheld licenses for U.S. tear gas products being exported to Bahrain, it is possible that the canisters were stockpiled or re-exported from other countries.[35]

King Hamad bin Isa al-Khalifa and Cambridge University-educated Crown Prince Salman bin Hamad al-Khalifa may hold the key to this conflict. The King commissioned Professor M. Cherif Bassiouni to investigate the civil disturbances beginning in March 2011.[36] Professor M. Cherif Bassiouni is an Emeritus Professor Law at DePaul University, where he has taught since 1964, and President Emeritus of the International Human Rights Law Institute, which he helped found in 1990. Professor Bassiouni essentially drafted Royal Order No. 28 outlining the task of the royal commission that includes four other internationally recognized members.[37]

The report by the panel, known as the Bahrain Independent Commission of Inquiry, found that "Bahrain's security services and Interior Ministry 'followed a systematic practice of physical and psychological mistreatment, which amounted in many cases to torture, with respect to a large number of detainees.'" Further, the panel called "the government's use of force and firearms excessive and, 'on many occasions, unnecessary, disproportionate and indiscriminate.' It cited instances in which masked men broke into the homes of dissidents between 1 a.m. and 3 a.m., 'terrorizing' inhabitants." [38]

The report also found that both Sunnis and Shiites were victims of the violence, but that Iran (a Shiite nation) did *not* instigate the unrest. The king, while disagreeing with that particular conclusion, responded by issuing a public address asserting that public officials who engaged in misconduct would be held accountable and replaced, and stressed that Bahrain's laws must be reformed in order to meet international standards. [39] In fact, the Physicians for Human Rights group acknowledged while the report was highly critical of the Bahrainian security forces using excessive force, torture and forced confessions, the group was nonetheless cynical and skeptical about Bahrainian adhering to its promises for reform. [40]

The Bahrainian protesters are, however, quite modest in their demands for reform. "It is not calling for revolution, or the execution of the ruler, or the overthrow of his family, as in Syria or Yemen. It has no arms. But it does call for deep political reforms—a constitutional monarchy with an empowered parliament, an elected government and an end to gerrymandering that has left Shiites disenfranchised." [41] It is too early to tell if these reforms will be made. Opposition leaders fear that the royal government may offer promises of jobs and housing, better salaries, a streamlined security apparatus and perhaps more aid from Saudi Arabia, rather than instituting concrete democratic reform in their country. [42] In fact, if these stopgap measures are adopted by the Bahrain government, it would not be too far off from other Arab monarchies.

3.   *Morocco, Saudi Arabia and Jordan*

King Muhammad VI of Morocco has appointed the Muslim Brotherhood's head of its Justice and Development Party as his Prime Minister. A new constitution was drafted and overwhelmingly approved by referendum on July 1, 2011. While making modest concessions to Parliament, the king has held onto most of his privileges thus staving off real reform. [43]

The Saudi Arabian royal rulers were also understandably alarmed by events in Bahrain, a fellow Sunni rulership, and sent in military enforcements. It has widely supported the idea (along with the king of

Bahrain) that the protests were fomented by Iran. In terms of its own country, Saudi rulers have quietly promised over $20 billion in social spending on its people, and also tightened controls on the press while permitting greater police controls over public gatherings.[44]

Jordan is also facing unprecedented protests over its 100-year old monarchy ruled by King Abdullah II. He has managed to stifle real civil unrest and "avoid the kind of turmoil that has upended other Arab countries by granting modest concessions like dismissing government ministers and preserving popular subsidies and by employing the security forces. Those forces have proved efficient in suppressing domestic and external challenges, and human rights groups have accused them of restricting freedoms of expression and assembly."[45] He has also addressed real concerns over graft and corruption by initiating investigations of public and business officials. Again, it is too early to tell whether these measures are sufficient to hold off systemic reforms in governance.

4.   Syria

The NATO-led military engagement in Libya is discussed in full in Chapter 8, and for purposes of this discussion, it is only salient to contrast it with the continuing uprisings in Syria, as yet an unresolved conflict at the time of this writing. The popular unrest which began in Tunisia in January 2011 spread to Syria in mid-March 2011. While President Bashar al-Assad first contemplated reforms, he lifted hopes by lifting a decades old state of emergency in April 2011. Quite unexpectedly, he then began launching massive crackdowns by rolling tanks into small towns and provinces, firing directly at protesters in Homs, Idlib and Dara'a.[46]

Syria has engaged in widespread violations of the cease fire agreement brokered by Kofi Annan, the special envoy from the United Nations and the Arab League. Syria has now slipped into an undeclared sectarian civil war. Friends of Syria, a group of 57 countries, have imposed financial sanctions on Syria which also includes an oil embargo and financial sanctions on Syria's Central Bank.[47] At this writing, French officials report nearly 10,000 dead, 44,000 refugees and 1.5 million Syrians in need of humanitarian aid.[48] Jordan has accepted over 180,000 Syrians since the conflict began and more than 72,000 are dependent on UN refugee aid.[49]

As the Civil War grinds on in Syria, leaving 40,000 Syrians dead at last count, President Hollande of France announced that the French Government "recognizes the Syrian National Coalation as the sole representative of the Syrian people and thus as the future provisional goverment of a democratic Syria and to bring an end to Bashar-al-Assad's regime."[50] This is an important step by France, the former colonial power in Syria, and it may lead to further political support, money and weapons for the rebel coalition.

The full ramifications of this conflict lie outside the scope of this analysis, but the continuing and violent nature of this repression distinguishes Syria from other countries swept up in the Arab Spring. The Syrian government seems impervious to change from the popular pressure of its own people and outside the reach of the international community. Syria is far more complex militarily than Libya was, and the UN Security Council has not passed resolutions instituting a no-fly zone in Syria, for example. Western powers have been cool to the idea of initiating a military campaign to stop the violence in Syria, making steps toward resolving the conflict very unclear.[51] The conflict also has grave regional implications as "Iraq's Shiite-dominated leadership is so worried about a victory by Sunni radicals in Syria that is has moved closer to Iran, which shares a similar interest in supporting the Syrian president, Bashar al-Assad."[52]

Syria is becoming a magnet for Sunni extremists, including those operating under the banner of Al Qaeda.[53] The Al Qaeda network may be viewed as opportunistic viruses attacking where there is sectarian revolt, government collapse and armed insurrection. Al Qaeda-linked terrorist cells are increasingly using suicide bombings to change the nature of the Syrian conflict and engage in a struggle that terrorists define as a sectarian conflict pitting Sunnis against Shiites. Thus, the world is teetering on the edge of yet another Al Qaeda-infiltrated conflict.

Notwithstanding that possibility, the U.S. Government is preparing for a post-Assad Syria. Apart from providing increased humanitarian aid and food supplies of $76 million to date, the U.S. State Department is studying ways in which to dismantle the thicket of U.S. and European sanctions against Syria in order to allow new investment to flow into the country following the exit of Assad. The U.S. Treasury Department has granted a waiver to permit the Syrian Support Group, a U.S. organization, to raise money for the rebels in Syria despite economic and financial sanctions that are already in place against Syria.

The Pentagon is also drafting contingency plans for operations in coordination with its NATO allies to manage the flow of refugees out of Syria into Jordan and Turkey, and to safeguard Syria's arsenal of chemical weapons. The U.S. Army's Central Command overseeing the Middle East region is creating "crisis action teams" that focus on military and other contingencies that may require the involvement of the U.S. military in some fashion. While immediate U.S. military action is not being considered at this point, there are contingences that are being carefully considered in preparing for a new Syria without Assad.

B.   Reflections on the Arab Spring

The perspective of the Iraqis may be useful in this context of examining the implications of the Arab Spring. In giving some hard-earned advice to the Libyans, the Iraqis touch on some difficult lessons learned from their experiments with democracy. In essence, "they had learned the hard way what they never understood living under decades of repression: that democracy is not just the absence of oppression, but that it also involves challenging concepts of tolerance, compromise and civic responsibility yet to take root in Iraq, or in Libya."[54] As further guidance, Iraqis urge that a presidential rather than a parliamentary system be chosen; that strong leaders who will not be corrupted be put in power; that all sectors of society stay engaged in the political process since ostracizing many Iraqis led to insurrection, and finally, give everyone a piece of land. Interesting, indeed. It also begs the question of whether Iraq would have had its own Arab Spring in revolt against Saddam Hussein had it not been for U.S. intervention in that country in 2003.

As a final footnote to this discussion, Iran has expressed grave concerns about the appropriation of the "Arab Spring" by Western powers. "The events taking place in Egypt, Tunisia, Yemen, Libya, Bahrain and certain other countries today are decisive and destiny making for the Muslim nations," [Ayatollah Ali Khamanei] said. However, he said, "if the imperialist and hegemonic powers and Zionism, including the U.S. tyrannical and despotic regime, manage to use the ongoing conditions in their own favor, the world of Islam will definitely face big problems for tens of years.'"[55]

In the Ayatollah view, the collapse of U.S.-backed governments in Egypt and Tunisia is an "Islamic awakening" that will change the dynamics with Israel and effectively reduce U.S. influence in the region. The Arab Spring has been characterized by Iranian leaders as similar to the 1979 Islamic Revolution in Iran, rather than the more recent 2009 green movement.[56] And for the first time, Iran has called on Syrian President Assad to recognize his people's "legitimate demands."[57] It should be noted, however, that the aim of the Arab Spring revolutionary overthrows of long-established governments in the region were directed at instituting real democratic reforms rather than ushering in an Islamic theocracy as Iran did.

The seeds planted by the Arab Spring may also be flowering very far away. For instance, Russian voters gave President Vladimir Putin a six-year term as president in March 2012 since he won 64.7 percent of the vote, thereby avoiding a run-off election. This extends his rule to an incredible 18 years.[58] However, the Russian elections and the victory for Putin have been marred by huge demonstrations protesting election fraud. In December 2011, for example, parliamentary elections set off widespread protests as well alleging more than 3,000 complaints of voting irregularities or violations.

In an open letter penned by Thomas Friedman, he writes:

> Dear Sirs: You may think that the situations in Egypt and Russia have nothing in common. Think again. Yes, these two countries have starkly different histories. But having visited both in recent weeks, I can tell you that they have one very big thing in common: the political eruptions in both countries were not initially driven by any particular ideology but rather by the most human of emotions–the quest for dignity and justice. Humiliation is the single most underestimated force in politics. People will absorb hardship, hunger and pain. They will be grateful for jobs, cars and benefits. But if you force people to live indefinitely inside a rigged game that is flaunted in their face or make them feel like cattle that can be passed by one leader to his son or one politician to another, eventually they'll explode. These are the emotions that

sparked the uprisings in Cairo and Moscow. They don't go away easily, which is why you're in more trouble than you think.[59]

Although the Russian people, like the Iranians involved in the Green Movement, did not succeed in bringing about regime change as did their counterparts in Arab nations, there is a restlessness that is reverberating among its citizens that may herald the winds of change.[60] However, change has not proven easy as the Putin Government has ordered the cessation of financial support of approximately $50 million per year offered by the U.S. Agency for International Development (USAID) by October 1, 2012. The USAID financing helped support pro-democracy groups and was viewed in some circles as encouraging political dissent. Although the Obama Administration is looking into creating a $50 million fund as an endowment for a private foundation under Russian law to support Russian civil society groups, this abrupt cut-off of assistance will negatively impact a number of fledging groups in Russia.[61]

On a much smaller scale, a certain dissatisfaction with government policies and leadership has also been expressed in the "Occupy Wall Street" movement in the United States. The goals of this grassroots protest movement are diffuse and over-inclusive and perhaps as a consequence have failed to coalesce into a political agenda. The thrust of this movement has largely been dissipated over time, but it nevertheless shows that even the most stable of democracies may be subject to large-scale demonstrations by unhappy voters. However, rather than seeing this as part of the Arab Spring, the Occupy Wall Street movement may simply be viewed as an outgrowth of a long-standing tradition of perennial protests again the World Bank and WTO at their annual meetings, Davos World Economic Forum summits, and most recently at the NATO Summit held in Chicago in May 2012.

C.   Terrorism@twitter.com

The significance of social media in the context of the Arab Spring has been discussed briefly above, but a second look at this phenomenon, particularly as its use spreads to terrorist cells, deserves a closer examination. Despite the wholesale rejection of Western culture, such as banning Western music, films, fashion, and even rejecting aid for famine victims, there seems to be an odd dissonance in embracing so-called "Twitter terrorism."[62]

Al Shabab in Somalia and other Al Qaeda franchises in the Arabian Peninsula and elsewhere are embracing English-language social media outlets like Twitter, Facebook, MySpace, YouTube, electronic chat rooms, and other web networks. The media war whether in the form of *Inspire*, an Al Qaeda English-language magazine, or accounts run by terrorist organizations is a strategic front of terrorist operatives. So much so, that it has attracted the attention of U.S. counterterrorism officials who are considering shutting down Al Shabab's Twitter account, @HSMPress, with close to 5,000 followers. This account is suspected of being used to recruit followers in the West.[63]

In fact, in a recent suicide bombing in Yemen, orchestrated by Ansar al Shariah, an Al Qaeda affiliate, the terrorist group announced on its facebook page (!) that the attack was aimed at Yemen's defense minister, Mohammed Nasser Ahmed. The attack was also in retaliation for a government campaign against its sanctuaries in southern Yemen where Ansar al Shariah is staging a secessionist movement from Yemen.[64]

The violence of terrorist attacks in Yemen cannot be underestimated. For example, a suicide bomber disguised as a solider blew himself up in the middle of a military parade rehearsal near the Presidential palace near Saba'een Square in Sana'a, the capital of Yemen. More than 90 people were killed and over 200 injured. Most of the casualties were members of the Central Security Organization, a paramilitary force commanded by Yahya Saleh, the nephew of the ousted former president. The carnage was indescribable prompting the current President, Abdu Rabbu Mansour Hadi, to address the nation in a televised address where he pledged to continue to fight Al Qaeda "until their eradication, no matter what sacrifices are required."[65]

Terrorists not only use social media as a pro-active tool, but they also deprive civilian populations of access to social media as a weapon of terror. For example, the Taliban has been systematically shutting off cell signal towers at 8 o'clock every evening in Afghanistan, severely cutting off relations with the rest of the world.[66] This is a grim reminder of the scope of the Taliban's influence. This influence combined with high-profile kidnappings that yield easy profits from distraught families keeps the Taliban substantially capitalized.

In sum, social media itself is a neutral force: it can be used for positive change as in the Green Movement and the Arab Spring, demonstrations in Russia and elsewhere, or it can be used for negative purposes such as recruiting and disseminating information about terrorism cells and activities.

Even in the West, social media can be used for destructive purposes as witnessed in the August 6, 2011 riots in London, Birmingham, Bristol, Liverpool, Manchester and other English cities. The police shooting of Mark Duggan in Tottenham in north London triggered the riots. (Apparently, the police intended to arrest him, not shoot him.) The unfortunate incident was met with a rush of Blackberry-fueled rioting that spread into general lawlessness and looting. Unlike race riots or social unrest demonstrations as seen in Britain in the 1980s, Los Angeles in 1992 or France in 2005, these riots were different, and not well-understood. By way of explanation, one commentator notes:

> There is clearly a cadre of young people in Britain who feel they have little or no stake in the country's future or their own. The barriers that prevent most youngsters from running amok—an inherent sense of right and wrong; concern for their job and education prospects; shame—seem not to exist in the minds of the rioters. Britain needs to try to understand why that is so... Perhaps it has something to do with the changing nature of the economy and consequent shortage of low-skilled jobs, or the long crumbling of family structures and discipline. ... The cracks in British society—economic and moral—have opened up, and they are deeper than they seemed.[67]

The Economist observes that,

> The riots took everyone by surprise. They were not, it seemed, political or anti-police, but mainly about looting. . . . Some people blame the politicians, claiming that the scandal over their expenses, undermined public morality. Some blamed the bankers, arguing that if people feel society is unfair they won't play by its rules. . . . The government-appointed panel that looked into the causes of the riot emphasized the effect of troubled families and the need for building character, 'including self-discipline, application, the ability to defer gratification and resilience in recovering from setbacks.'[68]

If true, this is deeply disturbing. Yet the same may be said of the so-called "flash mobs" in the United States where young people converge to loot a store or person (even in the presence of video cameras) and do so by using social media to organize the events. They seem to do so without fear of reprisal, or legal, social or parental discipline or consequences, without regard to the integrity of the persons or commercial entity involved, and with complete indifference to the pain, suffering and fear that they may create in others. The self-destructive nihilism they demonstrate reflects on a much smaller scale the angst that may have been felt by English youth.

Flash mobs reveal a certain moral decay. The causes of this decay may lie much deeper in a lack of parental controls, and a lack of education in moral, religious and social values. Re-education, while perhaps the only answer, will take a long time to address these issues. In the meantime, this social media-driven phenomenon poses a difficult quandary for the UK, the U.S., and beyond.

D. The Aftermath of the September 2012 Anti-American Protests

Although the significance of anti-American protests fueled by the release of a mysterious video entitled, "The Innocence of Muslims," to over 20 countries across the Middle East may fade over time, it sharply delineates the continuing cultural clash between Arab and Muslim countries and the West. The anger and resentment stretched from North Africa to South Asia to Indonesia resulting in the tragic deaths of U.S. Ambassador to Libya, J. Christopher Stevens, and three other U.S. officials in Libya on the 11th anniversary of the 9/11 attacks. Serious looting of the American Cooperative School of Tunis, where many children of African Development Bank officials go to school, also came as an unwelcome surprise. Over 700 laptops, musical instruments and other materials were looted and the building was set on fire.[69]

One explanation speculated that:

> Others said that the outpouring of outrage against the video had built up over a long period of perceived denigrations of Muslims and their faith by the United States or its military, which are detailed extensively in the Arab news media: the invasion of Iraq on a discredited pretext; the images of abuse from the Abu Ghraib prisons; the burning or

desecrations of the Koran by troops in Afghanistan and a pastor in Florida; detentions without trial at Guantánamo Bay; the denials of visas to prominent Muslim intellectuals; the deaths of Muslim civilians as collateral damage in drone strikes; even political campaigns against the specter of Islamic law inside the united States.[70]

More fundamentally, it may simply come down to a clash in the underlying principles of Western civilization and the perspective of Muslims where, "[t]he message here is we don't care about your beliefs-that because of our freedom of expression we can demean them and degrade them any time, and we do not care about your feelings."[71]

The silver lining in this, if it may be regarded as such, is the reaction of the Libyans to the death of U.S. Ambassador Stevens, a much beloved figure in Libya. Thousands of Libyans marched in Benghazi on September 21, 2012, demanding that the armed militias who may have been responsible for the armed attack on the U.S. Mission in Benghazi be disbanded. Protesters seized control of several militia headquarters and handed them over to the Libyan national army.[72] This may be a show of force by everyday Libyans so that their "Arab Spring" revolution is not co-opted by militias or jihadist elements.

The F.B.I. criminal investigation of the Benghazi attack is still months away at the time of this writing, and it is too early to reach any definitive conclusions at this point. U.S. Secretary of State, Hillary Clinton, has already suggested that a link exists between Al Qaeda in the Islamic Maghreb and the attack on the U.S. consulate. Mrs. Clinton intended to "underscore the rising threat that the Qaeda affiliate and other extremist organizations pose to the emerging democratic governments in countries like Tunisia and Libya."[73]   Further, there is now mounting evidence to lead to the belief that the planning and execution of the attack may have been transnational in nature, and was "not simply . . . a local spontaneous eruption of violence in response to an amateurish Internet video denigrating the Prophet Muhammad."[74] This incident has set off a political firestorm in the United States, the consequences of which are still unfolding.

A far more sobering view of the aftermath of the violence is the reluctance of Egypt's President Morsi to immediately condemn the violent attacks on the U.S. Embassy in Cairo when the walls of the embassy were breached by protesters. His "non-action" was designed to apparently appease the widespread domestic anti-American sentiment in Egypt. In a stern phone call from President Obama, the Egyptian leader was warned that relations with the United States would be jeopardized if he did not act to protect U.S. diplomats and interests.[75] President Morsi's apparent reluctance to support vital U.S. interests in his country after billions of U.S. dollars of assistance have been poured into Egypt over the past decades, and continue into the future,[76] is a sobering reality indeed. It reflects the ambivalence, or worse, contempt, which Egyptians may feel toward the United States after decades of misplaced diplomacy and foreign assistance.

E. Preliminary Conclusions

While it may be far too early to make any long-term conclusions about the significance of the Arab Spring, one thing is certain: it is a repudiation of the ideology of hate espoused by global jihadism. Ayman Mohammed Rabie al-Zawahiri, an Egyptian surgeon, became the leader of Al Qaeda with the death of Osama bin Laden on May 2, 2011, with his formal succession being announced on June 16, 2011.[77] In fact, he is even more isolated now since his deputy, Abu Yahya al-Libi, was killed in a CIA drone strike in June 2012.[78]

Ayman Mohammed Rabie al-Zawahiri's long-term torture in Egyptian prisons steeled his desire to overthrow the military, U.S.-backed regime of Hosni Mubarak. While I cannot speak for him, obviously, one may infer that it must be difficult for al-Zawahiri to triumph in the final result of the downfall of Mubarak's government. Instead of violence, peaceful protests were used. Instead of initiating shiari'a rule and a Caliphate to begin a seamless world domination by and through the orthodox Islamist principles that al-Zawahiri espouses, democratic elections were held and a democratically elected government was installed in Egypt.

Hosni Mubarak was tried in a court of law, and not killed summarily by a madding crowd. He was sentenced to life in prison for his involvement as an "accessory to murder" in the killings of thousands of protesters that brought down his government in 2011. His two sons and six high-ranking officials in his government were acquitted of related charges, triggering massive protests again in Egypt's Tahrir Square.[79] This seems to indicate that there is a newly expressed respect for the Rule of Law; however, these protests in Egypt seem to indicate something even more profound. Respect for the letter of the law does not seem to suffice. Egyptians are looking for something much more elusive yet fundamental: justice.

These actions are a repudiation of al-Zawahiri's ideology by millions of people living in an Arab world who sacrificed their lives, where necessary, to bring about these fundamental changes. Illegitimate tyrannical and corrupt governments were overthrown by non-violent means in order to achieve non-violent purposes. It was much closer to Gandhism than to jihadism, and therein lies the truth of the matter. As much as al-Zawahiri may have wanted this change, he neither contributed to it nor can he claim any moral right over its final outcome.

This is not to say that we are at the end of terrorism since the ideology of hate lives on in the franchised terrorist cells of Al Qaeda, a lasting legacy of Osama bin Laden. However, the light is dawning over the Arab world, and it would be well to remember Benazir Bhutto's admonition, "democracy is the best revenge."[80]

PART II

Transitioning from Global Terrorism:

A New Perspective

4

Creating the New Soldier

Professor Alan Beyerchen,[1] a distinguished historian at Ohio State University, has created a new taxonomy of four world wars based on Clausewitz's theories: World War I–a chemists' war that effectively used mustard gas, nitrates and chemical engineering to further war efforts; World War II–a physicists' war where the atomic bomb led to the decisive victory and the use of the electromagnetic spectrum in the form of radar and wireless communications were keys to winning the war; World War III (the "Cold War")–the information techonologists' war where net-centric warfare was key; and World War IV (The Fearful Symmetry)–the social scientists' war.[2]

Further, he theorized that shifts between phases of war are movements in underlying tectonic plates rather than volcanic eruptions. While one phase does not completely supplant the preceding one, the "emerging amplifier" is what gains a decisive victory. In other words, chemistry, physics and informational technology are not rendered defunct in the current context, but there is an emerging amplifier that will determine military success in the future.

Moreover, Beyerchen builds on Clausewitz's view of the non-linearity of war, a theory that, incidentally, has been related to dialectical materialism by both Engels and Lenin.[3] Beyerchen concludes that:

> Clausewitz perceives war as a profoundly nonlinear phenomenon . . . that demands that we retrain our intuition. . . . But for those trained in engineering and scientific fields, as are so many military officers and analysts, this retraining is likely to be a more wrenching and unwelcome experience. As the various scientists and mathematicians cited above

have suggested, the predominance of a linear intuition is endemic. . . .

Another implication of the nonlinear interpretation of Clausewitz is the need for a deepening of our understanding of his dictum on the relationship of war to politics. That "war is merely the continuation of policy by other means" is often taken to mean the primacy of a temporal continuum: first politics sets the goals, then war occurs, and then politics reigns again when the fighting stops. But such a view categorizes politics as extrinsic to war, and is an artifact of a linear sequential model. Politics is about power, and the feedback loops from violence to power and from power to violence are an intrinsic feature of war. . . . War is inherently a subset of politics, and every military act has political consequences, whether or not these are intended or immediately obvious. . . .

Clausewitz understands that war has no distinct boundaries and that its parts are interconnected. What is needed is to comprehend intuitively both that the set of parameters for "the problem" is unstable, and that no arbitrarily selected part can be abstracted adequately from the whole.[4]

Professor Beyerchen first uses Clausewitz's theories to reestablish the interconnectivity of politics with war, but he takes it one step further by relying on Clausewitz's non-linear view of history to create a new mandate of reasoning: namely, that we move from linear thinking to intuitive thinking. This is the first major step for the New Soldier to take.

Beyerchen's ideas were further expanded on by Major General (Ret.) Robert Scales of the U.S. Army. General Scales has theorized that World War IV (The Fearful Symmetry) will replace the political will of governments with the perceptions of the people in a "psycho-cultural war."[5] Thus, building on Clausewitz's basic insight that war is primarily influenced by people rather than technology, Scales argues that the Fearful Symmetry (World War IV) will be won by "winning the hearts and minds" of the people.

In a nutshell, the Fearful Symmetry will cause a shift in the *Center of Gravity* (a Clausewitzean concept) from the political will of a government (and its military leadership) to the perception of the people. Thus, wars will be fought on the battlefield of public perception where empathy demonstrated by soldiers may be more important than their ability to wield arms. Empathy will become an important weapon in this psycho-cultural war.

Moreover, cultural awareness and sensitivity along with the ability to create trust will be the decisive wining factors or the "emerging amplifiers." General Scales further argues that the soldier (e.g., the Army and Marine Corps in the U.S. military) will win the battle on the ground, and should be valued and invested in as a strategic and tactical asset over and above the tactical military technology provided by the Navy and the Air Force.[6]

Therefore, the new elements of victory in this asymmetric war begin with shifting the center of gravity. In other words, shaping perceptions should be elevated to a form of art. Arming and protecting the New Soldier fighting in World War IV (The Fearful Symmetry) means training the soldier, marine and airman in the new weapons of war: empathy, compassion and cultural understanding. By building tactical intelligence based on the soldier perceiving his or her surroundings in ways that are intuitive as well as psychological will best protect him or her. Teaching wisdom and intuitive decision-making in the military leaders of tomorrow will also help them forge new political and military alliances and build indigenous armies from the ground up.

In sum, General Scales offers the following insight:

> Empathy will become a weapon. Soldiers must gain the ability to move comfortably among alien cultures, to establish trust and cement relationships that can be exploited in battle. . . . Teaching commanders how to think and intuit rather than what to think will allow them to anticipate how the enemy will act. Convincing commanders to leave World War II-era decision-making processes in favor of non-linear intuitive processes will accelerate the pace and tempo of battle. The promise is enormous. But we will only achieve the full potential of this promise if we devote the resources to the research and education necessary to make it happen.[7]

Let us begin by first examining why the asymmetrical threats offered by modern forms of insurgency are so prevalent now. Clearly, conventional warfare used against the United States and its allies will not be successful. Therefore, there is no choice but to seek to use unconventional means of conflict. "The fundamental precept is that superior political will, when properly employed, can defeat greater economic and military power. Because it is organized to ensure political rather than military success this type of warfare is difficult to defeat. . . . The message is clear for anyone wishing to shift the political balance of power: only unconventional warfare works against established powers."[8]

Indeed, this approach is correct since insurgencies are the only type of wars that the United States has lost, not once but three times: Vietnam, Lebanon and Somalia. This type of asymmetrical warfare also defeated France in Algeria, and the former Soviet Union in Afghanistan (and possibly Russia vis-à-vis Chechnya). Further, the United States is still struggling in Afghanistan to resolve that military engagement.[9]

It is worthwhile to keep in mind three distinct aspects of insurgencies. First, they are small wars. In fact, the Spanish term "guerrilla" means little war and dates back to Spain's resistance to Napoleon's occupation of Spain from 1809-1813.[10]

Secondly, small wars are long in duration. The Chinese Communists fought for 28 years, the Vietnamese Communists for 30 years, and the Sandinistas for 18 years. The Palestinians have been resisting Israeli occupation since 1948.[11]

Finally, modern insurgencies aim for and achieve major changes in the political, economic and social structure of the societies in which such wars are prosecuted, for example, in the Afghan-Soviet war of the 1980s, the first intifada, and the Hezbollah campaign in southern Lebanon.[12]

Thus, these small wars may seem like wars without end, or "ghost wars" where the combatants, purposes and desired end goals may not be clear, but they are wars nonetheless. These wars are fought in complex physical, political and emotional terrains where none of the strengths and potentially all of the weaknesses of conventional war fighting states are taken advantage of and manipulated. This requires a change in the paradigm of war for the United States and its allies if the small wars are to end, and to end successfully.

In 1997, General Charles C. Krulak, Commandant of the Marine Corps, created the concept of the three-block war to describe the 21st century battlefield:

> It will be an *asymmetrical battlefield.* . . . [Emphasis supplied.] In one moment in time, our service members will be feeding and clothing displaced refugees, providing humanitarian assistance. In the next moment, they will be holding two warring tribes apart–conducting peacekeeping operations–and finally, they will be fighting a highly lethal mid-intensity battle–all on the same day, all within three city blocks. It will be what we call the 'three block war.' In this environment, conventional doctrine and organizations may mean very little. It is an environment born of change.[13]

In further describing the nature of each of the "blocks" in the three-block war, the first block is one of conventional kinetic warfare–traditional warfare that is fought by warfighting forces. However, unlike conventional warfare, the enemy "combatants" may not be governed by the law of war, and may deliberately use civilian casualties to further their cause. Thus, the conflict may be asymmetric in nature insofar as the warring sides may not be using the same rules of engagement.

Block Two is peacekeeping and other stabilization activities. Essentially, "[p]eacekeeping revolves around three inter-related principles: consent to the deployment of peacekeepers by all the parties involved in a conflict; impartiality on the part of the peacekeepers; and, the non-use of force–except in self-defense. The presence of peacekeepers is symbolic rather than coercive, and the success of their mission is highly dependent upon the permission of the belligerents they interpose themselves between. Peace enforcers make no such assumptions; they rely on force of arms in a hostile environment."[14]

Indeed, navigating the gap between peacekeeping and peace enforcement may be one of the gravest challenges of 21st century warfighting. Peace enforcement (using arms) may have disappeared, according to General (Ret.) Barry McCaffrey, after the death of 18 U.S. troops in Mogadishu, Somalia in 1993.[15] Now, "peacekeeping operations" have replaced "peace enforcement."[16] Even so, according to one estimate, there is less than one peacekeeper per 1,000 Afghans, a very discouraging ratio.[17]

Block Three is humanitarian assistance and reconstruction. Both Blocks Two and Three require that the military act in concert with the civilian corps including diplomats, Non-Governmental Organizations (NGOs), local and foreign government employees, and civilian employees of military forces. Neither of the blocks should be considered to be more important than the other, and all may need to be prosecuted simultaneously. The holistic and integrated nature of a three-block war is apparent in the latest insurgencies taking place in Iraq, Afghanistan and perhaps other venues as well. Indeed, the individual warfighter may need to conduct operations in all three blocks in a single day, as pointed out by General Krulak.

Thus, in fighting the three-block war, the warfighter must successfully transition "between its three elements as smoothly and seamlessly as possible, highlighting the relationship between peacekeeping and peace enforcement."[18] A full spectrum of operations must be smoothly transitioned to and from on a sliding scale. This is especially true since there are very few times where there is an actually defeat of the "enemy." In Afghanistan and Iraq, unlike Bosnia and Kosovo, there was no decisive defeat of all enemy combatants leading to a discrete end phase. Therefore, the three-block war should not be viewed as separate "blocks" but as a continuum where peaceful blocks may become combat zones, and vice versa.[19]

While the original concept of Block Three War may not have included economic reconstruction, it is a necessary follow-on corollary to humanitarian assistance. Humanitarian assistance is a stopgap short-term measure to alleviate human suffering in immediate terms. However, the underlying structural problems of a failure in development must also be addressed if sustainable peace is to be achieved.

As Michael Mazarr aptly points out, the military is not designed to address political grievances or failures in the development process. I agree. However, the problems with economic reconstruction in post-conflict areas is not a lack of political will, particularly among the international donor community or international organizations, or funds to finance such undertakings–it is the attacks by the enemy. In Afghanistan, for example, the Taliban, al Qaeda and other terrorist operatives "attack aid workers and destroy schools, wells and other economic projects."[20] Thus, the failure to properly securitize so-called post-conflict areas by military forces may be an easy target of blame, but as the above discussion sets forth, the three-block war is a continuum, and is not easily won.

How then do we prepare the New Soldier to fight the insurgencies of the 21st century? The same question was posed by General Krulak who provides the following insight:

> The lines separating the levels of war, and distinguishing combatant from 'non-combatant,' will blur, and adversaries, confounded by our 'conventional' superiority, will resort to asymmetrical means to redress the imbalance. Further complicating the situation will be the ubiquitous media whose presence will mean that all future conflicts will be acted before an international audience. . . .
>
> The inescapable lesson of Somalia and other recent operations, whether humanitarian assistance, peace-keeping, or transitional warfighting, is that their outcome may hinge on decisions made by small unit leaders, and by actions taken at the *lowest* level. [Emphasis in original.] The [Marine] Corps is, by design, a relatively young force. Success or failure will rest, increasingly, with the rifleman and his ability to make the *right* decision at the *right* time at the point of contact. [Emphasis in original.] . . . Most importantly, these missions will require them to confidently make well-reasoned and *independent* decisions under extreme stress–decisions that will likely be subject to the harsh scrutiny of both the media and the court of public opinion. . . . [Emphasis in original.] His actions, therefore, will directly impact the outcome of the larger operation; and he will become, as the title of the article suggests–the *Strategic Corporal.* [Emphasis in original.][21]

Indeed, the "three block war may very well be won or lost in the minds of our 'strategic corporals.'"[22]

Of course, as General Krulak points out, honor, courage, commitment and character remain bedrock values–his is the foundation upon which the New Soldier is created. Using character as a foundation, military forces must also learn how to cultivate intuitive decision making, a quality which may become decisive in this context. On the battlefield of the 21st century consisting of asymmetric threats of insurgencies, quick, effective decision making is critical to success.

General Krulak points out that decision making is composed of two different models: analytical and intuitive. "Analytical decison making uses a scientific, quantitative approach, and to be effective, it depends on a relatively high level of situational certainty and accuracy. . . . Unfortunately, the analytical model does not lend itself well to military applications once the enemy is engaged. At that point, military situations most often become very ambiguous, and the leader cannot afford to wait for detailed, quantitative data without risking the initiative."[23]

In contrast, "recognitional decision making depends on a *qualitative* assessment of the situation based on the decider's judgment and experience."[24] [Emphasis in original.] Rather than looking for an ideal solution, recognitional decision making seeks out a speedy one that will work under the given circumstances.

The key question here is whether the intuitive model of decision making may be taught, or is it simply intrinsic to the individual? Recently, "practitioners of the military art have come to believe that while heredity and personality may well have an impact on an individual's intuitive skills, these skills can also be cultivated and developed."[25]

During the World War II era, the Japanese instilled a "sixth sense" in their soldiers through months of intensive training in a cohesive unit, thus enabling their soldiers to make rapid, intuitive decisions. The Germans had a similar system of training for their officers whereby they were required to make rapid-fire tactical decisions under highly stressful situations. Of course, both nations lost the war, but there may be something to be learned from the tactics that they employed. General Krulak points out that, "Napoleon may be correct if he meant that intuition cannot be *taught* in the traditional sense, but both the Germans and the Japanese were successful in assuming that–through repetition–it could be *learned.* [Emphasis in original.][26]

Learning intuitive decision making may need to become a core value of organized national standing armies globally. The reason for this is grounded in the fact that asymmetric threats are no longer restricted to certain nations or peoples. Its effects are being felt globally. Further, while it may be a useful starting point to dedicate this type of training for officers rather than non-commissioned officers, "[w]e may need to face the paradox that our least experienced leaders–those with the least skill in decision making–will face the most demanding decisions on the battlefield."[27]

In sum, the three-block war requires not only knowledge of all three components of each block, namely, traditional warfighting, humanitarian assistance and post-conflict reconstruction, but also the means of fighting these conflicts by exercising intuitive decision making capabilities. Moreover, these warfighting tactics are not limited to the high-ranking officers for well-established militaries, but often must be deployed by lower ranking soldiers with the least training, skills, and personal life experience to aid him or her in meeting this monumental challenge.

Being trained to trust their own intuition must be rooted in the solid character of the individual warfighter. In order to develop this confidence, the New Soldier must be trained in repetitive decision-making skills under stressful situations so that individual decisions will be second nature, and emanate from his or her own sound character. While there may be a need to emphasize the "growth of integrity, courage, initiative, decisiveness mental agility and personal accountability,"[28] there also needs to be a moral compass guiding the actions of the New Soldier on the unknown terrains of the 21st century battlefield. In other words, a "culture" of intuitive decision making"[29] should be inculcated through the training of special operations-related military forces worldwide.

While some may argue that this type of training in situational awareness, including linguistic capabilities, has already been an integral part of military special operations-related preparedness. This is only partially true. Whereas situational awareness and making decisions based on a heightened awareness of the flashpoints of conflict, danger, and tactical military threats is, no doubt, an integral part of special operations-related training, in my view, it is limited both in its scope and purpose. This type of situational awareness is mainly geared towards making speedy and militarily effective decisions that move the conflict forward in a tactical way. This type of training may not include an intuitive sense of decision-making or the use of ethical principles to guide battlefield conduct to achieve strategic gains.

If, as General Krulak asserts that intuitive decision-making may be learned, the curricula of military training schools and facilities consequently need to be changed in order to incorporate it as a core discipline. In other words, intuitive decision-making must be taught order in for it to be learned.

This ethic is being absorbed gradually by the U.S. military. For example, the U.S. Army's Counterinsurgency Field Manual (FM 3-24) states:

> There are leadership and ethical imperatives that are prominent and, in some cases, unique to counterinsurgency [COIN]. The dynamic and ambiguous environment of modern counterinsurgency is frequently a small leader's fight however, commanders' actions at brigade and division levels can be even more significant. . . . [Soldiers and marines] must also rapidly adapt cognitively and emotionally to the perplexing challenges of counterinsurgency and master new competencies as well as new contexts. Those in leadership positions must provide the moral compass for their subordinates as they navigate this complex environment. . . .[30]

> COIN operations require leaders to exhibit patience, persistence and presence.[31]

Indeed, there may be some anecdotal evidence that the U.S. military is already trying to better understand and utilize the unconscious nature of sensing danger, including its emotional components. U.S. troops are now beginning to explore why and how some people sense danger and act on it long before others do which, in a life and death situation, could spell life over death.

For example, the sensing of "hunches" or a "gut feeling" as well as a cooling of body temperature, superb depth perception, sustaining intense focus for long periods of time, detecting odd shapes from a complex background are prompts which may be configured into brain activity or in a changed perception in emotions."The big question is whether these differences perceiving threat are natural, or due to training."[32] This question may be answered in due time. In the meantime, however, this type of sensory depth and emotional perceptions may all be added to the training of the New Soldier, and factored into his or her decision-making process on the battlefield of the Fearful Symmetry.

However, I am proposing a further paradigm shift. These battles and indeed, the war against Islamic-based global terrorism must be fought with compassion, empathy, integrity, courage and honor. Otherwise, we have already lost the conflict since we would have lost our bearings—a grounding in our own core values. The conflict will be lost without even being fought if we lose ourselves along the way. While integrity, honor and courage are all familiar within the military context as the backbone of military conduct and training, the qualities of compassion, empathy and wisdom may be less familiar to the military ethos. Exercising principles of compassion, empathy and wisdom by the New Soldier go far beyond even intuitively-based decision-making.

There is a heightened need for such rare qualities on the battlefield as a result of the nature of the conflict that we now face. It is no longer a question of winning a sharply-defined military conquest with politically certain outcomes. Now, the nature of the combat, the nature of the enemy combatants, and the goals and purposes of the conflict may be less clear and compelling from the conventional military conflicts in the past. The "fog of war" has, indeed, obscured these important markers.

While the qualities of compassion and empathy may resonate with pacificism, Gandhism, or a moral imperative to simply not engage in armed combat, this resemblance is superficial. I am not proposing that these other types of pacifist approaches to warfighting (or *not* engaging in armed combat altogether) be adopted. What I am proposing is that certain underlying qualities be incorporated into the warfighting capability of the U.S. military and its allies.

Why?

The terrains in which the insurgencies of the 21st century are being fought are not only physical but they are also psychological and emotional. It is no longer a simplistic equation of fighting and killing the "enemy." Who is the enemy, and what is the enemy fighting for? Where do his loyalties and alliances lie? Is he loyal to an ally of ours and if so, why? What is the desired outcome of the conflict for him, and for us? What are the consequences of the armed conflict and how does it affect the civilian populations? Where do their allegiances lie? These are all basic questions that have complex and shifting answers that change from day to day, if not moment to moment.

These considerations, and many others, need to be taken into account in prosecuting a "war without end." In order to so, and to do so in the most effective way, we must change the paradigm of the conflict. It is not so much about conquest, but of persuasion. This is fundamentally a war of ideas and ideologies in ways that are new, unknown and vastly intimidating. By exercising qualities of compassion and empathy, we increase our chances of persuading the people involved (most of them unwittingly) in the conflict in order to end it.

Further, it increases our chances of ending the conflict in a way that supports our goals as well as theirs. If the Afghans, for example, feel conquered or politically dominated, there is vast historical evidence that this conflict will not truly end. It will continue indefinitely, and further destabilize the region. Understanding their political goals and even their emotional needs, may help forge a lasting solution and a lasting victory for all sides. We can only win this conflict if they win as well.

This may seem to be a very strange suggestion to propose that we win only if our "enemies" win as well. The usual equation is that we win if *we defeat our enemy*. I agree that this formula has its utility, but we have moved away from the Newtonian universe of the predeterminant, inexorable laws governing celestial bodies in the universe and toward the Einsteinian universe of probabilities that are unpredictable and uncertain in the world of sub-atomic particles. We have moved away from the symmetry of the Cold War of two major political actors and systems in conflict with each other to the nano-universe of the Fearful Symmetry where anyone can become a terrorist in any place at any time. It is not predictable or knowable—it is unstable, unpredictable and unknowable. That is the true source of its power to terrify us.

Richard Haas was quoted earlier as having said that the "United States will no longer have the luxury of a '[y]ou're either with us or against us' foreign policy."[33] This is true as our alliances will rapidly change over time to accommodate new and shifting political goals and economic needs. The strict and doctrinaire pronouncements (and alliances) of the past will have limited utility in the future.

On a much deeper philosophical level, Martin Buber recognized that human existence may be defined by the way in which we enter into a dialogue with ourselves, with each other, with the world, and with God.[34] According to Buber, we may adopt two types of attitudes in dealing with the world: the *I-Thou* relationship and the *I-It* relationship. In the *I-Thou* relationship, the underlying relationship is one of subject-to-subject. In other words, human beings relate to each other not as objects but as subjects, and as having a unity of being. Thus, rather than perceiving other human being as having specific isolated qualities, we engage in a dialogue with each other involving each other's whole being. The *I-Thou* relationship is one of mutuality and reciprocity.[35]

In contrast, the *I-It* relationship consists of a subject-to-object relationship. In other words, human beings perceive of each other as having specific, isolated qualities, and view their relationship to the world as a world consisting of things. The *I-It* relationship is one of separateness and detachment.[36] Without venturing too far afield, the relevance of this discussion is to try to persuade decisionmakers, especially those in the military who are interested in the intuitive decision-making process, to perceive the conflict in a radically different way.

The conflict with fundamentalist Islamic-based terrorism is not only one of ideas but also one involving actual individuals. If these individuals are perceived as subjects (rather than as isolated objects), they may be more difficult to kill in hand-to-hand combat, fire missiles upon, torture, or treat in a dehumanized, degrading or indifferent manner. In fact, if these individuals are perceived as an integral part of a holistic whole that includes us, then we have subjectivized rather than objectivized our relationship to them.

What is the meaning behind this approach? It is the first step to creating empathy. More importantly, it fosters an understanding of the conflict from the emotional viewpoint of the "enemy." By this, I am not trying to suggest that the top leadership of Al Qaeda or even of the Taliban for that matter should or can be "subjectivized." There are certain "irreconcilables" who regrettably may only be eliminated as targets of war, or brought to justice for their criminal acts. However, the New Soldier may be better positioned and have more refined decision-making skills in separating the irreconcilables from the reconcilables. This may be a quality worth cultivating.

In fact, there may be some evidence that this paradigm shift is already beginning to occur, not in doctrine but in practice. For example, the United States and Afghanistan have signed a Memorandum of Understanding that ensures that night raids into peoples' homes must be ordered and conducted by Afghan troops with U.S. military forces in a supportive role.[37] This new effort is directed toward easing long-time tensions with civilians arising from casualties and home searches in U.S.-led or assisted ground operations. The U.S. military hopes that this resentment will abate, and that it will help build a "civilian surge" to support reconstruction and governance efforts in Afghanistan.[38]

One commentator offers the following prescription for ensuring success of the U.S. counterinsurgency strategy in Afghanistan:

> Tailoring COIN to Afghanistan is going to require four innovations. First, security, governance, and development must be integrated parts of the overall approach, and the requisite Afghan capacities for each part must be assessed and developed. Second, the fragmentation of governance and the agility of the insurgency require tailoring efforts to provincial and in some cases district conditions.. . . Third, a clear process of reaching out to the irreconcilable and identifying the reconcilable needs to be mapped out and explained to the public. Fourth, the sustainability of COIN depends on whether it is framed within a doctrine of state-building. Whereas the use of force is required in the short-term, the rule of law is required in the medium to long term.[39]

Recent reporting on the war in Afghanistan makes it clear that the aim of the U.S. military "is to combat the insurgency in a new way: Instead of targeting extremists strongholds, they will aim to protect communities from the Taliban."[40]

With specific regard to transforming Iraq-based tactics to Afghanistan, a reporter for the *Washington Post* notes the following:

> Helmand, Marines here are fond of noting, is the Afghan equivalent of Anbar, the once-lawless province west of Baghdad that was the focus of Marine operations in Iraq. Both are vast desert regions bisected by a river. The populations are tribal and religiously conservative. Criminal

activity–smuggling in Iraq and drug-trafficking in Afghanistan–is rampant. Cross-border infiltration of fighters and munitions from Syria was a massive problem in Anbar; Pakistan plays that role with Helmand. . . .

Although [Brig. Gen. Lawrence Nicholson] is now in a different country, with different traditions and a different insurgency, he nonetheless sees lessons from Anbar that can be applied to Helmand. At the top of his list is the need for more indigenous security forces... .

As a Marine patrol walked through the bazaar on a recent morning, its presence prompted a group of men sipping tea in front of a motorcycle repair shop to voice concern–not that the Americans had arrived but that they might depart before the Taliban had been vanquished. . . .

"We cannot trust the government or the Taliban," Zary Sahib, the leader of the town's mosque, told McCollough. "We can only trust you."[41]

Whether this sentiment is echoed by the majority of Afghans is not clear, but there is anecdotal evidence that the nature of the fighting in Afghanistan is changing significantly. It is being patterned after certain successes in Iraq. In fact, General Patraeus' "anaconda" strategy for Iraq may also be applicable in creating a new approach for Afghanistan. The anaconda strategy against Al Qaeda in Iraq involved six elements of kinetic warfare (i.e., armed combat), politics, intelligence, detainee operations, non-kinetics (e.g., education, job creation), and inter-agency efforts at stabilization and transformation.[42] Further, the nature of the Afghan mission has also dramatically shifted from routing out and killing extremists to protecting civilian populations and helping them reconstruct their war-savaged country.

In taking advantage of this shift in operational focus and mission, partnering with local inhabitants may be key. For example, the local inhabitants may have an intuitive sense of who may be reconcilable (or not), a very useful part of the tactics being employed in Afghanistan now. If local inhabitants and the human intelligence (HUMINT) capability they may offer, if harnessed effectively, could be made an integral part of the COIN strategy, locals could become actual stakeholders in this small but long war. Then, like an actual anaconda, the pressure exerted in an integrated COIN strategy against terrorist or destabilizing elements may become unbearable for such extremists.

As the U.S. Army Field Manual on COIN states, "[t]he insurgents persist by controlling the passive cooperation of the people around them."[43] If this support is undercut, then it may mean a subtle shift in the conflict that may become a game-changer. And, indeed, there is ample evidence that the local population in Afghanistan is exhausted and exasperated by this unending conflict.

As in the African proverb, when two elephants fight, the grass gets trampled. The locals are passively rather than actively engaged in this conflict since they must feel threatened, in some measure, by the Taliban, Al Qaeda and foreign military officers. Moreover, they do not know what the final outcome of the conflict will be. They may feel that the foreign forces will ultimately leave, but that the Taliban will stay.

British troops operating in Afghanistan have noted that the Taliban is not a "militarily and ideologically coherent force but a 'wide but shallow coalition of convenience' that relies on cooperation between groups that is 'opportunistic rather than strategic.'"[44] Moreover, local Afghans may not give the Taliban and other extremist elements active support, but often "acquiesce or turn a blind eye." The British note that "it is only when the cooperation, passive and active, of ordinary Afghans is removed that the insurgency will be fatally undermined. . . The squeeze on the Taliban must come from within as well as without."[45] Thus, if this sense of disaffection or negative energy expressed by the Afghan locals may be constructively channeled to support the end goals of COIN, then the nature of the conflict may change. In fact, it may change in a way that ultimately defeats the Taliban.

Otherwise, if U.S. and NATO-led forces continue engaging in sporadic skirmishes and setting up checkpoints that may be averted by the Taliban and jihadists, this war has no foreseeable end since there is no amplifier leading to a victory (or at least to a definitive conclusion). The conflict will continue in *stasis* indefinitely. The COIN Manual points out a simple truth, "[s]uccess in COIN depends wholly on the people."[46] This is the time for the New Soldier to capture the emotions and imagination of the people, the key to ending the conflict definitively.

Cultural Awareness as a Strategic Weapon

First and foremost, the nature of the asymmetric war needs to be redefined. Small wars, or what Rudyard Kipling called the "savage wars of peace,"[47] are ones where our "[f]uture opponents will avoid direct and conventional conflicts with America's overwhelming military power and purposely seek novel and asymmetric combinations of irregular warfare."[48] In fact, where symmetric adversaries are evenly matched and use similar technology, knowledge of each others' cultures is irrelevant.[49] However, in a small war, culture matters.

So, the U.S. military needs to reexamine the belief, heretofore true, that "success in war is best achieved through an overwhelming technological advantage."[50] The United States has so definitively captured the edge of winning any conflict through conventional and technologically sophisticated means, that a defeat of the U.S. using conventional means is no longer possible. Thus, the U.S. military has become virtually invincible in terms of modern conventional warfare. So, while using an overwhelmingly technological approach will guarantee victory in a conventional sense, it may and has led to defeat in an unconventional war. This was the bitter lesson of Somalia in 1994.

"In contrast, what is more important in Small Wars is a very comprehensive examination of the culture of the society or country that is the source of the conflict. Because Small Wars usually are interventions in an internal conflict and require efforts to reconstruct or establish political, social and economic institutions and mechanisms, an acute understanding of the society and its culture is essential. Small Wars are generally culture intensive conflicts, and the battleground, properly understood, includes the political and psychological elements of the populations and culture."[51]

Culture has been defined as the "combination of national history, myth, geography, beliefs, ethnic backgrounds and region.... Culture is the totality of socially transmitted behavior patterns, arts, beliefs, institutions, and thought characteristic of a community or population. Culture is a complex aggregate that includes knowledge, belief, art, law, morals custom and any other capabilities and habits acquired by a member of society."[52]

Cultural awareness also needs to be distinguished from situational awareness. Situational awareness is a full understanding of the aerial and ground intelligence technology and the physical surroundings in which the conflict is taking place. "In the military context, cultural awareness can be defined as the 'cognizance of cultural terrain for military operations and the connections between cultural and warfighting.' Cultural awareness implies an understanding of the need to consider cultural terrain in military operations, a knowledge of which cultural factors are important for a given situation and why, and a specified level of understanding for a target culture."[53]

However, during the culture-centric warfare aspect of asymmetric warfare, the "intimate knowledge of the enemy's motivation, intent, will, tactical method, and cultural environment has proved to be far more important for success than the deployment of smart bombs, unmanned aircraft, and expensive bandwidth. Success in the phase rests with the ability of leaders to think and adapt faster than the enemy and of soldiers to thrive in an environment of uncertainty, ambiguity, and unfamiliar cultural circumstances."[54] In the words of one young soldier, "I had perfect situational awareness. What I lacked was cultural awareness. Great technical intelligence . . . wrong enemy."[55]

It is clear that "cultural ignorance has been a challenge in the past for U.S. forces,"[56] and that developing greater cultural intelligence is what is needed now. Cultural awareness must augment situational awareness.

One reason cited for the absence of cultural knowledge in the U.S. diplomatic, military, intelligence or economic communities is "the almost total absence of anthropology within the national-security establishment."[57] In echoing a similar sentiment, David Kilcullen notes that:

> This is because, through the "military-industrial complex," a substantial portion of the American economy, and numerous jobs in almost every congressional district, are linked to the production of conventional warfighting capacity. It takes factories, jobs, and industrial facilities to build battleships and bombers, but aid workers, linguists, and Special Forces operators are vastly cheaper and do not demand the same industrial base. So, shifting spending priorities onto currently

unconventional forms of warfare would cost jobs and votes in the congressional districts of the very people who control that spending. This makes it structurally difficult for the United States fundamentally to reorient its military capabilities away from conventional war-fighting to divert a significant proportion of the defense spending into civilian capacity. Hence, absent a concerted effort by the nation's leadership in both the executive and legislative branches, the pattern of asymmetric warfare, with the United States adopting a basically conventional approach but being opposed by enemies who seek to sidestep American conventional power, is likely to be a long-standing trend.[58]

This is an interesting viewpoint that illuminates one possible economic reason driving U.S. military training and resource deployment toward technology-based fighting systems rather than toward cultural awareness training. There is another reason to add, and that is simply that the political, economic and cultural hegemony of the United States following the end of World War II made understanding other nations, cultures, or languages less relevant. It certainly was not a political or military priority.

Moreover, the United States may have been a victim of its own geography. European nations, for example, live cheek-to-jowl with each other and have vastly different languages, customs and traditions. Other nations may have many different languages and ethnic identities within it (e.g., India, Indonesia) requiring an elevated appreciation for cultural differences. In any case, the lack of cultural awareness is a strategic weakness that fundamentalist Islamic-based terrorists are taking advantage of by adapting and adopting "a method of war that seeks to offset U.S. technical superiority with a countervailing method that uses guile, subterfuge, and terror mixed with patience and a willingness to die."[59]

In order to create this New Soldier to win on a tactical level on the battlefield of The Fearful Symmetry, a new alliance with social scientists (traditionally kept at arms' length by military officers and leaders) may need to be forged. This New Soldier will need to learn new skills from different disciplines in the social sciences in order to navigate unfamiliar cultures and emotional terrains.

In fact, there is a new recognition that, "[c]ultural awareness has become an increasingly important competency for small-unit leaders. Perceptive junior leaders learn how cultures affect military operations. They study major world cultures and put a priority on learning the details of the new operational environment when deployed."[60]

Aside from using cultural awareness as a tactical weapon in fighting insurgencies and small wars, there is another dimension that has yet to be explored.

> War is a thinking man's game. A military too acculturated to solving warfighting problems with technology alone should now begin to recognize that wars must be fought with intellect. Reflective senior officers returning form Iraq and Afghanistan have concluded that great advantage can be achieved by outthinking rather than outequipping the enemy. They are telling us that wars are won as much by creating alliances, leveraging nonmilitary advantages, reading intentions, building trust, converting opinions, and managing perceptions–all tasks that demand an exceptional ability to understand people their culture, and their motivation.[61]

"Intelligence" within the military community has been restricted to the narrow confines of intelligence-gathering to obtain information about the enemy that may be used in gaining tactical or strategic advantages. This information-gathering effort is designed to support the military end of wining the conflict. However, intelligence gathering may need to be expanded to include from much wider sources to serve much wider purposes.

More importantly, the notion of "intelligence" needs to include the ability to wage the war intelligently by using all the tools and advantages at the warfighter's disposal. Much has been made of the military's use of "hard power," then "soft power," and now "smart power." The transition in the underlying popular lingo needs to be supported by an actual change in strategy and training. Intelligence should also mean ingenuity, intuition, inventiveness and "thinking outside the box." Agility on the battlefield of small wars means more than tactical maneuvering with weapons–it requires tactical maneuvering with the mind.

There is also a second missing dimension to fighting small wars– ethics. Ethics reflect a deeper cultural ethos. Quite disappointingly, one commentator concludes that "[t]he bottom line is that significant numbers of U.S. troops think and act in ways that violate their professional ethics and the laws of war."[62] This summary conclusion is particularly alarming in a counterinsurgency context.

Counterinsurgency ethics are particularly perplexing and complex because the primacy of civilian protection appears at odds with military service values that stress loyalty to fellow Marines and soldiers. It will take time for each service to articulate, inculcate and tend an ethic of counterinsurgency consistent with its culture."[63]

However, all soldiers in combat situations have a *jus in bello* obligation to protect the lives of innocent civilians–this duty is an ethical responsibility. *Jus in bello* refers to justice in war, or to right conduct in the midst of battle after the hostilities have already been declared.[64] This is a concept that applies to warfighters. (In contrast, *jus ad bellum* refers to the obligation of a state to enter into a war for a just reason such as self-defense or the defense of another. This obligation falls on heads of state and political leaders.)

Since counterinsurgencies are so different from those of conventional warfare, there is a transformational dimension of warfare that stems from the ethics of the battlefield. One commentator believes that protecting civilians from injury is the starting point for a "non-violent conflict transformation" for the New Soldier. This may already be taking place. The U.S. counterinsurgency efforts in Afghanistan and Iraq, for example, represent a profound paradigm shift. These operations were, over time, increasingly aimed at protecting civilians.

"Non-violent conflict transformation" is defined as "an approach to engaging in conflict that is rooted in understanding the complexity of the conflict and in finding creative ways to engage all parties in positive conversation that enables them to come to some level of engagement. It is a collaborative approach that looks to the future, focuses on relationships, and seeks to restructure relationships in order to meet everyone's needs."[65]

This transformation is important within the counterinsurgency context since it provides an avenue other than violence for the warfighter. This may seem counterintuitive, and it is not designed to render the warfighter incapable of waging actual combat. Instead, it enlarges the number of options available in waging a counterinsurgency campaign to include non-violent means as well.

Again, this may sound as thought I am reverting to a discussion of pacifism, Gandhism, and other non-violent means of waging a conflict. I am not. Rather, I am advocating for an enlarged scope of possible options and approaches to winning a conflict. Further, this is only applicable in relation to a warfighter interacting with civilian populations. This analysis would not apply to actual enemy combatants in an armed conflict scenario–the warfighter cannot be incapacitated from his warfighting capability.

However, in order to effect this transformation, the New Soldier would have to cultivate "creative thinking and deep listening skills."[66] In addition, understanding complexity, demonstrating empathy and respect for others involved in the conflict, and identifying non-violent means of interacting with the affected civilian populations are all skills that the New Soldier would have to acquire. This goes far beyond distributing candy, soccer balls or trinkets to local children.

This transformation will allow the New Soldier to move from peacekeeping to peacebuilding. If empathy forms the basis of the relationship with other involved in the conflict, then it evidences "a willingness to understand the situation of the other while not falling into their emotional state."[67] Moreover, empathy is the foundation of the *I-Thou* relationship.

At the outset, this kind of transformation within the rigid command structure of the military may seem to be a hopeless undertaking. However, the qualities of empathy, compassion, creativity, and imagination flow from moral courage and help create a new sensibility. This new ethos will permit the New Soldier to engage in more ethical decision making, pursue non-violent means of conflict resolution, and more effectively protect the lives and human rights of the civilians that he or she is there to protect.

In the end, the asymmetric threats posed by terrorists may be ameliorated over time as this new ethic will ultimately change the nature of the conflict. "Violence is known. Peace is the mystery. By its very nature, therefore, peace-building requires a journey guided by the imagination of risk."[68]

If a new ethical relationship is forged with the civilians involved in the conflict by the warfighter, a new heightened discipline of ethics will evolve over time. This new military ethics will be very recognizable since it flows from courage, duty and honor–the hallmarks of military service and sacrifice.

Indeed, there is reason to feel hopeful that this transformation is already starting to take place within the U.S. military itself. U.S. Army Field Manual 3-07 states that, "[c]onflict transformation focuses on converting the dynamics of conflict into processes for constructive, positive change. *Conflict transformation* **is the process of reducing the means and motivations for violent conflict while developing more viable, peaceful alternatives for the competitive pursuit of political and socioeconomic aspirations.** [Emphasis in original.] It aims to set the host nation on a sustainable positive trajectory where transformational processes can directly address the dynamics causing civil strife or violent conflict. It seeks to resolve the root causes of conflict and instability while building the capacity of local institutions to forge and sustain effective governance, economic development, and the rule of law."[69]

And further, "[c]onflict transformation recognizes that conflict is a normal and continuous social dynamic within human relationships and seeks to provide effective peaceful means of resolution. Conflict transformation is based in cultural astuteness and a broad understanding of the dynamics of conflict. Success depends on building creative solutions that improve relationships; it necessitates an innate understanding of underlying relational, social, and cultural patterns. Success relies heavily on understanding, recognizing that conflict can potentially stimulate growth and to leverage that potential to spur constructive change."[70]

Clearly, there is a recognition that conflict transformation is essential, and is based on "cultural astuteness." However, whether this transformation will actually take place through the efforts of military forces, among other actors, will only be revealed over time.

In sum, the New Soldier will need to be trained to move seamlessly from traditional warfare with a conventional enemy, to combating irregular threats, to providing humanitarian assistance to the innocent. Additional time will be required, not only to effectuate these profound changes to soldiering, but also in order to train soldiers in intuitive decision-making and wisdom. (This recommendation, of course, assumes that intuition and wisdom can be both taught and learned.) And, in following the Japanese model, discussed above, the New Soldier may need to be trained and deployed in smaller units in order to be effective.

The chart below inustrates some salient defferences between a traditional soldier and the new soldier.

Traditional Soldier V. New Soldier

	Traditional Soldier	New Soldier
Mission	Protect Population	Empower Population
Terrain	Physical	Psychological
Date Points	Quantitative (technology-based)	Qualitative (emotions-based)
Environment	Situational awareness	Psychological awareness
Decision-making	Logical	Intuitive
Linguistics	Limited ability	Enhanced ability
Cultural understanding	Limited	Enhanced
Responsiveness	Chain of Command	Public perception
Emotional Profile	Professionalism	Empathy, Compassion, wisdom
Objective	To win conflict by defeating "irreconcilables"	To win conflict by Partnering with "reconcilliables"
Impact	Securitize & stabilize Conflict zone	Transition & reconstruct conflict zone

stemming the tide of U.S. casualties caused by improvised explosive devices (IEDs), took some extraordinary steps.[71]

By November 2011, over 3200 U.S. soldiers and Marines had been wounded by IEDs in 2011 alone, up 22 percent from 2010. As it turns out, the insurgents' weapon of choice in Afghanistan is a plastic jug filled with ammonium nitrate fertilizer. The finished product is made from fertilizer that Taliban insurgents soak in hot water to remove the calcium carbonate which sinks to the bottom of the container. The dried powder looks like laundry detergent, has no metal or moving parts, and is exceptionally difficult to detect. Blasting caps are made from ballpoint pens or glass tubes filled with acid. Although the fertilizer is banned in Afghanistan for this very reason, most of the fertilizer is sourced from Pakistan.

Lt. General Barbero called Fawad Muhktar, the chairman of the Fatima Group which owns the fertilizer plants in Pakistan, and asked for a meeting. The first meeting took place not in Pakistan but in Arlington, Virginia, where Mr. Muhktar was dropping off his son to school. While cognizant of his concerns, Mr. Muhktar countered that only 1 percent of his fertilizer fell into the hands of insurgents. The rest was being used for farming and agricultural purposes.

Undaunted, Lt. General Barbero organized his own conference in Arlington, VA to persuade over 120 industry executives, chemists and military officers to change the formula for fertilizer to make is less attractive for bomb-making. Creative solutions were sought out and discussed, the most promising being the addition of coated urea fertilizer granules to the ammonium nitrate. The combination has a strong affinity for water and is hard to separate which must be done in order to create a dry powder explosive. Other options of adding dyes or radio tags to the ammonium nitrate or banning the use of ammonium nitrate in Pakistan were discussed. The point is that creative "out of the box" solutions were sought in a proactive way that involved many of the stakeholders, including a representative at the conference from the Fatima Group. Clearly, it may be argued that the extraordinary actions taken by Lt. General Barbero constituted a "New Soldier" approach to resolving the conflict by disarming the "enemy," not by just winning the war by use of force.

Assuming the best case scenario that this intuitive tactical and strategic military approach of the New Soldier is fully adopted and implemented by U.S. military forces and its allies, does this mean that these forces will ultimately win the global war on terror (The Fearful Symmetry)? Probably not.

However, this may be the emerging amplifier that is the next dialectical leap in our own evolution. If we can learn to face the most unrelenting, deadly and uncompromising hatred and commitment to our violent destruction of global terrorists and respond with empathy, compassion and intuitive decision-making on the battlefield, this may be the greatest lesson that human history may have to offer. In fact, I would argue that this new non-linear, intuitive soldiering will assimilate the best of Eastern and Western traditions including, arguably, those lessons from Islam that teach empathy and compassion.

No doubt, most will view this argument as hopelessly naïve, and I would agree in large part. Further, since I cannot support this argument with empirical evidence that adopting this approach will, in fact, help resolve or end the Fearful Symmetry, it may lack practical relevance as well.

In my view, however, the only true end to the Fearful Symmetry and the pathway to move into the next historical phase is for the global terrorists to love–not us, but themselves. By disavowing their self-destructive, self-abnegating and self-indulgent nihilism and replacing it with a sense of self-respect followed by the respect for others, they will decisively end the Fearful Symmetry. This is quite a challenge, and there is no evidence that there is even a remote possibility that this challenge will be met. But by restoring hope, we restore faith in the belief that we can and must live peaceably together, and that tomorrow will surely be better than today. At that point, we can move past the Fearful Symmetry and usher in a new era of history that will begin when this one ends.

5

"Re-Visioning" Stability and Peace Operations

The asymmetric threats posed by fundamentalist Islamic-based separatists and global terrorism are grave dangers to the international community and the existing world order. Confronting these threats in a systematic way is a difficult, complex, multilateral and multi-faceted challenge. This challenge has four discrete dimensions: military, political and diplomatic, economic, and cultural. Military strategies apply primarily to global Islamic-based terrorists and secondarily to separatists (but with different objectives and tactics in mind); political and diplomatic action apply to separatists; economic measures apply to separatists; and cultural efforts to win over the terrorists apply to both, again, with different goals, objectives and tactics in mind for reasons described more fully below.

A. Military Action. The discussion above described the relative failures in

Table 5.1 Four Dimensions of Confronting Asymmetric Threats

	Military	Political/ Diplomatic	Economic	Cultural
Separatists	Limited Engagement	Yes	Yes	Yes
Global Terrorists	Yes	No	No	Yes

imposing military solutions by external parties to forge a new "peace." (The exception to this generalization may be post- World War II Germany and Japan according to the RAND study cited earlier–however, there are many dissimilarities between those two countries after their respective defeats following World War II and present-day Iraq and Afghanistan.) In light of this important historical lesson, using military solutions with separatist Islamic-based terrorist movements may not be a compelling or particularly effective course of action. Thus, it may be argued that diplomacy, political solutions and effective economic development strategies (rather than military options) should be pursued in this context. In fact, this may be an optimal time to consider a change in strategy with respect to an Islamic separatist-based brand of terrorism.

With respect to Islamic-based global terrorists, however, a two-fold military strategy seems to be warranted. The first is to vigorously continue and expand law enforcement efforts, described below, and second, to create a "New Soldier" for the battlefield of the Fearful Symmetry.

1. National and International Law Enforcement. First and foremost, it is critical to strengthen linkages among all nation-states, intelligence and policing agencies and international organizations, media, and other non-state actors to contain, if not actually win, the so-called "global war on terror." Stemming the exponential growth of the Hydra-headed monster of global terrorism is a daunting task that requires cohesive, well-coordinated planning, information-sharing and decisive action among these and other actors. Aside from national and international intelligence operations, containing and preventing the spread of traditional arms along with nuclear and chemical weapons, the identification and prohibition of financial flows to terrorists, criminal prosecutions both nationally (with extradition arrangements in place, as required) and internationally, where appropriate, there are undoubtedly many other aspects of containing terrorism that should be vigorously pursued. Most importantly, creating new methods of detecting terrorist activities, cells, and plots should be highly prioritized and adequately funded by the international players acting in concert with another.

The nature of this "military action" is primarily one of intelligence gathering, law enforcement and the administration of justice rather than engaging in formal military operations *per se*. Whether these actions actually stem the flow of terrorist activities themselves is an open-ended question, but it is highly unlikely that this level of law enforcement action alone will be sufficient in winning the global war on terror.

Moreover, there is a related dimension of analysis to consider. The missing dimension of analysis goes back to the theory of Carl von Clausewitz, a Prussian military philosopher who was an observer of and a participant in the Napoleonic wars. His seminal work, *On War*, simply states the following dictum:

War is the continuation of politics by other means.[1]

This simple observation has proven problematic for many U.S. administrations who may have been tempted to not pursue diplomatic channels as vigorously as possible simply because the U.S. military is and continues to be so powerful and effective with respect to its military operations. Thus, rather than seeking diplomatic and political solutions, military options are pursued instead.

Indeed, one commentator notes that, "[t]oday, war is no longer an instrument of last resort. . . . In other words, today's environment turns the Clausewitzean paradigm upside down, contemporary conflict is no longer an extension of politics, politics is an extension of conflict."[2]

However, despite whatever "sins of omission" in failing to pursue diplomatic solutions that may have been committed by U.S. policymakers and others during the Cold War era, this still does not explain the rage of global terrorists. It is very clear that global Islamic-based terrorists are not interested in creating stable nation-states or economies. Therefore, negotiated political solutions or economic incentives to create stronger market-based economies are not persuasive courses of action. With global jihadists, a law enforcement based solution may be the only option.

The only addition to the description above of prescribed law enforcement activities that may have some value in this context is to identify new tools with which to win, not the war against global terrorism, but the peace. The Iraq example may serve to highlight the problematic nature of peacekeeping and stabilization operations after the kinetic warfare aspect of the military operation has been successfully concluded.

This is especially the case where separatists' movements converge with the agenda of global jihadists. While not detracting from the brave and exemplary conduct of all the soldiers and marines in the battlefields of Iraq, Afghanistan and elsewhere, there may be the need to create a new kind of soldier that can win the uneasy "peace" in these highly volatile and unstable environments. Peace, of course, is a highly relative term since terrorist and separatist-based violence is endemic in these and other places.

B. Diplomacy and Political Action. As indicated above, global terrorists do not have any interest in creating stable political or economic structures. Moreover, negotiating with them can seriously undermine national political processes and the overall global balance of power. Therefore, this is not a real option– unless the so called "terrorists" are elected to parliament!

1. Diplomacy. With respect to fundamentalist Islamic-based separatist movements, there is room for diplomatic efforts and an ongoing political dialogue to resolve underlying issues that may, for example, be related to establishing their sovereignty, land rights, political representation, and releasing political prisoners. Going back to the earlier analysis of recognizing the efficacy of engaging in diplomacy before, during and after actual war is waged (a Clausewitzean principle)–this means that international diplomacy needs to be fundamentally redefined and restructured.

Diplomacy should be the first and very well-integrated step in a larger political process that addresses underlying issues of political representation, land issues, legal grievances, criminal prosecutions, economic empowerment, education and health along with other matters. Diplomatic efforts with Islamic separatist-based terrorist movements could begin with special political envoys or international mediators. The key here is the trust placed in such individuals by the parties in conflict.

The diplomatic effort must, however, be fully committed to by all affected parties, and the roles of each participant should be fully described, designated and agreed to in advance. A structured process that delineates well-publicized and agreed-to benchmarks by the key parties in the diplomatic process is critical. Without the requisite political will to commit to a diplomatic resolution, no substantive results will be possible.

In fact, a breakdown in the diplomatic process may lead to a feeling of further betrayal, thus spurring more terrorist-based activities in order to achieve what are essentially political goals. Therefore, it is critical that a win-win scenario be made possible so that each side (or every side, depending on the complexity of the conflict) may claim victory.

As described earlier, a diplomatic effort that is an integral part of a disciplined peace process is very complex, a multi-actor, multi-tiered, multi-faceted and multi-phased process. Along with the political will necessary to make such a process successful in the short-term and enduring in the long-run, sufficient resources in terms of funds, time, and perhaps even empathy from all the actors must be devoted to this effort.

Finally, in order to fundamentally restructure the diplomatic process on a global basis, the political will of the entire international community needs to be a key factor. In other words, diplomatic efforts to resolve conflict should not be left to the isolated, unilateral or sporadic efforts of the United States or other Western powers. Neighboring states to the conflict area and even a broader multilateral effort should be engaged in the diplomatic process.

Perhaps an independent consultative group (for example, an NGO-based effort) should take the lead with respect to identifying neutral parties that can effectively be trained to lead a negotiated peace process. So, in other words, neutral South African parties (particularly those well-versed in the truth-and-reconciliation process, for example) may be trained to lead the peace process in the Philippines. The possibilities are enormous but are totally dependent on the will of the international community to commit to the effort of conflict prevention and resolution. The international community must be persuaded that it is in its best self-interest to resolve and prevent conflict, and take active steps in order to ensure that a brokered peace results from these efforts. If successfully persuaded, these international peace "brokers" can be continually deployed to both resolve and prevent conflict.

Ensuring the success of this type of diplomatic effort is dependent on two factors: (1) trust in the process itself and in the parties to the process, and (2) meeting the specifically-negotiated commitments of the peace process. Trust is needed before the diplomacy is embarked upon, and meeting the commitments of the negotiated outcome is required after the diplomatic process is completed. If the requisite political will exists to commit to these two requirements at the outset of the negotiations, then a positive outcome is almost assured. If not, then the quagmire of conflict, mistrust, continued impoverishment, and missed opportunities for peace will, no doubt, continue into the foreseeable future.

2. A Political Process. A recapitulation of the essential factors in an overall structured political process follows, along with a fuller explanation of its implications.

> ➤ *Stabilize the conflict area through multilateral and/or regional military intervention (such as UN peace-keeping forces where needed) in order to end civil war, strife or unrest.*

> ➤ The first choice to be made is whether the peacekeeping operation and/or a follow-on nation-building exercise should be unilateral or multilateral. The RAND study concludes that multilateral peacekeeping efforts are more time-consuming and complex than unilateral operations, but are less expensive for the participants. Further, multilateral operations tend to produce more thoroughgoing political transformations, and greater reconciliation among the parties. However, multilateral efforts must have a unity of command in order to achieve these results.[3]

> ➤ The second choice is whether to dismantle existing institutions wholesale or reform them from within. A unilateral U.S. effort to reform post-World War II Japanese institutions from within was very successful, while a multilateral effort to dismantle German institutions and recreate them from whole cloth was less successful.[4] If multilateralism is chosen, Afghanistan currently has no existing viable institutions, and everything needs to be built from the ground up. In Iraq, a unilateral effort by the United States to re-create dismantled institutions has yielded mixed results, and it may be too problematic to know if a multilateral approach would have been more effective in this context.

> ➤ The RAND study further indicates that the UN may be a suitable choice for most peacekeeping operations in terms of its

multinational character that adds to its legitimacy, having lower operating expenses, and using a team of seasoned professionals who understand the challenges of nation-building that have succeeded in the past. However, there are two other options to consider. The first is more expensive, but it would be a multilateral operation involving the United States, the European Union, and NATO such as in the cases of Kosovo and Bosnia. (The regional character of these institutions may limit its geographic reach, but perhaps this may be changed in the future.) The second option is also multilateral, but is also less capable in the view of RAND, and that is to use regional organizations such as the African Union and ASEAN for peacekeeping and peace-brokering purposes.[5] Perhaps a useful investment would be to provide training and capacity building for these institutions along the lines suggested above.

> *Structure a coherent and well-developed agenda with well-known, publicized and accepted benchmarks for an internationally brokered peace process that includes, inter alia, a truth and reconciliation process for healing purposes.*

> The first important step that needs to be taken by the parties to a potential peace accord is to identify: (1) the issues creating the conflict; (2) the affected parties; (3) the negotiating parties, and (4) the tools, means, and political processes by which to forge a lasting peace. This is a difficult undertaking since the issues may be complex and mired in decades-long grievances, attacks and retribution for past wrongs, whether perceived or real.

> The intervention of an outside neutral party experienced in such peace negotiations may be a helpful starting point. Further, planning a political map for political and economic empowerment so that educational, economic and political opportunities are restored as quickly as possible may also be a good tactic to consider. However, the complexity of this task is daunting since the answer, for example, may lie in restoring physical infrastructure to the conflict area to permit its integration with the rest of the country–and this may be a difficult undertaking for the host government if it is struggling itself with its national budget.

- ➢ As discussed above, trust and the political will to commit to the peace-making process at the outset and in terms of meeting conditions subsequent is critical to the success of the negotiation. In my view, the more well-known the benchmarks of the diplomatic process are, the greater the opportunity to enforce the accountability of the parties by the affected people in the post-conflict zone.

- ➢ Secondly, a continuing process of dialogue and accountability to ensure that benchmarks are being adequately met, or to ensure that such benchmarks are modified in response to changed circumstances or needs, is also an important component in facilitating the success of peace-keeping measures. Rather than signing a peace accord and leaving the negotiation table, it may be a wiser course of action to monitor the progress being made to the commitments of all parties, and make adjustments accordingly.

- ➢ Adequate enforcement measures of the outputs of the diplomatic negotiation also need to be integrated into the original negotiation process. If there is a failure in the outcome of the peace dialogue, then peace-keeping negotiations may need to be resumed. This aspect needs to be taken into account at the outset, and prepared for as an outside contingency.

- ➢ Accountability for past injustices is a powerful force in moving the parties towards a final and lasting reconciliation. This is, however, a very difficult, complex and inherently controversial matter, and it is one that needs to be carefully considered and committed to, if undertaken by the parties. War crime tribunals, special forums, and truth and reconciliation commissions are powerful tools in airing past grievances, seeking forgiveness, and forging a lasting reconciliation among the parties.[6]

- ➢ The RAND report also suggests that making economic reparations immediately after the end of a conflict is counterproductive. RAND suggests waiting until the economy has stabilized and grown before attempting to make reparations.[7]

- ➢ ***Strengthen the infrastructure of the failed or collapsed state as a commitment of the international community acting in partnership*** *with the groups in conflict, NGOs, neighboring countries, regional and multilateral organizations, the media and other non-state actors.*

> Strengthening the infrastructure of the affected conflict area is principally an economic undertaking that will be discussed in the next section. However, the RAND report also makes clear that the participation and commitment of neighboring states is vital to creating an enduring peace process.[8]

The above discussion sets forth a complex matrix of interrelated responsibilities of the parties to any peace-making mission, and it is a challenge under the best of circumstances. It requires foresight, compassion, trust, creativity and the requisite political will of all the parties in order to be successful.

C. Economic Measures. It is clear that political stability or economic growth is not possible without security measures being in place. Once security measures stabilize the conflict area, other issues may be addressed. The above discussion sets forth a fairly complex and highly-interrelated agenda for planning appropriate military, diplomatic and political action. These actions must, in larger part, precede economic measures being put in place. All these components (including cultural initiatives, to be discussed below) should be part of a coordinated whole.

Bolstering the peace process with supporting economic measures is necessary, but it is certainly no guarantee against future terrorist action. But we ignore global poverty at our peril. Further, there is a linkage between failing states, poverty, weak institutions and corruption and an increased vulnerability to harboring terrorist networks.

One commentator notes that, "[d]enying terrorists the sanctuary they seek in failed states may become a central feature of the war on terror. . . . Yet, strengthening weak states to the point where their weakness is no longer an 'attractive nuisance' for terrorists may require a decades-long commitment of financial and humanitarian aid, technical and military assistance, and institution-building. A massive state-building effort, even with unlimited resources, would likely require years of incremental progress before it produces meaningful results."[9]

In other words, decades of poor governance that profoundly ignores the need to provide for basic human sustenance tends to result in weakened or failing states, increased militancy, and a receptiveness to terrorist operatives and networks. Moreover, general lawlessness supports the growth of crime syndicates, illegal drug and trafficking networks and other illegal activities that can potentially be used to finance global terrorism.[10]

Rather than embarking on an elaborate agenda of economic measures that should be taken in order to bolster and strengthen a peace-keeping process, and to do so in a factual vacuum, it may be more useful to put certain considerations into an historical context. Professor Kimberly Marten argues that recent nation-building efforts or what she calls "complex peace-keeping operations" are both similar to and dissimilar from historical colonial antecedents.[11] In essence, she argues that the emphasis on creating market-based economies and liberal civil societies are not new but an echo from the past.

In other words, former colonial powers acquired territories and possessions with the view towards instilling a certain kind of economic development in these areas for purposes of:

- ➤ Accessing raw materials and commodities;

- ➤ Selling finished or manufactured goods to captive markets;

- ➤ Expanding trade opportunities for domestic companies of the colonizer;

- ➤ Creating international investment opportunities;

- ➤ Creating a foreign tax base to make the colonies self-financing;

- ➤ Alleviating poverty domestically and in their colonies;

- ➤ Achieving economic dominance in Europe.

Aside from the *mise en valeur* policy of European colonizers, they also wanted to instill Western values (including religious values), languages and institutions in their colonies. This may be viewed as colonial-based "paternalism," but the humanitarian impulse to indoctrinate or "civilize" foreign subjugated societies in the elements of representational local governance, civic values and the principles of rationality were all strong motivating factors behind colonization. Thus, the basis for economic development and the propagation of Western-styled institutions, manner of governance, and societal ethical and religious norms laid the foundation for "modernizing" these societies. Professor Marten argues, therefore, that the similarity in instilling a Rule of Law agenda in the context of modern complex peacekeeping operations harkens back to a distant colonial imprint.

Modern peacekeeping operations are also dissimilar from their imperialist antecedents as well, according to Professor Marten. Such operations are not designed to capture closed economic markets or exert colonial-style political governance over them. The recent efforts at peacekeeping are also limited in two important ways: first, these efforts are limited in terms of how much change may be imposed by external forces, no matter how well-intentioned such efforts are; and second, and perhaps more importantly, these efforts are limited by the political will of the outside peacekeepers or peace builders.[12]

Wholesale conquest and the imposition of long-term occupation over conflict areas is simply not on anyone's political agenda at this time. Professor Marten recommends using multilateral forces to legitimate the effort (and remove the post-colonial imprint), and limit those forces to providing security alone.

She states:

> The colonial operations carried out by liberal states at the turn of the twentieth century and the complex peacekeeping operations of more recent years had one key component in common, despite all their differences. They were characterized by the desire of outsiders to control political events happening on the ground abroad. Whether for self-interested security motives or genuine humanitarianism, western liberal democratic states wanted these foreign regions to adopt more of the values and institutions of the western liberal democratic world. In more recent times, this goal was shared by significant portions of the peace-kept populations, but a substantial fraction of the target population has in each case opposed the international presence, which is why the use of robust military force has been necessary.

While the balance of reasons for undertaking these operations shifted between the two eras, favoring state self-interest in the former period and humanitarianism in the latter, the desire for foreign control over political and social institutions was a constant.[13]

Professor Marten points out that the lack of political will (in other words, competing political goals and agendas) interfere with and impede the successful and permanent conclusion of peacekeeping operations. Thus, she argues for a limited goal in peacekeeping in light of:

The history presented here suggests that given the difficulty liberal democracies have in imposing coherent political influence over foreign societies, the limited goal of establishing security over the medium term is more likely to be achievable. In the colonial era, attempts to instill supposedly western values throughout the empire ultimately backfired, as the population recognized the inconsistencies in the policies of the imperialist states. In many cases it appears that it was the brutality of the imperialists, rather than their humanitarianism, that most influenced the later development of politics in postcolonial territories. While complex peacekeeping operations have not been so brutal, the inconsistencies within the liberal democratic values that they have proclaimed, as well as the inevitable lack of cohesive follow-through on planning, have demonstrated that the notion of imposing liberal democracy abroad is a pipedream.[14]

Therefore, she concludes that:

The comparison of recent peacekeeping operations to the era of colonialism as practiced by liberal democratic states has highlighted the fact that imposing control over a foreign society is not possible using liberal democratic means. No matter how noble our intentions, we face limitations in our capabilities and in the effects that our actions can have. . . . In places like Haiti, a large expenditure of resources in the end created no change, and a decade later the international community was called back in again. The people were replaced, but the system was not. Instead of trying to change societies, we should change our expectations. A return to the goal of keeping the peace, rather than imposing change, will lead to more realistic policies that have a better chance of reaching their goals.[15]

This is sound advice, but it is short-sighted since it does not further the means for resolving the conflict giving rise to the need for peacekeeping in the first instance. Simply providing security measures in a traditional peacekeeping operation is only the first step in establishing an umbrella for other actors (state and non-state) to move in with a highly defined and coordinated agenda for action. While economic growth measures that were designed to stabilize and expand the economies of developing nations may have, in large part, failed, continuing to ignore its implications may simply *not* be an acceptable course of action for the international community.

Thus, based on the foregoing discussion, economic measures are only relevant with respect to Islamic-based separatist movements. Since global jihadists are dedicated to destabilizing (and possibly overthrowing) stable liberal nation-states, the adoption of an economic agenda for change is irrelevant to them. Except for the limited engagement of identifying, terminating, prosecuting and preventing terror financing (a component of military action that involves law enforcement), economic measures, as described above, are only relevant with respect to Islamic-based separatists.

Professor Marten also mentions the absence of political will with respect to liberal democracies enforcing the peace with respect to conflict areas. She points out the liberal democratic values and approaches cannot impose change in conflict areas from without. However, a missing dimension of this analysis is the lack of political will of the people in the conflict areas themselves. Again, this is a failure of the state insofar as the governed are not able (or are not willing) to hold their leaders accountable in the overall development process.

Going back to the foregoing analysis, viewing the concept of security as integral to overall sustainable development would be a welcome departure from current international development policies. Changing the current policies of development institutions to include security as a vital aspect of development may effectively redefine and help strengthen the political will of liberal democracies. In other words, if security as a development concept is incorporated into the conceptual thinking and planning of multilateral development institutions along the same lines as "food security" was incorporated into their thinking in the 1970's, this might be a concrete step forward. This step will help commit liberal democracies to revitalizing the development process–by ensuring security, they will ensure a new stable framework in which the development process may unfold.

D. Cultural Initiatives. Finally, the last component of this complex matrix is undertaking cultural initiatives that should be directed to separatists as well as global terrorists. In revisiting an earlier discussion, the essay argues that while Western-styled institutions, structures and approaches may have been adopted by many developing nations (with unequal successes and results), the underlying ideological foundation generally was not. Perhaps a fuller discussion of why this may have occurred would be appropriate in this context.

The principal difference between the developed and the developing worlds is most often cast in economic terms (or the so-called "haves" and "have-nots"). Again, the salient difference between the two groups is viewed in terms of their relative economic power to pursue (i.e., purchase) their individual happiness. However, there is at least another difference which may, ultimately, be more significant. That difference lies in the absolutist objectivity of the developed (so-called Western) world versus the relativist subjectivity of the developing (so-called non-Western) world. In other words, developed societies have the demonstrated capability to create, understand, and rely on a belief system of abstract ideals (e.g., equal justice for all, equal application of the law, due process, democratic representation and governance). (The dictum, "We are a nation of laws, not men," may be appropriate in this context.)

The subjective, personal element where loyalties are given not to abstract concepts but to families, patrons, rulers, ethnic or religious identities or leaders tend to be much more prevalent in developing societies. Thus, while it is difficult to make overbroad generalizations in such a complex matter, perhaps the underlying ideological foundation in most of the developing world is simply incompatible with the Western-oriented values of strict rationalism, empiricism and materialism. In essence, therefore, the struggle between the developed and the developing worlds is not only one of economic accumulation but also one of a struggle of ideas around which societies are organized.

For example, the Western view of a nuclear family consisting of parents and their children may be inconsistent with the broader and more inclusive one comprising the more complex family structures found in many places in Latin America, Africa, Eurasia and Asia. Therefore, familial obligations (whether viewed as being law-based or based on societal obligations) may be much broader as well. Thus, the emotional ties and commitment to a much broader family structure may be very relevant in dictating certain kinds of conduct.

In other words, *the failure* of a corporate insider in Jordan, for example, to release confidential information to his family and friends concerning a stock offering may be seen as a betrayal. It may be the perceived duty of such a corporate insider to provide his family and associates with the information and the means by which to enrich themselves. After all, such gains may fund a son's (or a daughter's) tuition to college.

Thus, adhering to a legal regime where insider trading is a criminal offense may be seen as incomprehensible, alien, bizarre, and in conflict with the mores and expectations of Jordanian society. It may be a pat assumption for Western experts and consultants to feel that such a leap of faith on the part of the Jordanians is logical, necessary, or inevitable. It may be more helpful to establish a dialogue on the rationale for criminalizing insider trading and coming to terms with the underlying cultural mores that are affected (or offended) by this proposed new legal practice. If Western consultants assume that the criminal nature of insider trading is self-evident, then the interests of their mission to bring legal change, as well as the broader interests of the Jordanians, may not be not well-served.

Moreover, it may be wise to keep in mind that there are many structural changes that are taking place in Western societies that are, for example, broadening the concept of the family well past the traditional notion of two parents and their children to include blended and other family structures. In other words, the "Newtonian" legal universe of immutable, predictable laws and relationships has been transformed into an "Einsteinian" legal universe where the actors, rights and duties are relative, fluid, unpredictable, and unstructured. Naturally, this is bound to meet with resistance and distrust, primarily from Western legal practitioners.

In addition, it may be worth remembering the rationalist ideals of the Enlightenment were later tempered by the ideals of the "romantic rebellion"[16] that followed. Romanticism gave new supremacy to values of subjective experience rather than to unchanging rational ideals.

> Romanticism therefore values the particular insight, the visionary glimpse into imaginative union with the universe, the emotional certainty and joy that arises from a feeling of intimate association in an envisioned patterned order. It distrusts any systematic knowledge, any inherited systems of belief, anything not generated by one's own imagination. It rejects any sense of rational limits to what the human imagination might know. The power of the imagination is potentially infinite: "Less than all cannot satisfy man," cried [William] Blake.[17]

Thus, the ideals of subjectivity, emotionalism and the elevation of individual emotions to a new poetic and artistic ideal is not foreign to Western cultures after all. Moreover, the idea of intuitively and empathetically understanding differences in thinking and feeling among cultures is an idea that goes back to creating a new soldier waging a new kind of war in the Fearful Symmetry. Rather than promulgating Western-influenced cultural values of tolerance, acceptance and political inclusion, the most persuasive value of indoctrinating such cultural values should originate with moderate Muslims.

For example, the Saudis have recently initiated a terrorist "deprogramming" effort. NBC News was recently given exclusive access to Saudi Arabia's new Al Qaeda rehabilitation center, a minimum security resort outside Riyadh. Here, clerics try to deprogram militants, teaching them social skills as they swim, play football and video games before being released. Apparently, the recidivist rate of returning to a life of terrorism is nil at this point.[18]

Another example is that of Singapore. "Terrorist detainees in Singapore undergo a program incorporating psychological, social and religious rehabilitation. The religious counseling program is driven by volunteers from Singapore's Muslim community. There are no beatings or torture. There have been no deaths. Two-thirds of the terrorists arrested since 2001 have been released and have reintegrated into society. None has strayed back into terrorism so far. Singapore's program is often cited by international experts, including William J. Dobson of the Carnegie Endowment for International Peace, as a model for the detention and rehabilitation of terrorists."[19]

While these efforts at rehabilitation may be viewed with a certain degree of skepticism, it may be worthwhile to note that the RAND Corporation has proposed concrete steps in creating moderate Muslim networks, and disrupting radical networks.[20] These and similar efforts may help win over young Muslim terrorists.

Moreover, another RAND study[21] recommends reintegrating former terrorists and extremists found in renegade state militias, insurgent forces or armed gangs (including "child soldiers" co-opted into combat at early ages) by providing education, job training and placement. Of course, this is also a facile solution since it is often the lack of educational and employment opportunities in the first place that may lead to radicalization. However, as a long-term solution, it is certainly a worthwhile pursuit. The study recognizes that the longer such ex-terrorists remain rootless, the more of a problem recidivism and related problems become—in other words, such individuals drift from one conflict zone to another.

The RAND study also cautions that while the familiarity of ex-terrorists with combat and armed conflict seem to make them viable candidates to join reconstituted state militias, police forces and other legitimate state security structures, this may not be the wisent option. Security reform is a difficult undertaking and often the security-related structures are corrupt, ineffective, politicized and unprofessional. If this is the case, then integrating ex-terrorists or child soldiers in such structures may be adding to the problem rather than solving it.[22]

In essence, the indoctrination of other cultural values such as tolerance, respect, acceptance and resolving conflict peacefully rather than violently should be directed to all Islamic-based extremists by members of their own community to start with. A constructive dialogue needs to be put in place and should be aimed not only at Islamic separatist-based movements but at global jihadists as well. The first question that will need to be answered for them is, "why pursue this course of action?" What do terrorists (or would-be terrorists) have to gain by participating in belief systems and structures that no longer have any validity for them? This loss of faith and the disaffection that they feel is very real and needs to be addressed now.

While the most effective course of action seems to be action taken by other Arabs (individually, collectively, and as nation-states), perhaps there are other means to be pursued as well. For example, NGOs may have a critical role to play here in terms of understanding, empathizing and legitimating the feelings of distrust, despair and disaffection that these young Muslims feel. Providing alternate courses of action (particularly through non-violent means) may be a useful starting point to help them think differently–merely providing job opportunities certainly will not be enough in light of the fact that the newest recruits are already well-educated and employed individuals.

Providing cultural initiatives to help redeem the promise lost to young Muslims is a challenge for moderate Muslims along with the international community. Clear leadership is necessary from both communities and is vital to winning the Fearful Symmetry.

6

Creating a Platform for Reconciliation and Transition

The previous discussions were devoted to an analysis of what gives rise to violent extremism in general, and to fundamentalist Islamic-based terrorism in particular. The last chapter laid out a proposed four-filter analysis of how to direct international efforts to stabilize and reconstruct societies destabilized by such extremism and Islamic-based terrorism. In fact, the relative degree of the terrorist threat may actually affect the continued viability of certain nations such as Afghanistan, and perhaps for other countries in North Africa as well. Now, it is time to turn to the actual policy matrix and U.S. military and civilian deployments that have taken place over the past several years that are designed to address these concerns. An examination of this post-9/11 effort is important in this context since it forms the real-life backdrop for this discussion.

At the outset, it is important to examine the definitional challenges of this effort. "Peacekeeping" is the term that is most generally associated with operations to contain hostilities once the kinetic stage of warfare has ceased. However, this term is misleading since such peacekeeping operations are generally very dangerous, and take place in highly volatile, dangerous environments that are not the least "peaceful." Further, the term was also associated with UN-led efforts beginning in the late 1950s when UN peacekeeping forces were deployed to enforce a cease fire agreement. Many of there operations were perceived as being less than successful which stigmatized the operations.[1] Further, the term "peacekeeping" was highly ambiguous since it captured several interrelated elements of enforcement, securitization and stabilization.

In 1992, the UN created the term "peace enforcement" to describe operations in unstable situations where peacekeepers are allowed to use force to maintain peace because of a greater possibility of conflict or a threat to their safety. "Peacebuilding" was adopted as a term for activities that are designed to prevent the resumption or spread of conflict, including disarmament and demobilization of warring parties, repatriation of refugees, reform and strengthening of government institutions (including re-creating police or civil defense forces), election-monitoring, and promotion of political participation and human rights. Organizing and providing security for humanitarian relief efforts can be a part of peacekeeping and peace enforcement operations."[2]

Peacekeeping may also be referred to as "peace operations" or by the U.S. Army term of "stability operations,"[3] which cover a wide range of activities in Iraq and Afghanistan. For example, stability operations may include peace enforcement and peacekeeping, humanitarian assistance, counterterrorism, counterinsurgency, counter-drug and other related post conflict operations. The foregoing discussion illustrates that there is quite a bit of definitional confusion among the terms "peacekeeping," "peacebuilding," "stability operations," "stabilization and reconstruction," and "nation-building."

The U.S. Imprint on Stability Operations

Certain doctrinal changes were ultimately made by the U.S. military that led to clearer policy support for stability operations. On November 28, 2005, the U.S. Department of Defense (DOD) issued its directive on, "Military Support for Stability, Security, Transition and Reconstruction (SSTR) Operations."[4] This new directive radically redefined the mission of DOD to include, in relevant part:

"It is DoD policy that:

4.1. *Stability operations are a core U.S. military mission that the Department of Defense shall be prepared to conduct and support.* [Emphasis supplied.] They shall be given priority comparable to combat operations and be explicitly addressed and integrated across all DoD activities including doctrine, organizations, training, education, exercises, materiel, leadership, personnel, facilities, and planning.

4.2. Stability operations are conducted to help establish order that advances U.S. interests and values. The immediate goal often is to provide the local populace with security, restore essential services, and meet humanitarian needs. The long-term goal is to help develop indigenous capacity for securing essential services, a viable market economy, rule of law, democratic institutions, and a robust civil society.

4.3. Many stability operations tasks are best performed by indigenous, foreign, or U.S. civilian professionals. *Nonetheless, U.S. military forces shall be prepared to perform all tasks necessary to establish or maintain order when civilians cannot do so.* [Emphasis supplied.] Successfully performing such tasks can help secure a lasting peace and facilitate the timely withdrawal of U.S. and foreign forces. Stability operations tasks include helping:

4.3.1   Rebuild indigenous institutions including various types of   security forces, correctional facilities, and judicial systems   necessary to secure and stabilize the environment;

4.3.2. Revive or build the private sector, including encouraging   citizen-driven, bottom-up economic activity and constructing   n e c e s s a r y infrastructure; and

4.3.3. Develop representative governmental institutions."[5]

The breadth and scope of these tasks is overwhelming.

Further, U.S. Army Field Manual (FM) 3-07 was issued on October 6, 2008, updating the version released on February 20, 2003.[6] This manual makes it clear that:

"Stability operations are usually conducted to support a host-nation government or a transitional civil or military authority when no legitimate, functioning host-nation government exists. Generally, military forces establish or restore basic civil functions and protect them until a civil authority or the host nation is capable of providing these services for the local populace. They perform specific functions as part of a broader response effort, supporting the complementary activities of other agencies, organizations, and the private sector. When the host nation or other agency cannot fulfill their role, military forces may be called upon to significantly increase its role, including providing the basic civil functions of government.

By nature, stability operations are typically lengthy endeavors."[7]

Moreover, FM 3-07 makes an important and clear distinction: "For many agencies and organizations, stability operations are considered as part of broader efforts to reestablish enduring peace and stability following the cessation of open hostilities. For military forces, however, stability tasks are executed continuously throughout all operations. Executed early enough and in support of broader national policy goals and interests, stability operations provide an effective tool for reducing the risk of politically motivated violence. It does this by addressing the possible drivers of conflict long before the onset of hostilities. Providing the authority and resources to conduct these stability operations as part of peacetime military engagement may be the most effective and efficient method to mitigate the risk of lengthy post-conflict interventions."[8]

In sum, the doctrinal matrix that governs U.S. security strategy which shapes the conduct of stability operations includes the *National Security Strategy*, the *National Defense Strategy*, and *The National Military Strategy of the United States of America* (known as the *National Military Strategy*). (Related strategies include the *National Strategy for Combating Terrorism, the National Strategy for Homeland Security, and the National Strategy to Combat Weapons of Mass Destruction*.)[9] The *National Security Strategy* addresses stability operations, and the *National Defense Strategy* addresses fragile states and the national security threat they may pose to the United States.

Additionally, in 2005, former President George Bush signed National Security Presidential Directive 44 (NSPD-44) which outlined his vision for promoting the security of the United States through improved coordination, planning, and implementation of reconstruction and stabilization assistance.[10] Moreover, NSPD-44 formally acknowledged that the stability of foreign states served the broader national interests of the United States.

President Bush designated the U.S. Department of State to be the lead agency responsible for these operations, and directed the former Secretary of State, Colin Powell, to coordinate and lead integrated U.S. Government efforts in preparing, planning, and conducting reconstruction and stabilization activities. NSPD-44 also mandated the Secretary of State to coordinate with the Secretary of Defense to ensure the integration and synchronization of any planned or ongoing U.S. military operations, as needed.[11]

Accordingly, based on an April 2004 decision of the National Security Council principals committee, former U.S. Secretary of State Colin Powell created the Department of State, Office of the Coordinator for Reconstruction and Stabilization (S/CRS) in July 2004. S/CRS has now been reorganized as the State Department's Bureau of Conflict and Stabilization Operations (CSO). Historically, the bureau has two institutional capabilities consisting of the Interagency Management System (IMS) for reconstruction and stabilization, the whole of government planning framework, and the Civilian Response Corps (CRC). The IMS is a management structure designed to assist policymakers, chiefs of mission, and military commanders who manage complex reconstruction and stabilization activities. The IMS structure assists them by ensuring coordination among all U.S. Government stakeholders at the strategic, operational, and tactical levels.[12] The CRC provides the standing civilian corps to support stability operations in the field, and may be replaced with the Expert Corps shortly.

Also, in support of its mandate to coordinate closely with DOD, the CSO deploys Humanitarian, Stabilization, and Reconstruction Teams (HSRT) to the field to participate in post-conflict planning where U.S. military forces will be engaged. Further, the CSO deploys Advance Civilian Teams (ACTs) with the U.S. military to initiate humanitarian, stabilization and reconstruction tasks on the ground. ACTs may also form the foundation for the civilian component of Provincial Reconstruction Teams (PRTs), or similar inter-agency field organizations.[13] Better joint civilian-military planning is desired in order to make such interventions as successful as possible. Civil affairs offices in the U.S. military provide language expertise, regional specialization and other skills to support stabilization operations.

In addition, the Special Operations Command (USSOCOM) is a unified effort by the U.S. Army, Air Force and Navy to plan, direct and execute special operations in counterterrorist and related operations worldwide. USSOCOM consists of the U.S. Army Special Operations Command, the Navy Special Warfare Command, the Air Force Special Operations Command, the Joint Special Operations Command, and the Joint Special Operations University. Many worldwide nongovernmental organizations are also active in stabilization and reconstructions activates in post-conflict areas.[14]

Thus, DOD Directive 3000.05, signed by the U.S. Secretary of Defense, as discussed above, in combination with NSPD-44 signed by former President George W. Bush, both of which were executed in 2005, created the underlying doctrinal and institutional framework for U.S. military-led stability operations.

Aside from the U.S. State Department's CSO Office, the U.S. Agency for International Development (USAID) Office of Transition Initiatives provides flexible short-term foreign assistance to help build peace, democracy and promote human rights. USAID's former Administrator, Andrew Natsios, formulated nine principles of reconstruction and development which also helps further define the policy matrix for the U.S. Government in undertaking the stabilization and reconstruction of fragile countries.

Natsios builds his nine principles based on the Nine Principles of War. The principles of war were formulated in the U.S. Army, Field Manual 100-5, (1994), and outlines objective, offensive, mass, economy of force, maneuver, unity of command, security, surprise, and simplicity as the U.S. military's nine principles of war.[15] These nine principles are the same as those set forth by von Clausewitz in his treatise, *On War*.[16]

Natsios notes that, "military thinking has evolved and now incorporates the phrase 'stability operations' as a term of art to describe post-conflict nation-building efforts. Despite this shift, the military continues to use the Nine Principles of War as an intellectual basis for all military operations, including stability operations. . . . The Nine Principles of Reconstruction and Development have evolved from a similar institutional experience. They distill fundamental lessons from this experience and bring greater clarity to the operating principles that inform the mission of USAID."[17]

The nine principles Natsios sets forth are:

> ➤ Ownership (build on the leadership participation, and commitment of a country and its people);

> ➤ Capacity Building (strengthen local institutions, transfer technical skills, and promote appropriate policies);

> ➤ Sustainability (design programs to ensure their impact endures);

> ➤ Selectivity (allocate resources based on need, local commitment and foreign policy interests);

> ➤ Assessment (conduct careful research, adapt best practices, and design for local conditions);

> ➤ Results (direct resources to achieve clearly defined, measurable, and strategically focused objectives);

> ➤ Partnership (collaborate closely with governments, communities, donors, non-profit organizations, the private sector, international organizations, and universities);

> ➤ Flexibility (adjust to changing conditions, take advantage of opportunities, and maximize efficiency);

> ➤ Accountability (design accountability and transparency into systems and build effective checks and balances to guard against corruption).[18]

Natsios attempts to fit the USAID experience into the military paradigm in an effort to mesh the two perspectives and organizational cultures into a compatible framework. However, one should remain cognizant of the fact that the values underlying the divergent experiences of the U.S. military and USAID are vastly different. This attempt at synchronizing the two, while laudable, may have limited utility in this context.

U.S. Participation in International Peacekeeping

U.S. military participation in international peacekeeping efforts has been uneven and sporadic ranging from operations in Bosnia (1992-2004), Haiti (1994-96), and Somalia (1992-94).[19] Since April 30, 2006, U.S. military personnel were serving in five U.N. peacekeeping or related operations located in the Middle East, Georgia, Ethiopia/Eritrea, Liberia, and Haiti. While this history provides a very rich background in terms of understanding policy, strategic and tactical choices made by the U.S. military in prosecuting wars in Iraq and Afghanistan,[20] in my view, it would be too wide a diversion and too discursive a discussion to merit treatment here. However, it does form a backdrop to this discussion, and certain elements will be highlighted, as appropriate.

Table 1: U.S. Efforts at Nation-Building (1898-2003)

Type	Successes	Failures	Ongoing
Unilateral	Panama (1989)	Cambodia (1970-73)	
	Grenada (1983)	Vietnam (1964-73)	
	Japan (1945-52)	Dominican Republic (1964-65)	
		Cuba (1917-22)	
		Dominican Republic (1916-24)	
		Haiti (1915-34)	
		Nicaragua (1909-39)	
		Cuba (1906-09)	
		Panama (1903-36)	
		Cuba (1898-1902)	
Multilateral	Germany (1945-49)	Haiti (1994-96)	Iraq (2003-Present)
			Afghanistan (2001-Present)
			Kosovo (1999-Present)
			Bosnia-Herzegovina (1995-Present)

* Source: "Transforming for Stabilization and Reconstruction Operations," Table 8 at 117, ed. Hans Binnendijk & Stuart Johnson, CTNSP, National Defense University (November 12, 2003), available at http://www.ndu.edu/ctnsp/S&R_book/S&R.pdf (last visited on July 12, 2009.)

Provincial Reconstruction Teams (PRTs)

The following discussion will focus on the creation, organization and effectiveness of Provincial Reconstruction Teams (PRTs). The model combines a military-civilian joint field presence and has many interesting implications which are still unfolding. The utility of this model in serving as a stability and reconstruction team to initiate key tasks in post-conflict societies will be critically examined.

The downstream effects of *Operation Enduring Freedom*, a U.S.-led military coalition launched on October 7, 2001, against Afghanistan's Taliban government, toppling it after only two months of actual combat. The United Nations Security Council resolution 1386 established the International Security Assistance Force (ISAF) on December 20, 2001 to help the Afghan Interim Authority to maintain security in and around Kabul.[21]

ISAF was formed in January 2002 as an *ad hoc* coalition operation of some 5,000 troops from 18 nations under British command. ISAF troops patrol Kabul and its immediate surrounding areas under a U.N. Chapter VII authorization, and has expanded its operations throughout the country. As of April 2006, about 170 U.S. military personnel support NATO's ISAF operating in Afghanistan.[22]

ISAF is unique from a NATO operational perspective since it is the first time that NATO has invoked Article 5 of its articles of association which requires collective action once one of its members (in this case, the United States) is attacked.[23] Further, this is its first "out-of-area" mission beyond Europe.[24] While combat-related restrictions have been placed on ISAF forces operating in Afghanistan by their contributing European members, the ISAF intervention in support of stabilization and reconstruction of Afghanistan has been key.

NATO assumed command of ISAF on August 11, 2003, just over 18 months after its formation, and after the cessation of the initial hostilities. The underlying UN Security Council Resolution 1836 (September 23, 2008), permitting this takeover states that NATO shall provide security, law and order, promote governance and development, help reform the justice system, train a national police force and army, provide security for elections, and assist the local effort to interdict the narcotics industry.[25] ISAF includes troops from all 28 member states of NATO, including from certain non-member states such as Australia, New Zealand, Sweden, Jordan and Azerbaijan.[26]

Figure 1. Chain of Command for PRTs in Afghanistan

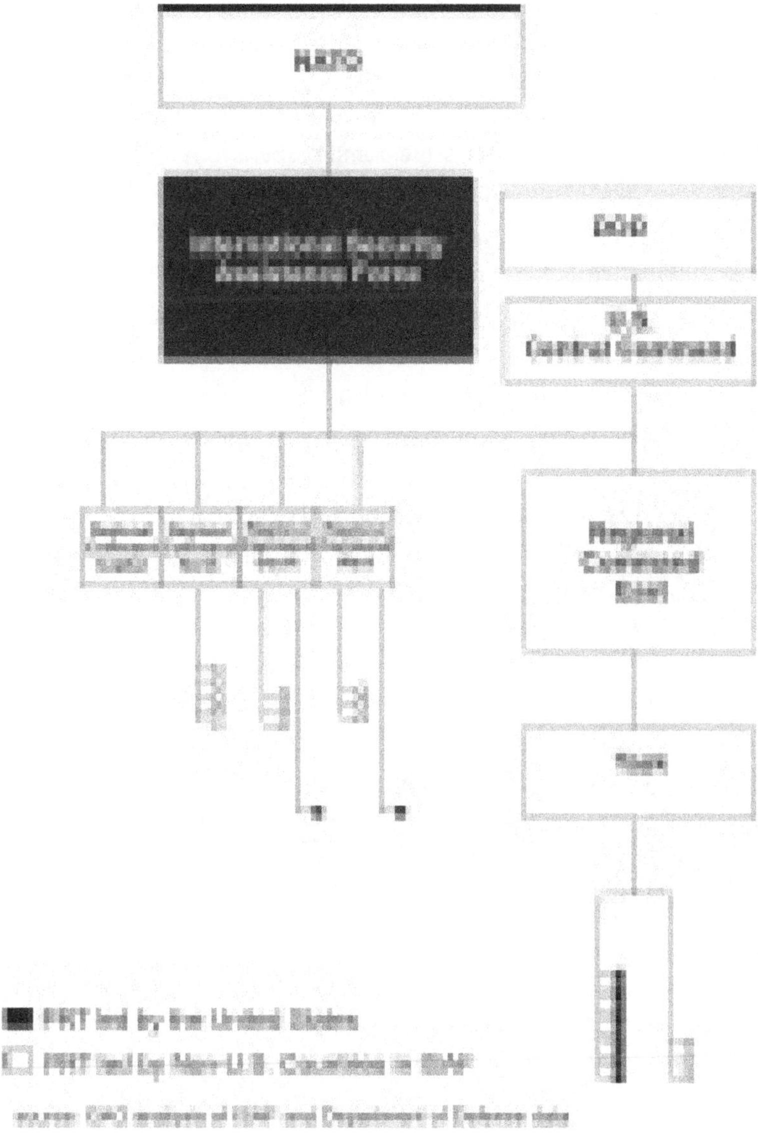

See "Provincial Reconstruction Teams (GAO-09-86R) (October 1, 2008), available at http://www.gao.gov/new.items/d0986r.pdf (last visited on July 16, 2009).

U.S. troops do provide some assistance to the ISAF (i.e., logistical, intelligence, and quick reaction force support), but they do not engage in ISAF peacekeeping.[27] NATO's involvement in the Afghanistan conflict permitted it to launch 26 provincial reconstruction teams (PRTs) in the country.

NATO planned the ISAF mission in Afghanistan in 2001 to evolve in five stages. Stage One (assessment and preparation) took place during 2003-04, when NATO moved into the French and German-forces dominated northern area of the country. Stage Two (geographic expansion) began in May 2005 when NATO moved into western Afghanistan with Italian and Spanish forces being in the lead. Both regions remain fairly stable. Stage Three (stabilization) came into operation on July 31, 2006, and was designed to move NATO into the southern part of the country where the Taliban is based. Stage Four (transition) began on October 5, 2006, when the United States transferred 10,000-12,000 of its troops to ISAF to serve under the NATO commander. By 2006, NATO's ISAF had covered all of Afghanistan in its operations, and is considering beginning Phase Five, or the redeployment stage.[28]

The security environment in Afghanistan continues to be very complex. Indeed, one report highlighted the fact that, "[c]ivilian-military coordination at the strategic level is not just complicated by the presence of two coalitions conducting military operations with different objectives–warfighting and stabilization. The complexity is compounded by the absence of an overall lead agency or lead nation. The [United Nations Assistance Mission in Afghanistan] UNAMA is in charge of civilian reconstruction and advises the Afghan government on its National Priority Programmes, the U.S. is in charge of rebuilding the Afghan National Army (ANA), Germany is responsible for police training, Italy has taken the lead on judicial reform, the UK is in charge of the counter-narcotics programme, and Japan is in charge of disarmament, demobilization, and reintegration (DDR). This lack of overall coordination was one of the factors that led the U.S. to launch the PRTs."[29]

It was during the summer of 2002, that U.S. military forces developed the idea of provincial reconstruction teams which would spread the effects of the ISAF without expanding ISAF itself. Originally designed as "Joint Regional Teams (JRTs)" by the U.S. Central Command (USCENTCOM), a U.S. Army combatant command with an area of responsibility that covers Afghanistan. "JRTs" was later changed to PRTs at the request of Afghan President Hamid Karzai. The PRTs provide support to the central government, and not to local warlords.[30]   In his opinion, warlords rule regions; governors rule provinces.[31]

PRTs were established in Afghanistan at the end of 2002 and were integrated military-civilian organizations composed of military officers, diplomats, reconstruction subject-matter experts relevant to establishing stability in fragile or weak states. A PRT in Afghanistan generally consists of between 60-100 personnel, commanded by a military officer generally with the rank of Lieutenant Colonel or Commander. The team has various specialized experts such as engineers, medical staff, information and public diplomacy officers, and National Guard members to provide security. In Iraq, the team leader was a civilian official who reported directly to the U.S. Department of State, with the deputy usually being a military officer. These U.S. PRTs are focused on providing support in the functional areas of the Rule of Law, local capacity building, and good governance.

In focusing on Afghan PRTs, DOD was given responsibility for all logistical support and providing force protection for all PRT members, including civilians.[32] USAID was the lead agency for reconstruction; and DOS was responsible for political oversight, coordination and reporting. Both military and civilian leadership in PRTs must approve all reconstruction projects and coordinate such projects with local government offices and local ministries.[33]

While PRTs were given flexibility in accomplishing their objectives, the lack of explicit USG guidance led to confusion concerning the respective roles of military and civilian members of the PRTs. Thus, "in the absence of broadly accepted guidance, the importance of personality, individual leadership style, and previously established relationships had inordinate influence on the effectiveness and impact of the PRT."[34]

Moreover, a shortage of staff and limited technical and managerial support from Kabul also undermined the effectiveness of PRTs.[35] A more complicated problem was the inability to fill civilian positions with senior experienced personnel. Many civilian slots remained vacant over time and where civilian employees were assigned to the field, they often lacked the requisite knowledge and experience to be effective members of the PRT. Indeed, military staff members often had 16-20 years of experience before joining a PRT. In such cases, military members took the lead in both reconstruction projects and political engagement by default.[36]

In sum, while a PRT is uniquely positioned and capable of bringing a USG-led or internationally coordinated effort to prevent civil strife and violence, it is only able to do so within a narrow band of engagement. PRTs are most effective where instability is still so prevalent that NGOs are prevented from intervening, but not where violence is so extreme that combat operations predominate.[37]

On a broader scale, NATO established a common vision and strategy for PRTs as part of the International Security Assistance Force (ISAF) Operations Plan. However, NATO does not have authority over lead-nation civilian efforts within a PRT.[38] The continuing confusion over the role and political objectives of PRTs is grounded in the difference of approach in the multiple partners in the ISAF. "The United States, UK and a group of active members of the Alliance perceive the entire mission in Afghanistan as a war, whereas the UN, the EU and some troop contributors to the ISAF approach the situation using crisis management and/or peace-building as a starting point. Are we trying to win a war or build peace?"[39] Good question.

The role of PRTs also touches on a highly charged issue of the militarization of aid. Humanitarian aid delivered through military channels has an implicit risk: humanitarian aid may be perceived by local and international participants as being part of a military campaign. Consequently, this may result in a diminution of humanitarian space in conflict and post-conflict zones. In a Finnish study examining different national models for PRTs (*e.g.,* U.S., German, Nordic, and Turkish), a general but not definitive conclusion was that the UK model provided the "best practices" model.[40]

The UK PRT created an "integrated command group" consisting of personnel from the UK Ministry of Defence, the Foreign and Commonwealth Office and the Department of International Development.[41] This was also the model favored by many international NGOs for reconstruction efforts in conflict zones.[42]

Thus, PRTs were first introduced in Afghanistan in late 2002, and were intended to have an "ISAF-like" effect outside of Kabul by creating "nodes" of stability while maintaining a "light footprint" of the military forces.[43] PRTs replaced the Coalition Humanitarian Liaison Cells (CHLCs) and the U.S. Army Civil Affairs Teams (CAT-As).[44] Originally a U.S.-led effort, PRTs were a new model of military-civilian integration permitting civilian personnel to work in highly dangerous environments under the protection of military forces.

As of March 2008, there were 26 PRTs in Afghanistan and 28 PRTs in Iraq. Beginning in October 2006, the PRTs were made part of the NATO-led ISAF mission. Of the 26 PRTs in Afghanistan, 12 PRTs are under U.S. command. U.S.-led PRTs include: Asadabad, Gardez, Ghazni, Jalalabad, Khowst, Mehtarlam, Farah, Qalat, Sharana, Nurestan, Jalalabad, and Panjshir. ISAF multinational PRTs include: Baghlan (Hungary), Chaghcharan (Lithuania), Fayzabad (Germany), Herat (Italy), Kunduz (Germany), Mazari Sharif (Sweden), Maymana (Norway), Qala-e Naw (Spain), Kandahar (Canada), Lashkar Gah (United Kingdom), Tirin Kowt (Netherlands), Wardak (Turkey), Parwan (US/South Korea), and Baymian (New Zealand).[45]

Interestingly, the PRTs in Iraq are different in organization and command structure from those in Afghanistan. For the PRTs in Iraq, U.S. Department of Sate personnel lead the team which consist mainly of civilian and contractor staff. The PRTs in Afghanistan are composed of 50-100 personnel with a U.S. military lead with only about three or four U.S. Government civilian or contractor staff.[46]

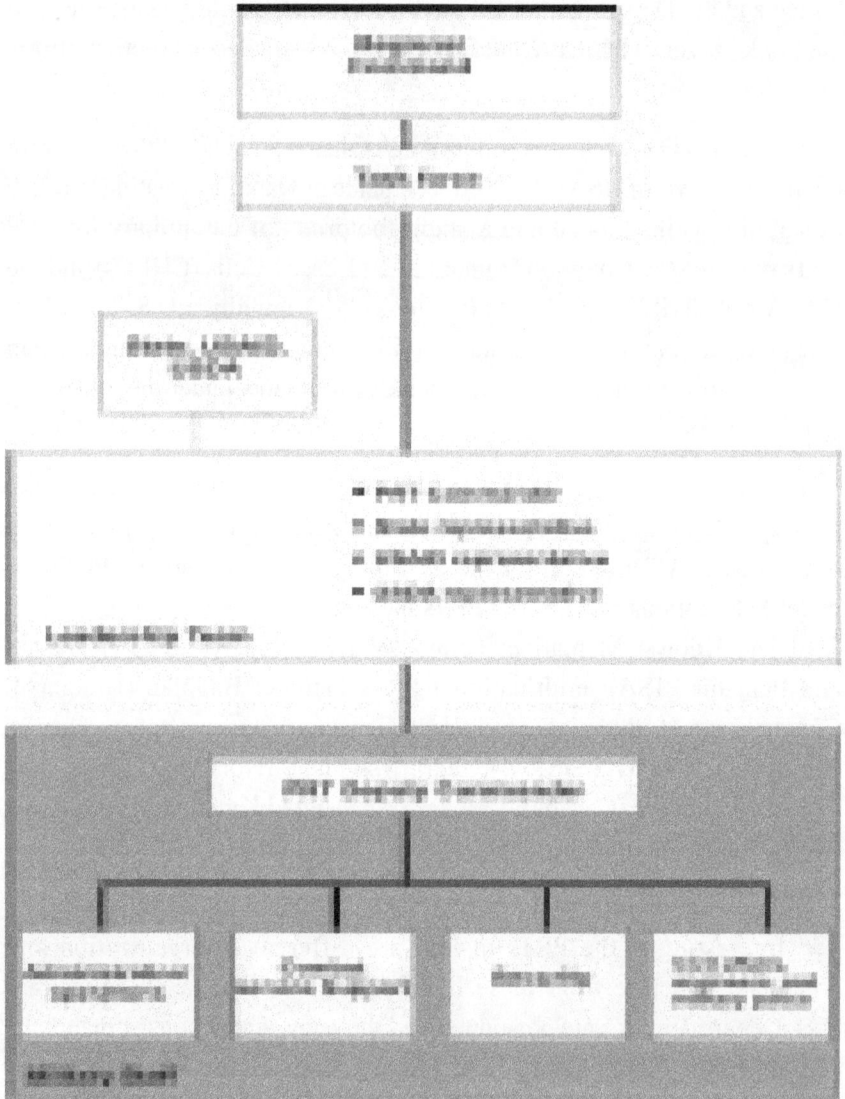

Source: GAO, "Provincial Reconstruction Teams (GAO-09-86R) (Washington, D.C., October 1, 2008), available at http://www.gao.gov/new.items/d0986r.pdf (last visited on July 16, 2009).

"PRTs gradually evolved a three-fold mandate: providing local security; conducting small-scale reconstruction; and facilitating the expanding presence of the central government. PRTs were sufficiently flexible to be tailored to unique operational environments, permitting commanders to exercise initiative and creativity. Although often characterized as civil-military teams, U.S. PRTs in Afghanistan remain overwhelmingly military in composition, with 80 to 100 soldiers under the command of a field grade military officer, most dedicated to force protection. The sole civilian components are individual representatives from State, USAID, and the Department of Agriculture."[47] (The terms of reference for PRTs operating in Afghanistan were issued in 2005.)[48]

"In Afghanistan, PRTs perform development, reconstruction, and governance activities, and serve a monitoring and reporting function. Afghanistan has one of the world's highest maternal mortality rates and a life expectancy at birth of about 44 years. To help meet the country's significant needs, PRT projects include schools, health clinics, and roads efforts to build provincial governments' capacity by helping provincial officials develop basic management skills; and facilitating communication between the provincial and central governments. PRT representatives also participated in consultations on the Afghanistan National Development Strategy, the Afghan government's 5-year development framework. In addition, according to State and USAID officials, PRTs serve a monitoring and reporting function, as PRT members report to their agencies on local conditions." [Footnote deleted.][49]

A PRT Executive Steering Committee provides guidance and oversight over all PRTs in Afghanistan. "The committee, which meets once a month, is made up by the Afghan Minister of the Interior (chair), the Minister of Finance and the Minister of Reconstruction and Rural Development; the commanders of ISAF and the CFC-A (both co-chairs), the Special Representative to the United Nations Secretary General, United Nations Assistance Mission to Afghanistan (UNAMA), NATO's Senior Civilian Representative, ambassadors of PRT contributing countries and potential contributing nations, and representatives of other nations as they become contributors to PRT operations."[50]

Two working groups report to the Executive Steering Committee, and meet on a weekly basis to discuss operational issues. "This working group has the following membership: Ministry of Interior (chair), UNAMA's civil-military coordinator, CFC-A Task Force Victory, ISAF HQ, US Embassy and embassies of PRT-supporting nations or prospective PRT-supporting nations."[51]

"The NGO Civil Military Working Group meets once a month to facilitate communication among NGOs, international military forces and the Afghan government on operational issues, and address NGO concerns. It is chaired by the UNAMA Civil-Military Coordinator and composed of representatives from NGOs, NGO coordinating bodies (the Agency Coordinating Body for Afghan Relief (ACBAR), the Afghan NGOs Coordination Bureau (ANCB) and the South Western Afghanistan and Balochistan Association for Coordination (SWABAC), ISAF and CFC-A PRTs, other military forces, and representatives from UNAMA and the Afghan government. Its purpose is to share information, prioritize issues of concern for NGOs and the military, resolve and prevent conflicts between military and humanitarian actors, and document and distribute lessons learned on civil-military coordination." [Footnotes deleted.][52]

Assessing the Effectiveness of PRTs

In assessing the effectiveness of PRTs in bringing about stabilization and reconstruction efforts in Afghanistan, it is clear that PRTs are having a positive impact in Afghanistan. Although PRTs are making a small but positive contribution there are a number of drawbacks to their current structure, composition, deployment and relations with the civilian corps that need to be critically assessed.

One Danish report concluded that, "the PRTs are successful because they have helped to extend the authority of the Afghan government beyond Kabul, facilitated reconstruction and dampened violence. At the same time, it is clear that they cannot address the underlying causes of insurgency in Afghanistan. The PRTs only make sense as part of an overall strategy in which they serve to buy time while other instruments are employed to tackle the military threat posed by the Taliban and Al Qaida; the infighting between the warlords; the increased lawlessness and banditry; and the booming opium poppy cultivation and the drug trade. A comprehensive strategy that couples the deployment of more PRTs by NATO with determined action against these causes of instability is therefore required."[53]

The report also concludes that the U.K. model PRT operational in Mazar which is focused on securitization rather than reconstruction (a thrust of the U.S.-led PRTs) is more successful, and therefore, preferable.[54] I would argue that while there may be merit in this assessment, there is certainly room for both securitization *and* reconstruction. The manner and strength of the deployments of PRTs with different missions, respectively, is a matter perhaps best left for coordination by the ISAF, working with U.S. military forces to 2014, and perhaps beyond.

TABLE 2. Comparison of Three PRT Models

(U.S., U.K., German)

	U.S.-led PRT	U.K.-led PRT	German-led PRT
Principal Focus	Quick impact reconstruction	Security Sector reform, active patrolling	Force protection, enabling civilian reconstruction
Military involvement on reconstruction	Considerable involvement	Limited involvement	Limited involvement
Degree of civil-military integration	Integration, civilian personnel embedded in military teams	Joint leadership, operational autonomy, separate reporting mechanisms	Separate leaderships, weekly coodination meetings
Responsiveness to UN and NGO suggestions	Limited	High	High

Source: Peter Jakobsen, "PRTs in Afghanistan: Successful but not Sufficient," DIIS Report 2005:6), (2005), at 28, available at http://www.diis.dk/graphics/Publications/Reports2005/pvj_prts_afghanistan.pdf (last visited on July 13, 2009).

First, with regard to assessing the utility and success of PRTs, it is becoming increasingly clear that the civilian component both in terms of personnel and funding must be strengthened and augmented. Civilian participation, while key, lack resources and often play an advisory rather than a leadership role.[55] PRTs need a broad range of expertise on a variety of development-related areas, and establishing the rule of law. Civilians must be able to play a leadership role in order not just to stabilize the region but to also to begin the process of reconstruction. One report, in fact, advocates that the Afghanistan PRTs be civilian-led like the PRTs in Iraq.[56]

Secondly, there needs to be better civilian-military coordination. Just at the Goldwater-Nichols legislation[57] mandated "jointness" among individual U.S. military services (Army, Navy, Marine Corps and Air Force), the same kind of jointness between the military and the civilian corps needed to be strongly advocated and implemented, if not actually legislated into being. Full integration of civilian efforts into military strategic interventions in Afghanistan are a necessary component of the stability operations, and needs to be addressed on an institutional level among DOD, DOS and USAID among others. Taking a "whole-of-government" approach by the U.S. Department of State has been viewed very favorably by certain commentators who also recommend that a cross-government approach be legislated by U.S. Congressional appropriations for PRTs.[58]

Moreover, certain observers have noted that the merger of military with civilian functions under the same "roof" so to speak may result in the loss of so-called "humanitarian space."[59] In other words, most nongovernmental organizations (NGOs), and international organizations (IOs) often prefer not to be associated in funding, leadership, mission or actual physical location with military operations.

Many NGOs foster the views that military actors are not "humanitarian" and add further, that in providing humanitarian assistance to civilian populations in post-conflict areas, the military does so in order to provide force protection, further the national foreign policies of the governments that they represent, or are meeting their international obligations. Humanitarian missions may be viewed as an aspect of "psychological operations" whereby needy populations are furnished with food, water and other basic human needs assistance in order to further a political gain or advantage rather than for humanitarian purposes alone. Moreover, military personnel often have no training in promoting sustainable development and generally lack a long-term development focus.[60]

Such organizations may argue that:

A clear distinction between civilian and military roles is vital for the preservation of humanitarian space. In a conflict or other nonpermissive environment, if the local population is unable to differentiate between foreign civilian and military actors, all international entities may be perceived as belligerents. If military elements operate in civilian clothes a drive unmarked, nontactical vehicles while engaging in relief and reconstruction activities–as they did in Afghanistan during the summer of 2002–the boundary between civilian and military efforts can become blurred, if not erased altogether.[61]

This argument is often vehemently offered by NGOs and their counterparts in bilateral relief agencies, and in my view is short-sighted. As the U.S. Institute for Peace special report quoted from above itself remarks, "[h]umanitarian space is not an 'all-or-nothing' phenomenon. In many of the countries where the humanitarian community operates, 'humanitarian space' has a fluid quality."[62]

And further it states that, "[a]ssistance agencies make themselves targets simply by providing relief to the population. As the emphasis shifts from emergency response to reconstruction and development, principles of impartiality and independence lose their applicability. . . . Mere association with the central government's objectives and its efforts to provide for its citizens and extend its writ throughout its sovereign territory is often sufficient to invite retaliation. From the perspective of many in the military, this is the primary reason for the loss of 'humanitarian space' in Afghanistan and Iraq, and not the supposed blurring of civil and military roles caused by military involvement in civil action and reconstruction activities."[63]

While I do understand the perspective of NGOs personnel and others involved in humanitarian missions in post-conflict areas, and the passion with which they feel that a clear distinction in both mission and operations should be maintained by the civilians and the military operating in such arenas, this view neglects an important dimension of the conflict. The harsh reality is that such operations (whether seen as strictly humanitarian, or as psychological operations, or as occupying a spectrum between the two) are unfolding in highly dangerous environments. The force protection offered by the military is critical, unless such NGOs are proposing to wait until the full and final cessation of all hostilities before commencing their humanitarian and reconstruction work. This approach is not feasible in the forbidding terrains in Afghanistan and other conflict-ridden areas.

The important humanitarian and related work offered by civilian missions and personnel are indispensable to the efforts at quelling the insurgencies, and moving the post-conflict areas on a pathway forward. One commentator points out that, "[t]he presence in war zones of military personnel and humanitarian staff is one of the most effective means of guaranteeing not only the delivery of the relief aid but also the protection of civilians from hostilities."[64]

Further, this aspect of the conflict goes back to a Clausewitzean principle that war is part of a continuum, and may not have a discrete beginning and end. Thus, humanitarian operations may need to commence before armed hostilities have actually ceased. This may be an inconvenience that we will simply have to accept in prosecuting a long and "small war" that does not seem to have a true ending point.

Thirdly, in assessing the success of PRTs, there seems to be a clear consensus that there need to be far more PRTs in the field. As one commentator points out, establishing 22 PRTs in three or more years after the fall of the Taliban Government is proceeding at a "snail's pace when dealing with an insurgency."[65] And PRTs should also place a greater emphasis on capacity building in Afghanistan that improve local governance and help link local officials with the central government, thereby enforcing federalism and a better central organization of the country.[66] Others argue that, "PRTs operate without an overarching concept of operations, . . . do not have a unified chain of command, and often do not coordinate or exchange information on best practices."[67]

While these are serious criticisms aimed at improving the performance and impact of PRTs, it should be clear that these actions are taking place in highly compromised and dangerous environments. The lack of sustainable or discernible progress should not be surprising in this context; however, the U.S. public in particular, and the international community in general, cannot be expected to wait indefinitely for tangible results. While the dedicated efforts of the individuals (both civilian and military) operating in PRTs are courageous and necessary, the impact of their actions need to have a palpable effect in ending the conflict, and in securitizing, stabilizing and transitioning the post-conflict societies in question. Only when a platform of stability is created can the important tasks of reconstruction begin in earnest.

Thus, with regard to measuring the actual progress in the stabilization and reconstruction efforts (a broader focus than simply measuring the relative success of the PRT model in the field), there is a report that was issued by the U.S. Institute of Peace (USIP) that described a matrix of discrete elements that should be applied in making this assessment. Starting with the premise that establishing an objective process for evaluating the progress of stabilization and reconstruction efforts, the report stated that the "main barriers to progress is political, not conceptual."[68] Often, there are political pressures that are brought to bear on actors in the post-conflict scene to "declare that political objectives have been obtained," before this is really the case.[69]

In other words, "individual agencies are inclined to report their success at implementing programs rather than on their impact on stabilization."[70] This is particularly true since an agency's success may be measured in terms of the funds it obligates rather than on whether the funds were actually disbursed and, if so, what impact the funds disbursement had on achieving stabilization goals. The USIP study advocated creating a system of metrics, or measurable indicators of progress, to provide a critical assessment tool to the U.S. Government. This tool could then be linked to clear, well-integrated goals and to strategic forward planning.

While this study emphasizes measureable progress from the viewpoint of the U.S. Government (and perhaps other national actors acting within the PRT framework), it does not examine the measure of success as seen from the vantage point of the Afghanistan Government. While a consultative process with counterparts in the Afghan Government is, no doubt, a daily occurrence in PRTs, it may be wise to also measure progress in terms of meeting the political goals and expectations of the host government. The host government's indicia of success also need to be incorporated into the measure of success overall for the international community.

One of the most elusive elements to discuss in this context is the aspect of political will. In other words, what is the Afghan Government or even more broadly, the Afghan people willing to support in terms of their own securitization, stabilization and transition from a war-torn society to one moving forward? This is the aspect of success that is the most difficult to measure, and frankly, I have not seen it as a measure of success from the point of view of international or bilateral donors during the course of my professional career. Perhaps this is an aspect that needs to be part of the way in which this conflict is perceived, and the way in which this conflict will end.

In conclusion, while PRTs are a good example of creating local foreign-based teams of both civilian and military personnel with specialized areas of expertise, it is a beginning and not an end. Although strengthening PRTs is a necessary component of the current efforts to stabilize and reconstruct Afghanistan, this measure alone may not be sufficient to end the conflict. Unless a new cultural awareness and sensitivity to the underlying drivers of conflict are brought to bear in Afghanistan and other post-conflict areas, there may not be that much tangible success in the end. The underlying factors of conflict will continue to be insufficiently identified, and fail to be dealt with in a consequential manner. And we may expect this pattern to continue into the future.

Moreover, the PRTs model demonstrates that there is a progressive merger of many different and seemingly incompatible actors and approaches to this conflict. First, there is a subtle merger between civilian and military missions, functions, and roles. Traditional roles of civilian agencies are now being performed or supported by military forces. This has major repercussions in terms of the underlying domestic and international law governing these acts, and the politics giving rise to such laws.

Secondly, the internal cultures of the agencies fulfilling these roles (civilian, military agencies, Non-Government Organizations, and International Organizations) will and are being dramatically affected. The downstream implications of this may not yet be clear, but there is an important change in organizational cultures that is already underway.

In terms of expanding PRTs beyond the Afghan context, three themes emerge. First, a common vision and strategy for all international partners working together is key in any PRT endeavor. Second, understanding the drivers of conflict and creating tailor-made programs to address the causes of conflict and instability in a culturally specific context is also necessary. Lastly, PRTs are only effective in so-called "non-permissive" environments where humanitarian NGOs and other actors are prevented from intervening in a meaningful way due to a high level of violence in post-conflict environments.

A Change in Focus in Afghanistan

Taking a wide angle view of the conflict in Afghanistan, there is a very distinct change in the mission focus which began fairly narrowly in 2001 in terms of capturing and/or killing Osama bin Laden and his top lieutenants, and overthrowing the Taliban leadership. The U.S. military later took on an SSTR agenda of securitization, stabilization, transition and reconstruction in 2005. None of these elements were first thought of as part of the Afghanistan-related war effort when *Operation Enduring Freedom* began on October 7, 2001.

Even with respect to securitization, the mission has evolved from "securitizing" Afghanistan from the perspective of defending the national interests of the United States to one that takes into account the "human security" factor of the civilians caught in the conflict. By supporting the individual security interests of innocent civilians as the top priority of the U.S. military operating in Afghanistan, the nature of its mission has shifted substantially, yet subtly. By adding the larger agenda of initiating reconstruction activities, the scope of the human security element has been enlarged further.

One commentator remarks unequivocally that:

Peace and relief operations, therefore, represent a tremendous paradigm shift in military thinking and culture.[71]

This conclusion is based on the following observation:

There has been a dramatic shift in approach to the protection of human rights to the effect that the military has been called upon to protect civilians in situations of gross human rights violations and grave breaches of [international humanitarian law] IHL by way of 'humanitarian interventions' to safeguard innocent civilians. Thus, military forces are declining to be instruments for pursuing power policy, but are increasingly becoming guarantors of foreign policy primarily aimed at stability and peacemaking, which is pursued by States, coalitions such as the African Union (AU) and the UN. Although military personnel have been trained and organised primarily to conduct combat operations, the same expertise has given them a unique capability to undertake many of the functions involved in peace and relief operations. Combat troops are trained to close with and destroy an enemy. Yet, in peace and relief operations, they find themselves trying to maintain a peaceful environment without the use of force. Their mission is essentially to keep, enforce, and promote peace and to safeguard the geostrategic changes, hence a transition from an era of confrontation and strategic bipolarity to a more cooperative and multipolar world.[72]

Indeed, the underlying legal doctrine supporting IHL principles stem from the Fourth Geneva Convention of 1949. Article 3 provides in relevant part that, "[p]ersons taking no active part on the hostilities . . . shall in all circumstances be treated humanely, without any adverse distinction founded on race, colour, religion or faith, sex, birth or wealth, or other similar critieria. . . . [and] the following acts are and shall remain prohibited at any time and in any place . . . (a) violence to life and person. . . . (c) outrages upon personal dignity, in particular, humiliating and degrading treatment."[73]

By assuming a mission to protect civilians, the U.S. military is moving beyond the negative injunctions set forth in the Fourth Geneva Convention and toward a duties-based legal regime. In other words, an argument could be made that the U.S. military has assumed a "duty" to protect the Afghan citizen beyond what is required by the Convention. If this argument is accepted, there has been a subtle movement in action (if not in policy or doctrine) towards civilian protection that goes beyond the requirement that civilians during wartime be "humanely" treated, and not subjected to any violence or outrages to their personal dignity.

Interestingly, this approach mirrors, in principle, the "Responsibility to Protect (RtoP)." In 2005, the UN World Summit endorsed this "groundbreaking" doctrine, "that sovereign States have the primary responsibility to protect their citizens but if a State is unable or unwilling to protect its own citizen, the responsibility falls on the international community."[74] While I am not making an argument that the RtoP principle has been adopted *de facto* (as a matter of fact) or *de jure* (as a matter of law) by the U.S. military, there is an interesting resonance between the two.

Finally, the decentralized nature of the combat units and their smaller size also means that lower-ranking military offices may be taking on leadership roles, and this has ramifications that will be explored later in the text. In fact, there may be evidence that this approach is an effort to provide "bottom-up" securitization, reconstruction and trust-building rather than "top-down" nation-building efforts planned centrally from Washington, DC, or from Kabul.

In light of the changed nature of the mission, and the means by which the mission is being implemented, there is ample room and reason to introduce the New Soldier. The New Soldier concept is designed to address the larger "human security" aspect of the conflict. Deploying the New Soldier as a warfighter with a heightened cultural awareness and sensitivity may be one means of seeking to end this intractable conflict. Cultural intelligence may be key in winning this conflict, and may be the "amplifier" that definitively brings this conflict to a successful conclusion.

Further, in making PRTs more relevant to the "SSTR" policy platform, it seem clear that securitization and stabilization are among the first priorities for PRTs in terms of initiating a stable cease-fire, and ensuring the safety of local nationals. While "reconstruction" has been addressed by U.S.-led PRTs, in particular, in terms of initiating activities that rebuild the destroyed physical infrastructure of Afghanistan (e.g., roads, bridges, airports, schools, hospitals, government buildings), very little attention has been given to the "T" or the *"transition"* in SSTR.

Defense Directive 3000.05 "Military Support for Stability, Security, Transition and Reconstruction (SSTR) Operations," discussed above, has the word "transition" in its title, but the DOD policy document does not give any background of what "transition operations" are or how they should be carried out. While DOD Instruction 3000.05, "Stability Operations," (September 16, 2009),[75] inter-departmental guidance for the Pentagon, it does not address liaising with foreign government counterparts or with non-USG actors in general. This policy vacuum is very telling, and I propose that it be filled with transition activities that should be implemented by the New Soldier.

The U.S. Agency for International Development (USAID) on its website reports that, "In July 2009, USAID's Office of Transition Initiatives (OTI) launched a country program in Afghanistan to support the U.S. Government's stabilization and reconstruction initiatives. A new part of this effort is to bring stability to violence-prone areas of the country. The initial objective of the Afghanistan Stabilization Initiative (ASI) is to address instability by creating conditions that build confidence and trust between the Government of the Islamic Republic of Afghanistan (GIRoA) and local Afghan communities. In close coordination with the International Security Assistance Force, ASI aims to improve the economic and social environment in Afghanistan through small community-enhancement projects. In addition, ASI will support the GIRoA by providing increased public access to information about its social, economic, and political activities and policies."[76]

While this description is a bit obscure, it seems that the USAID program is focused on small community projects (of an indeterminate nature), and the dissemination of public information on political activities and policies. While State/CRS defines its mission as helping to "stabilize and reconstruct societies in transition from conflict or civil strife so they can reach a sustainable path toward peace, democracy and a market economy,"[77] there is no definition of what this transition consists of.

Since there is no current policy directive from DOD or from USAID that explains or defines, "transition," it is not clear whether "transition" is meant to be political, economic, legal, or military in nature. Perhaps it is all of them. I will argue that the role of the New Soldier in the context of "transitioning" post-conflict societies beyond the stabilization phase may be viewed very broadly. The New Soldier (acting as an integral part of the PRTs in the field) may, in fact, be deployed to: (1) build trust; (2) build peace; and (3) build reconciliation.

The role of politics and diplomacy in transitioning post-conflict societies has already been addressed earlier, and only a few points need be highlighted here. Let me make one distinction clear at the outset, however, I am not arguing that the New Soldier be viewed or deployed as a de facto international "diplomat" since soldiers are not legally authorized with appropriate and sufficient delegated authority to engage in this type of diplomacy. However, since the New Soldier is among the first responders to the scene of conflict and/or post-conflict areas, he or she may be in a unique and highly favorable position to initiate a *process* leading to diplomatic negotiation.

While the actual diplomatic process of ending the conflict officially may be initiated by special political envoys, professional international mediators, or by actual diplomats of the international community that have the political will and proper authority to act in this capacity, there is still room for the New Soldier to operate in this context. Indeed, the New Soldier may be in a highly favorable position by using his or her specialized "active" listening skills, his knowledge of local conditions, and his familiarity with local actors who carry weight with the community to ascertain the true nature of the underlying conflict.

The conflict that expresses itself in extremist fundamentalism resulting in terrorist acts may actually be deeply rooted in past grievances, historical inequities, or personally driven agendas. The New Soldier may have unique insight into the "drivers" of the conflict, the players, and how best to seek a reconciliation of opposing interests, factions, tribes, warlords, or other relevant actors. This is not to suggest that all actors and all opposing interests in a conflict of this nature may ultimately be reconciled–that would be an overly optimistic and naïve view–but making the initial determination of who may be an "irreconcilable" is a major starting point. Understanding which person should be subject to an armed confrontation, or subject to capture for prosecution under relevant law enforcement regimes, or subject to a peace and reconciliation effort is vital knowledge in this context.

Further, understanding the essentials of the conflict, and its underlying causes, requires skills that are highly intuitive and emotions-based. I realize that this may be foreign territory for most warfighters, but it is a skill that I believe may be cultivated. Using empathy can become a weapon of war if it is used to identify the sources of the conflict, and seek empowering and trust-building ways for resolving the conflict.

In fact, the experienced New Soldier may rely on his or her own life experiences to build a strong bond of communication and empathy with the participants in the conflict. This bond, once forged, may help bring about a stronger, more lasting result if it is based on mutual understanding and respect. Humor may also be a key to unlocking hidden hostilities by finding a way to humanize rather than dehumanize the actors involved in the conflict. This is the transition where "hard power" becomes "soft power" which then becomes "smart power."

One of the points made earlier is the possibility of using independent consultative groups, NGOs, or neutral parties to lead a negotiated peace-finding process. In other words, South Africans and Rwandans, for example, that are well-versed in the truth-and-reconciliation process may be neutral parties to begin the discussion in Afghanistan, the Philippines, or other regions of strife. In fact, the truth-and-reconciliation process may be a good starting point to identify grievances, and start the healing process.

Of course, the first element of this undertaking is trust. Trust must be cultivated by the New Soldier, by the independent negotiator (if there is one), and by the locals within the affected conflict-ridden community itself. There must be the requisite political will to achieve trust on all sides. Airing grievances and finding a safe place in which to express deeply felt and hidden emotions in a constructive, non-violent way builds trust and helps to initiate the healing process. Further, this becomes a building block for peace and later, for political reconciliation. This is the stage at which the politically-driven reconciliation process may begin leading to actual political gains or achieving discrete political goals.

Needless to say, it may also become very easy to become bogged down in the process of "listening," so this process must be initiated consciously with specific targets, goals and political outcomes in mind. (I am not proposing "therapy for terrorists.") However, a constructive, well-structured dialogue that is linked to specific, objective, well-publicized and politically accepted goals by all participants may be the beginning of an actual "transition" in SSTR operations.

This "transition" is so difficult to bring about because it actually takes place in an emotional terrain where it remains unseen. Unlike seeing a bridge being build over a river, this "bridge" is an emotional one that is far more difficult to build and sustain. Regardless of its insubstantial (or ethereal) nature, it is a critical foundation that will ensure that the same conflict does not erupt again. Ending the conflict dispositively will ensure the success of the final outcome of SSTR operations. Otherwise, we may be left fighting "ghost wars" forever.

Further, in building on the transition initiatives that have already been undertaken by USAID in Afghanistan, there may also be room to build the capacity of local counterparts in Afghanistan by using the PRT structure. One study points out that, "[o]ne of the most important goals of PRT operations is to build the capacity of [the] provincial government. Although programs aimed at teaching governance skills serve a valuable purpose, they are no substitute for directly involving local leaders in the process of project development, budgeting and oversight. A process that vests local leaders with a degree of executive authority creates a perception of legitimacy in the community, and local stakeholders who help design and implement projects feel invested in their long term success."[78]

While capacity building may be fraught with all sorts of underlying political landmines, using the New Soldier to build local capacity in governance and democratization may vest the provincial government with both the skills and the will to politically reconstruct Afghanistan. This may be another very important facet of making a "transition" to a stable and viable post-conflict society in a political dimension.

Thus, the New Solder may be a vital instrument in creating a broad-based foundation for dialogue, reconciliation, and transition to a stable, securitized post-conflict society. The New Soldier may be trained and deployed to build trust, peace and reconciliation. Thus, the current function of "peace operations" may also include "peacebuilding" activities that can incrementally lead to sustainable peace and help rebuild the post-conflict society.

The use of diplomacy along with actively seeking out creative, innovative and non-violent means of exploring conflict resolution by the New Soldier may help facilitate the creation of a platform–a platform for sustainable political, economic and legal transformation of a post-conflict or collapsed society. This platform may then be used by actual diplomats, social scientists, civil engineers, architects, designers, air traffic controllers, city planners and countless others to commence their important work. The New Soldier should be regarded as another means of achieving an end.

The New Soldier, if deployed, could be instrumental in stabilizing fragile states, reconstructing war-torn and collapsed societies and, perhaps most importantly, transitioning them to a politically and economically viable nation-state. Thus, the next part will explore how to operationalize the concept of the New Soldier. In so doing, we will be shifting from Afghanistan to Africa, another region deeply affected by fundamentalist Islamic-based terrorism.

A Postscript to PRTs in Afghanistan

The above discussion was focused on the "lessons learned" of the recent U.S. and NATO-based PRT experience, however, the U.S. military is already moving past the PRT structure in Afghanistan. It is in the process of moving away from conventional combat missions designed to clear Afghan villages of Taliban elements and militant insurgent attacks, thereby allowing local forces and government agencies to rebuild the local economy and governmental institutions.[79] The U.S. military is currently elevating the role of Special Forces in Afghanistan to advising the Afghan military and engaging in raids to kill top insurgents.[80] In other words, the U.S. military is moving away from a counterinsurgency campaign to a counterterrorism one.

The Pentagon is expected to create a new two-star command to oversee the entire Special Operations effort in Afghanistan. The changeover, scheduled for summer 2012 will place Maj. General Tony Thomas, the deputy commander of the U.S. Joint Special Operations Command which oversees the counterterrorism effort worldwide, in command.[81]

The new Special Operations Joint Task Force-Afghanistan (SOJTF-A), will bring all elements of American, NATO and Afghan special operations under a single organization, and will be led by Maj. Gen. Tony Thomas.[82] The new command is essentially designed to improve coordination among U.S. NATO and Afghan special forces, allowing "units to share information, resources and enablers and ensures a more efficient use of these resources." Further, "as a unified command, SOJTF-A presents [U.S. and coalition] command with one collective voice" for special operations according to a Pentagon spokesperson. But that collective voice does not mean that Afghan special forces will now be under the command of American or coalition leaders. However, linking ISAF forces with Afghan forces has raised issues especially in cases where Afghan attack NATO or coalition troops in so-called "green-on-blue" attacks, addressed later in the text.[83]

In due time, the three-star corps headquarters that currently commands day-to-day operations and is held by a U.S. Army officer, will be turned over to a Special Operations officer.[84] This will decrease the heavy U.S. military "footprint" in Afghanistan, thus easing political pressures at home while still exerting military force on insurgents and counterterrorism efforts in that theatre.

While PRTs were an expedient vehicle for power projection in Afghanistan and elsewhere, it remains a military tool that may be deployed in certain geographic regions for certain purposes: it is not a military solution that fits all counterinsurgency needs.

The Endgame in Afghanistan

Presidents Barack Obama and Hamid Karzai signed the Strategic Partnership Agreement (SPA) on May 1, 2012 in the Presidential Palace in Kabul, Afghanistan.[85] The SPA outlines the details of U.S. troop withdrawal from Afghanistan from 2014-2024.[86] But the endgame in Afghanistan is far from clear.

The Taliban has many Pashtun members. So it is very likely that the Taliban will continue to hold sway in southern and eastern Afghanistan, especially if sanctuary to its militants is provided by Pakistan.[87] On the other hand, the Afghan army is composed of many Tajiks, Uzbeks and Hazaras mainly concentrated in the northern and western provinces of Afghanistan. These ethnic groups comprised the former Northern Alliance that warred with the Pashtuns during the 1990s.[88] The natural allies of the former Northern Alliance are India,[89] Iran and Russia whose strategic military interests in the region will keep them engaged.[90] That may leave the United States betwixt and between two opposing factions in Afghanistan whose differences are deep and deeply felt. Moreover, any potential alliance between the U.S. and Iran in this effort (and perhaps with Russia as well) is highly problematic.

More alarmingly, the U.S. Special Operations forces has stopped its training of Afghan Local Police and special operations forces as of September 2012, pending a stricter vetting of new Afghan recruits. This is in response to a rash of attacks on U.S. and NATO troops in Afghanistan, or the so-called "green-on-blue" attacks where Afghan forces kill the foreign troops that are training them. More than 45 U.S. and NATO service members have been killed in 2012 by insider attacks. Roughly 20,000 or 7 percent of Afghan forces will be affected by this stand-down; however, the vast majority of the 350,000 Afghan National Army soldiers and Afghan Police members will not be affected.[91]

Taliban insurgents infiltrating the training grounds, ISI involvement, and infiltration by the Haqqani network have all been cited as reasons for these "green-on-blue" attacks along with other factors for the killings stemming from personal disputes, stress or cultural clashes.[92] The extent to which this pause in training new Afghan recruits will affect the U.S draw down by December 31, 2014, remains to be seen. However, these joint training exercises were a linchpin of the final stages of the U.S. military involvement in Afghanistan, now jeopardized by the last wave of violence visited on U.S. and NATO troops.

As another disappointing footnote to this discussion, much of U.S. economic assistance was directed toward Afghanistan in the hope that it would help stabilize the country by providing it the financial means to jumpstart its economy. Although this economic support was taking place while intractable insurgency and related political problems persisted, the expectation was that it would support the economic development of Afghanistan. However, in the final analysis, U.S. financial support was largely ineffective and may have only served to exacerbate underlying problems of corruption and graft.

The example of the Kabul Bank may illustrate this conclusion best. The near collapse of the Kabul Bank totaling a sum of nearly $900 million, or the equivalent of the Afghan Government's total annual revenues, will be a cost that must be borne by the governments of Afghanistan, the United States, and other foreign donors.[93] The founder and former chairman of the Kabul Bank, Sherkhan Farnood, spent almost $150 million of the Bank's money to buy villas and to construct office buildings in Dubai in his own name.[94]

Kabul Bank also financed shell companies to embezzle funds from the Afghan Government, and other insiders were given interest-free loans so that they could buy stakes in the bank. It is not even clear whether Mr. Farnood will face criminal or other charges for his activities.[95] As it stands, the matter is far from being resolved and has the net effect of exemplifying "how the United States is leaving behind a problem it underwrote over the past decade with tens of billions of dollars in aid and logistical support: a narrow business and political elite defined by its corruption, and despised by most Afghans for it."[96]

Another egregious example of graft in Afghanistan is Afghan Army's former Surgeon General, General Ahmad Zia Yaftali. He stands accused by NATO investigators who allege that he stole tens of millions of dollars' worth of drugs from the country's main military hospital where scores of Afghans died from simple infections since they could not afford to bribe the nurses and doctors to treat them.[97] The United States financed the day-to-day operations of the hospital.

By 2010, 97 percent of Afghanistan's gross domestic product resulted from international assistance, according to the World Bank.[98] (I suppose the other 3 percent came from illegal drug sales.) The culture of dependency on foreign aid has led to a sense of anxiety among Afghans who fear the departure of foreign military troops, humanitarian aid workers and the billions of hard currency that they brought with them. "As aid is withdrawn, the World Bank forecasts that growth could fall to 5 or 6 percent for the next few years. But the slowdown could be more severe if security worsens, if Afghans cannot maintain their new infrastructure or if the government fails to garner royalties from contracts for the country's mineral wealth."[99]

In fact, the United States has recently discovered over $1 trillion in unmined mineral deposits in Afghanistan.[100] In 2004, U.S. geologists working on reconstruction efforts found old charts and data at the library of the Afghan Geological Survey in Kabul left behind by Soviet mining experts during the Soviet occupation in the 1980s, and abandoned there after the Soviet withdrawal in 1989.[101] Iron, copper, niobium, a metal used in producing superconducting steel, rare earth elements used in cell phones and other digital instruments, and large gold deposits were found in astonishing quantities.

However, this news was not met with enthusiasm but with a certain resigned pessimism stemming from the intractable and undeniable corruption in Afghanistan. At the urging of the United States, one Afghan Minister of Mines was replaced after being accused of accepting a $30 million bribe from Chinese officials who are actively seeking access to rare metals.[102] More alarmingly, "A recent [U.S.] Defense Department analysis said criminal mining syndicates were smuggling chromite over the border, paying protection money to the Pakistan Taliban and the Haqqani insurgent network."[103]

The concern is that its mineral riches may be used to finance further tribal and ideological warfare, following in the "Dutch disease" syndrome of the Democratic Republic of Congo (minerals), Zambia (minerals), Nigeria (oil), and Sierra Leone (diamonds). This is the phenomenon where natural resources do not enrich a country, but fuel conflict and further impoverishment.

Rather than following Sierra Leone's example where diamonds (or so-called "blood diamonds") have financed a violent insurgency by the Revolutionary United Front, Afghanistan should look to Botswana who used its diamond revenues to build roads, power grids, schools and other economic infrastructure, or to Malaysia which used its mineral revenues to create jobs in export zones.[104] Although Afghanistan has signed onto the Extractive Industries Transparency Initiative,[105] there is no real evidence to support the belief that it has the requisite government institutional framework or private industry in place to support a vibrant mining industry.

In sum, while Afghanistan has the necessary resources, financing and international political support in place, it is truly a question of the political will of its own people that will determine its own destiny.

PART III

The Role of U.S. and International Actors:
A New Integrated Approach

7

Managing Global Instability:
Exploring the Role of the U.S. Government

Contingency operations are currently taking place in various conflict areas of dangerous, unpredictable and highly volatile environments where local government institutions have weakened or collapsed. However, providing security alone is not sufficient. Instituting and enforcing security measures by the military is merely the first step that permits other actors to take an active role in implementing critical strategic and tactical measures in initiating stability, security, transition, and reconstruction operations. Coordinating a comprehensive whole-of-government approach becomes vital in this context in facilitating the local actors to move past the conflict.[1]

While the pivotal importance of the military's role in peacekeeping is generally acknowledged, it also recognized that this role must be fully integrated with the political, diplomatic and economic efforts of the groups in conflict, international organizations, Non-Government Organizations (NGOs), the media, and other non-state actors.[2] The question is how to coordinate such complex and interrelated functions being carried out by different institutional actors with varying objectives, timelines and mandates. This topic specifically addresses one of the most serious challenges of the U.S. Government (USG) in a post-9/11 world. Before we address this complex and multi-faceted subject, however, certain prefatory issues must be defined and examined first.

The initial question is where are such "failing or failed states" located, and what causes such states to fail in the first instance? Although the topic of failed states has been addressed earlier in the text, it is being revisited here in a USG-specific context. Second, why should the USG take on the task of preventing conflict in such conflict or post-conflict zones? Finally, will USG intervention foreseeably reduce the conflict and move the failed or failing state toward the path of stabilization and reconstruction? Or, in other words, what should the USG's short-and the long-term political objectives in undertaking conflict prevention be?

In light of this challenge, the discussion below will address the following:

> Examine the initial questions, discussed above, to set the stage for a fuller discussion of the national interests that may propel the United States into undertaking such a complex, difficult and long-term goal of inter-agency cooperation in this context.

> Critically review the current obstacles and roadblocks to achieving interagency cooperation that is specifically designed to address long-term issues of preventing conflict in failing and failed states.

> Propose a practical, solutions-based approach in achieving the goal of interagency cooperation as a way forward.[3]

A.   Setting the Stage: Why Do Certain Nations Fail?

At the outset, it is important to recognize that there is no one single accepted USG definition of what constitutes a failing or failed state.[4] The Department of States (DOS) uses the term fragile states as those "unable to provide physical security and basic services for their citizens due to lack of control over physical territory, massive corruption, criminal capture of government institutions, feudal gaps between rich and poor, an absence of social responsibility by elites, or simply grinding poverty and the absence of any tradition of functioning government."[5] The U.S. Agency for International Development (USAID) defines fragile states as including failed, failing, and recovering states.[6] USAID also proposed the "Fragility Framework" as the means for analyzing governance in fragile states.[7]

(1) Definitions

The National Security Strategy (2010)[8] and the National Military Strategy (2011)[9] do not define "failing or failed states." The National Military

Strategy, however, warns of the danger of failed states by stating, "[s]tates with weak, failing, and corrupt governments will increasingly be used as a safe haven for an expanding array of non-state actors that breed conflict and endanger stability, particularly in Africa and the broader Middle East."[10]

Perhaps the most complete definition of failing states is contained in the U.S. Army Doctrine Field Manual FM 3-07 *Stability Operations,* which sets forth the following definitions:

> "A *fragile state* **is a country that suffers from institutional weaknesses serious enough to threaten the stability of the central government.** These weaknesses arise from several root causes, including ineffective governance, criminalization of the state, economic failure, external aggression, and internal strife due to disenfranchisement of large sections of the population. . . . [11]

The term fragile state refers to the broad spectrum of failed, failing, and recovering states. The distinction among them is rarely clear, as fragile states do not travel a predictable path to failure or recovery. The difference between a recovering and failed state may be minimal, as the underlying conditions, such as insurgency or famine, may drive a state to collapse in a relatively short period. It is far more important to understand how far and quickly a state is moving from or toward stability. The fragile states framework, developed by the U.S. Agency for International Development, provides a model for applying U.S. development assistance in fragile states. This framework serves to inform understanding for intervening actors, providing a graphic tool that describes the conditions of the operational environment. . . . [12]

Fragile states can be defined as either vulnerable or in crisis. A ***vulnerable state*** **is a nation either unable or unwilling to provide adequate security and essential services to significant portions of the population.** In vulnerable states, the legitimacy of the central government is in question. This includes states that are failing or recovering from crisis. **A *crisis state* is a nation in which the central government does not exert effective control over its own territory.** It is unable or unwilling to provide security and essential services for significant portions of the population. In crisis states, the central government may be weak, nonexistent, or simply unable or unwilling to provide security or basic services. This includes states that are failing or have failed altogether, where violent conflict is a reality or a great risk." (Emphasis in original.)[13]

The lack of USG-wide accepted definitions of what constitutes failing or failed states reflects, and perhaps perpetuates, the difference in perspectives of the various U.S. government agencies dealing with failed states. These agencies and departments include, but are not limited to, DOS, USAID, and the Departments of Defense (DOD), Agriculture (USDA), Justice (DOJ), Commerce (DOC), and Homeland Security (DHS). In spite of these differences, "the challenge for military and civilian leaders is to forge unity of effort among the diverse array of actors involved in a stability operation. This is the essence of *unified action*: the synchronization, coordination, and/ or integration of the activities of governmental and nongovernmental entities with military operations to achieve unity of effort."[14] (Emphasis in original.)

Moreover, two more important distinctions need to be made, first, the need to create a *whole of government approach* that integrates the collaborative efforts of the departments and agencies of the United States Government to achieve unity of effort toward a shared goal.[15] Indeed, a successful whole of government approach requires that all actors—

➢ Are represented, integrated, and actively involved in the process.

➢ Share an understanding of the situation and problem to be resolved.

➢ Strive for unity of effort toward achieving a common goal.

➢ Integrate and synchronize capabilities and activities.

➢ Collectively determine the resources, capabilities, and activities necessary to achieve their goal.[16]

In thinking ahead, the USG also needs to partner with its allies, intergovernmental and nongovernmental organizations, private sector entities and others in forging a *comprehensive approach* to dealing with failing and failed states.[17]

(2) Identifying Failing and Failed States

Aside from definitional issues, there is also no generally accepted agreement on which nations have failed or are at risk of failing. Popular indices of measuring such failures include, for example, the Brookings Institute Index of State Weakness; the George Mason University State Fragility Index; the World Bank at Risk States Index; the U.S. Department of State Foreign Assistance Framework; the U.S. Institute of Peace Measuring Progress in Conflict Environments (MPICE) framework; and the National Intelligence Council Internal Stability Watchlist.

In a collaboration between *Foreign Policy* and the Fund for Peace, the 2011 Failed States Index lists the following nations as the top twelve "failed states," namely, Somalia, Chad, Sudan, the Democratic Republic of the Congo, Haiti, Zimbabwe, Afghanistan, the Central African Republic, Iraq, Côte d'Ivoire, Guinea and Pakistan.[18] The U.S. has fought valiantly in Afghanistan and Iraq who rather disappointingly rank seventh and ninth, respectively, on this list. Also, alarmingly, Pakistan rounds out the top dozen. Does this mean that the USG owes the same duty of intervention in all the failed states on this list?

Thankfully, not, for the reasons discussed below.

(3) The U.S. Response to Failing and Failed States: Federal Laws and Interagency Coordination

The strategic level chain of command for dealing with failing states is defined in the *Reconstruction and Stabilization Civilian Management Act of 2008* (the "Act").[19] Section 1604(a)(1) of the Act provides that:

> "If the President determines that it is *in the national security interests of the United States* for United States civilian agencies or non-Federal employees to assist in reconstructing and stabilizing a country or region that is at risk of, in, or is in transition from, conflict or civil strife, the President may . . . notwithstanding any other provision of law, and on such terms and conditions as the President may determine, furnish assistance to such country or region for reconstruction or stabilization. . . ."[20] (Emphasis supplied.)

Finding a legally mandated "national interest" that justifies engaging in an overseas contingency operation,[21] and the political will to exercise it is quite a task for this, or any other, U.S. Administration. In reality, not all failing or failed states pose a national security threat to the United States.

Somalia, for example, has been listed as #1 on the Failed State Index for the past four years, and has not had a functioning national government in over 20 years. While this alone may not necessarily pose a compelling national security threat to the United States, Somalia is problematic insofar as international pirating operations are being launched from its territory.[22] In contrast, mass killings in the Democratic Republic of the Congo and the Sudan have not elicited a U.S. national security response to date.[23] (Historically, the same was true in Rwanda and Burundi.)[24]

States fail for a multiplicity of difficult, thorny, inter-connected and disconnected reasons that are difficult to organize into neat categories. Clearly, a fuller discussion of why states fail lies outside the scope of this essay.[25] One organizing principle to consider is that state failures only rise to the level of affecting U.S. national interests when there is a nexus between the activities of the collapsed or failing state and U.S. strategic political, military or economic interests. So, generally speaking, imploding states like Zimbabwe, Central African Republic, or Guinea do not pose a national security threat to the U.S., but Afghanistan, Pakistan and even Somalia do pose a real or existential threat.

One of the reasons that it has been difficult to develop U.S. national policy on failing and failed states is because the problems underlying such failures are generally so intractable. Notwithstanding the difficulty of formulating a national strategy, however, "[o]ne of the standing critiques of the Obama administration's foreign policy is that, though the president has spoken frequently of the danger posed by state failure, he has never formulated a coherent policy to prevent or cure it."[26]

Regardless of the underlying political and practical considerations that may be in play, once a national security interest determination is made under the Act, the President is authorized to use funds made available under the Foreign Assistance Act of 1961, as amended, subject to a 15-day notification to Congress as required by Section 634 of the Foreign Assistance

Act. Further, the President must also furnish a written policy justification to Congress's foreign affairs and appropriations committees subject to the provisions of Section 614(a)(3) of the Foreign Assistance Act, prior to using such funds.[27]

This Act also formally recognizes and establishes the Office the Coordinator for Reconstruction and Stabilization (S/CRS) within DOS, an office that was created in June 2004 by former Secretary of State, Colin Powell. The Act gives the Coordinator for Reconstruction and Stabilization the "mandate to lead, coordinate, and institutionalize United States Government civilian capacity to prevent or prepare for post-conflict situations and help reconstruct and stabilize a country or region that is at risk of, in, or is in transition from, conflict or civil strife."[28]

The Act formally references National Security Presidential Directive 44 (NSPD-44) which gives the Secretary of State, with the Coordinator's assistance, the lead role in developing reconstruction and stabilization strategies. The Secretary is also given the responsibility to coordinate with the Department of Defense on reconstruction and stabilization responses, and to integrate their planning and implementing procedures.[29] Further, NSPD-44 specifies that the "Secretaries of State and Defense will integrate stabilization and reconstruction contingency plans with military contingency plans where relevant and appropriate."[30]

Thus, NSPD-44 gives a fairly detailed roadmap for the U.S. State Department to take the lead in coordinating USG responses for reconstruction and stabilization and interagency processes related thereto; resolving relevant policy, program and funding disputes among USG departments and agencies; and working with expatriate and foreign individuals and organizations related to such activities.

The U.S. State Department has also flushed out its own responsibilities in its first "2010 Quadrennial Diplomacy and Development Review (QDDR): Leading Through Civilian Power," where it announced that the Civilian Reserve Corps may be replaced with an Expert Corps that will work with experts outside the USG to deploy quickly to the field where contingency operations are taking place.[31] Also pursuant to the QDDR, DOS announced the formation and reorganization of a number of its bureaus on

January 5, 2012. Principally, for purposes of this discussion, the Office of the CRS (S/CRS) became the Bureau of Conflict and Stabilization Operations to be led by a new Assistant Secretary. The mandate for this new Bureau is to advance U.S. national security by "driving integrated, civilian-led efforts to prevent, respond to, and stabilize crises in priority states, setting the conditions for long-term peace."[32]

This organizational change may address one of the structural problems with the former Office of the CRS which was expected to report directly to the U.S. Secretary of State. No doubt, this became unwieldy over time, and has been addressed by this reorganizational change where an assistant secretary of state will now provide an intermediate level of supervision, review and direction before any decision-making is taken up with the Secretary of State.

USAID also announced recently that it was changing the name of its Office of Military Affairs (OMA) to the Office of Civilian Military Cooperation (CMC). "This change reflects the office's evolving role in facilitating civilian-military cooperation, and better conveys the mission of the office—to improve communication, mutual understanding and cooperation between USAID and the Department of Defense."[33]

In addition, innumerable other USG agencies and independent organizations have issued thoughtful and thorough guidance on coordinating interagency efforts in dealing with complex operations, including the Col. Arthur D. Simons Center for the Study of Interagency Cooperation.[34] Nevertheless, despite a wealth of statutory and handbook guidance, there are still significant obstacles and barriers to facilitating successful interagency cooperation in dealing with failing and failed states. The following discussion will address some of these issues.

B. Problems in Interagency Coordination

Problems related to interagency coordination efforts in dealing with failing and failed states are essentially three-fold in nature: (1) structural; (2) cultural; and, (3) practical.

(1) Structural Problems

General William "Kip" Ward in looking back on his experience as Commander of the United States Africa Command (AFRICOM) describes its mandate as being "interagency-oriented."[35] AFRICOM, in his words, reflected the "3-D" approach of the diplomacy, defense and development efforts of DOS, DOD and USAID which were designed to take place in mutually supportive and complementary ways.[36] But he points out that:

> Often turning requirements into security assistance programs in Africa requires considering options that combine defense (Title 10 [of the U.S. Code]) with non-defense (Title 22 [of the U.S. Code]) appropriations. Rarely are these arrangements sustainable over time. . . . This strict compartmentalization of funding sources can impede unity of effort, especially since much of the Title 22 budget tends to be earmarked for very specific purposes. The answer is not to call for changes to the legal differentiation between Title 10 and Title 22, which exists for important historical reasons regarding the separation of military and non-military matters. Rather, other U.S. government agencies need both adequate resources and increased flexibility and versatility to turn short-fused opportunities into potentially long-term and successful programs that when combined with DOD efforts represent a holistic approach to security among U.S. partners.[37]

For purposes of clarity, Title 10 of the U.S. Code of federal laws is designed to provide the legal basis for the roles, missions and organization of DOD and its respective service branches, and to authorize its military operations. Title 22 sets forth federal laws on foreign relations including subjects such as diplomatic and consular relations, foreign assistance, arms control, etc. Moreover, the Foreign Assistance Act (Pub. L. 87-195, 75 Stat. 424, enacted September 4, 1961, 22 U.S.C. § 2151 et seq.) is a federal law that reorganized the structure of existing U.S. foreign assistance programs, separated military from non-military aid, and created a new agency, the United States Agency for International Development (USAID) to administer those non-military, economic assistance programs. On November 3, 1961, President John F. Kennedy signed the Foreign Assistance Act and issued Executive Order 10973 (November 3, 1961).

As General Ward correctly points out, these legal authorities cannot be easily merged since these are separate functions that are separately authorized and funded by Congress. Further, oversight over the 3-D agencies are exercised by many different committees in the U.S. Congress that have varying roles and perspectives on the functions, programs and relations among DOD, DOS and USAID. Thus, this stove-piping in roles, functions, legal authorities, funding and Congressional oversight obviously creates problems in achieving a unity of effort in creating a whole of government approach.

General Ward also mentions the pivotal Goldwater-Nichols legislation[38] that mandated sweeping reforms of the U.S. military including instilling the military doctrine of "jointness" and "inter-operability" among military service branches. The legislation was designed to address inter-service rivalry and the lack of cooperation during the Vietnam War and afterward. General Ward applies the Goldwater-Nichols Act to the current interagency context by stating, "[a]s with Goldwater-Nichols' impact on jointness, interagency integration is about how disparate agencies work together to accomplish their respective missions under unity of effort."[39]

If one were to argue that NSPD-44 sets up the roadmap for jointness among military and non-military agencies in a similar manner as the Goldwater-Nichols legislation, does it truly accomplish this goal? One commentator bluntly concludes that "[w]hile the Goldwater-Nichols Department of Defense Reorganization Act of 1986 required and over time improved cooperation and inter-operability among the armed services, no similar dynamic has forced fusion of the civilian agencies, let alone between civilian and military agencies."[40] Thus, the answer may be a disappointing "no" based not only on structural but also on cultural differences.

(2) Cultural Differences

While different U.S. military service branches have separate cultures that are reflected in their disparate roles and functions, there is an underlying commitment to the same strategic vision. The same cannot be said of other federal departments and agencies as dissimilar as DOS, USAID, USDA, and DOJ, among others.

One factor that strongly differentiates the military approach from the civilian one is based on different learning cultures. The U.S. military has doctrine, civilian agencies do not. The U.S. military also has a sophisticated approach to learning the lessons of experience, embedding it in a system of professional education that is tailored to promotion and advancement within the U.S. military. These lessons are archived and disseminated so that successor generations of soldiers and airmen may benefit from this corporate knowledge. In fact, the U.S. Army created the Center for Army Lessons Learned to manage this process.[41]

By contrast,

"The key civilian agencies involved in foreign policy in the U.S.—the Departments of State, Treasury, Agriculture, Homeland Security, and Justice and the U.S. Agency for International Development—do not have robust institutional cultures of learning. Most learning is done on the job. It is neither cumulative nor closely related to career development. It is not systematic and tends to be based on personal and anecdotal experience and absorbing the institutional culture of the home organization. Unlike the military, civilians have no doctrine; no accepted tactics, techniques and procedures; and no clear chain of command, so lessons learned are much more difficult to nest institutionally. Moreover, no civilian agency has complex operations as its core mission, so lessons from complex operations tend to get diluted and blended down into traditional diplomacy, development and defense core missions."[42] (Indeed, USAID eliminated its training and evaluations office in 2005, and is now trying to re-create it.)[43]

Thus, the cultural differences between military and non-military U.S. actors are real and systemic and cannot be easily or quickly overcome. Indeed, in light of the DOS's recent announcement that it will be replacing the statutorily-mandated Civilian Reserve Corps[44] with an Expert Corps, it may not be fair to pre-judge the change and deem it a failure before it is even implemented. However, it will take time, effort and a change in culture, mission, and chain of command in order to fully and permanently effectuate these interagency organizational, structural and cultural changes that are already underway. In the meantime, however, practical considerations are adding a layer of urgency and new complexity to the problem.

(3) Practical Considerations

An irrefutable fact is beginning to change the complexion of the problem of interagency coordination in dealing with failing and failed states. The risks of war are dramatically shifting away from military personnel and toward civilian employees and contractors. In 2011, 418 U.S. soldiers died in Afghanistan.[45] By comparison, 430 employees of U.S. contractors were reported killed in Afghanistan in 2011; 386 worked for DOD; 43 for USAID and one for the Department of State.[46]

Under the Defense Base Act, 42 U.S.C. §§ 1651–1654, U.S. defense contractors are required to report the war zone deaths and injuries of their employees, including subcontractors and foreign workers to the Department of Labor, in part, to make insurance claims for death and medical compensation of the killed or injured workers. In the words of one commentator, "No one believes that we're underreporting military deaths, . . . [but] everyone believes that we're underreporting contractor deaths." Thus, many contractors' deaths are not reported and their survivors may be left uncompensated for these deaths. "By continuing to outsource high-risk jobs that were previously performed by soldiers, the military, in effect, is privatizing the ultimate sacrifice."[47]

Why is shifting the risk of war, or in other words, of being in harm's way from soldiers to civilians so important within this context? First, because it is what civilians fear the most. It is not, generally speaking, part of their undertaking in the contractual relationship with their employer: it is an unfortunate and undesired consequence. To put it more succinctly, "[e]ven dying is being outsourced here."[48]

Secondly, it changes the nature of interagency cooperation if the risks of injury and death are to be shifted dramatically away from the military. Indeed, this shift seems to reflect a growing trend in Afghanistan over the past several years, and it also reflects the same trend in Iraq where civilian deaths exceeded military ones as long ago as 2009.[49] This inherently changes the nature of the dialogue on interagency cooperation when the risks are being redistributed to and assumed by civilian employees and contractors.

In fact, a recent U.S. government audit estimated that the cost of providing security for U.S. development work in Afghanistan will increase sharply when it begins using a security enterprise run by the Afghans. Steven Trent, the acting Special Inspector General for Afghanistan Reconstruction (SIGAR) wrote a letter to the U.S. Agency for International Development (USAID) advising it that the cost of providing security for USAID-funded projects could increase as much as 46 percent.[50] SIGAR calculated that the net cost of an Afghan guard would range from $710.00 to $830.00 per month representing a 25-46 percent net increase in cost. Trent also advised that if the Afghan Public Protection Force (APPF) is not fully functioning by the March 20, 2012 deadline to disband private security companies, USAID projects worth about $900 million were at "significant risk of termination." The report was rejected "in its entirety" by USAID's Mission Director in Kabul Afghanistan.[51]

Afghanistan's new security structure nominally took effect on March 20, 2012 through the Ministry of the Interior which runs the APPF. The Ministry will be charging clients for firearms, ammunition, training, uniforms and administrative costs. In addition, the Ministry has agreed to extend the licenses for certain private security companies for licensing fees of $120,000 annually plus a bank deposit of $400,000 as security for the performance of the company and from which fines may be deducted by the Afghan government.[52] The initiative to form a 25,000 member security force was in response to President Karzai's mandate since he apparently regarded private security companies operating in Afghanistan as an affront to its sovereignty. However, the APPF is not fully operational to date.[53]

To illustrate how difficult securing development projects in Afghanistan is, the example of the Kajaki Dam, a hydroelectric power plant in the Helmand Province about 100 miles northwest of Kandahar, may serve this purpose. The dam was built in the 1950s by a U.S. firm, Morrison-Knudsen.[54] In 1975, USAID installed two generators that fell into disrepair after the Soviet invasion in 1979. USAID hired the Louis Berger Group, a Washington-based consulting firm in 2003 to refurbish two turbines.[55]

The Afghan government hired a Chinese firm to add a third turbine who did not get started in the project until 2007. By 2008, British troops were deployed to Kajaki to provide escort to convoys of trucks carrying parts for the turbine. After the British left, the roads deteriorated, the Chinese left, and Louis Berger was forced to use helicopters to deliver cement and other supplies to finish the project. The two rehabilitated turbine now produce about 33 megawatts of electricity, only 30 percent of which reaches Kandahar since about 40 percent is lost to transmission inefficiencies and theft.[56]

USAID reportedly rejected an offer by a German firm to install the third turbine, and failed to install transmission lines to carry the electricity, a job that is now impossible to complete due to security concerns. After spending more than $47 million on the project, in the view of one expert working for the NATO command in Kandahar, the lack of electricity in Kandahar is "the principal symbol of the government's inability to deliver services to the people."[57]

Thus, security is inextricably linked to development which is the foundation of stability and economic progress. The difficulties of establishing security, stabilization, transition and reconstruction framework are glaringly apparent in the Afghan context. In sum, the above discussion outlines some of the structural, cultural and practical challenges in developing a sustainable interagency approach to contingency and related operations.

C. Interagency Cooperation in Complex Environments: A New Roadmap

Stuart W. Bowen, Jr. was appointed Inspector General for the Coalition Provisional Authority in January 2004, and, since October 2004, has served as the Special Inspector General for Iraq Reconstruction (SIGIR). He has proposed that the U.S. Congress create a U.S. Office for Contingency Operations (USOCO) that would house the Office for the Coordinator for Reconstruction and Stabilization in DOS (and now a separate bureau); the Office of Transition Initiatives now located in USAID, the Office of Technical Assistance now located in the Department of the Treasury, and the International Criminal Investigative Training and Assistance Program (ICITAP), now located in the Department of Justice. He also recommends that certain DOD stability operations initiatives be moved to the USOCO. Finally, he also recommends that a new Contingency Federal Acquisition Regulation (CFAR) be created in order to make procurement for contingency operations more user-friendly for both contractors and government personnel.[58]

This is a well-thought out springboard for a more targeted, but perhaps more ambitious, initiative to create an interim interagency approach to contingency operations. This approach resolves certain tensions while giving USG actors a sufficient amount of time to implement USG-wide structural changes and to smooth out cultural issues, as discussed above, to the extent possible. Rather than creating a new USG office that permanently relocates a number of existing USG offices which still leaves the structural and cultural problems discussed above in place, I propose creating a temporary entity with expansive powers, the U.S. Center for Peace Operations (USCPO).

The mandate of USCPO should be two-fold: (1) long-term humanitarian peace operations that are able to take place in permissive environments where the level of violence is manageable enough for peace building to take place; and (2) short-term overseas contingency operations to be coordinated with DOD, DOS and with international partners, as necessary. USCPO will take a *whole of government* approach that incorporates the collaborative efforts of USG departments and agencies in order to achieve unity of effort as well as a *comprehensive* approach that incorporates the views, resources and strengths of USG allies, NATO, intergovernmental and nongovernmental organizations, and private sector entities.

New legislation authorizing such an entity will need to be proposed and passed along with delineating clear oversight responsibility from appropriate Congressional committees. However, the funding should be derived from the Overseas Contingency Operations (OCO) account that DOD has traditionally used to identify exceptional funding requirements for contingency operations.

For the first time, both DOS and USAID requested OCO funding in the Administration's FY 2012 International Affairs budget request. The budget requests were specifically targeted to provide diplomatic security and SIGIR oversight of USAID-funded programs in Iraq; to support capacity building, large infrastructure development and a counternarcotics strategy in Afghanistan; and support the Pakistani government in eliminating insurgent sanctuaries as well as shifting the funds for the Pakistan Counterinsurgency Capability Fund from DOD to DOS.[59]

In terms of the structure and composition of the USCPO, my first thought was to suggest a U.S. government corporation in order to institute a governing board of directors. However, I must refrain from making this suggestion as USG corporations are traditionally allowed to sue and be sued under a recognized broad waiver of sovereign immunity,[60] and this may open up the USCPO to possible unwanted lawsuits that may be nearly impossible to defend in such difficult operating environments. So, perhaps a board-like structure of advisors will suffice, especially to make recommendations as explained below.

The USCPO would become the new operating center for peace operations of the USG with appropriate staffing to do so. Employees from other USG departments and agencies that play a supportive role could be detailed to the USCPO temporarily at the outset while permanent staffing takes place. Subject-matter experts from USG agencies and from the private sector should be sourced for staffing needs.

The first task of the USCPO would be to establish "doctrine" or "policy" regarding the definition of failing, failed, and fragile states that would become the operative definitions for the USG. As it stands, definitional problems and issues are at the base of the doctrinal and policy confusion surrounding a coherent USG response (or lack thereof) to failing and failed states. In fact, establishing doctrine regarding overseas contingency operations should be a core function of the USCPO.

With respect to overseas contingency operations, a military operation is either designated by the Secretary of Defense as a contingency operation or becomes one as a matter of law under 10 U.S.C. § 101(a)(13). This is where a USCPO board of directors or advisors could recommend to the Secretary of Defense that a specific overseas contingency operation be authorized for the USCPO to lead and direct the operation.

The composition of the USCPO board of directors or advisors should include the *ex officio* participation of at least the following federal agencies, DOD, DOS, USAID, DOJ, USDA, and Treasury. Additionally, some thought should be devoted to including private sector board members drawn from defense, development and humanitarian aid sectors to further enrich the dialogue in making well-thought out proposals and recommendations to the Secretary of Defense in considering whether to designate certain conflict zones as appropriate for USCPO overseas contingency operations. Private board members could bring their perspectives from field experience, working with foreign government counterparts, and the general business concerns of organizing, implementing and successfully concluding complex overseas operations.

This may seem to conflict with the role of the Special Operations Command (SOCOM), but it could be structured as a partnering arrangement to cover a full spectrum of theatre operations ranging from combat only (SOCOM), non-permissive (USCPO military-trained employees organized into expeditionary units), and permissive (USCPO civilian employees).

SOCOM is currently led by Admiral William McRaven who is advocating a larger role for SOCOM and has proposed the Global SOF [Special Operations Forces] Alliance.[61] The Alliance will bolster current SOCOM forces now numbering at about 66,000 or about 2 percent of the U.S. military. Certain United States Combatant Command (COCOM) commanders and DOS officials have expressed reservations about diminishing their role in such theatres, and are fearful of the possible diplomatic fall-out from an operation like the kind that resulted in the death of Osama bin Laden. This was a Navy SEAL operation overseen by Adm. McRaven, and one for which he has received wide commendation in political circles, including the White House.[62]

In draft legislation channeled through the Pentagon in late April 2012, Admiral McRaven proposed using $25 million in SOCOM funds to buy uniforms, build barracks and transport foreign troops in areas of conflict in Asia, Africa, and Latin America, thus expanding into areas where Special Operations forces have not traditionally operated for the past decade or so.[63] Training and equipping military forces in Yemen, the Horn of Africa, Kenya, Libya, Mali, Mauritania and even Nigeria were contemplated by this proposal. The proposed legislation also included special fast-track acquisition authorities that would permit moving materiel, equipment and elite troops into "hot spots" of terrorism or other disruptions. The proposal envisaged SOCOM officials working closely with U.S. ambassadors in the affected countries in order to fully support U.S. foreign policy goals.

In what has been characterized as "a rare rebuke," U.S. House, Senate, State Department and other cabinet-level officials rejected the proposal on May 7, 2012, as causing "unnecessary confusion and friction."[64]   Adm. McRaven was advised to use the existing Global Security Contingency Fund that was formed jointly in 2011 by Secretary of State Hillary Clinton, and former Secretary of Defense, Robert Gates. Accordingly, Admiral McRaven's proposal has been modified in a short-term solution using the Global Security Contingency Fund.[65]   However, Secretary Clinton did implicitly recognize the New Soldier aspects of creating a new type of joint military and civilian force by stating at SOCOM headquarters in Tampa, Florida on May 23, 2012, that "[w]e need Special Operations Forces who are as comfortable drinking tea with tribal leaders as raiding a terrorist compound. . . We also need diplomats and development experts who understand modern warfare and are up to the job of being your partners."[66]

Regardless of these concerns, however, the role of the Special Operations forces continues to grow in influence, and its training and tactical methods are being adopted by the U.S. Army at large to meet counterinsurgency and counterterrorism needs in the future. General Ray Odierno, the U.S. Army's Chief of Staff, has already begun to institutionalize the training and tactics of Special Forces used successfully in Iraq and Afghanistan.[67] Some conventional units of the U.S. Army will be officially placed under Special Operations commanders, and others are to be assigned to parts of the world seen as emerging security risks such as Africa. In fact, the first unit to be designated for this new regional approach will be a full brigade to train for mission sin support of the U.S. Army's Africa Command (AFRICOM).[68]

Creating new formal relationships between U.S. Army general purpose units and Special Forces Command will initiative a seachange in the command and combat structure. New training for joint operations between a conventional unit and a Special Operations unit will begin in June 2012 at the Joint Readiness Training Center at Fort Polk, Louisiana. This training is anticipated to be expanded to the National Training Center in Fort Irwin, California in the autumn of 2012.[69]

Whatever the merits of the Global SOF Alliance or the Global Security Contingency Fund, the USCPO would not conflict with U.S. military strikes, but would provide a slightly longer-term engagement that is designed to move the post-conflict society into peace building operations. USCPO would be better designed to partner with NATO or African Union Standby Forces to help prevent conflict in failing and failed states while supporting the U.S. national security interest in that conflict area. USCPO could have its own training and education protocols, and focus on the transformation of U.S. military capabilities to better support and integrate its operations with humanitarian missions and peace building operations. It could establish its own "lessons learned" center for the USG that focuses on joint concept development and experimentation, joint training and joint interoperability and integration.

The USCPO should also focus on historical case studies developing "lessons learned" on an USG-wide basis. Further, evaluations of how successfully the complex operations fared should be done automatically at the conclusion of an engagement. Foreign policy implications along with defense-related concerns on military readiness, responding to nonconventional threats, and future force projection should be part of a full spectrum analysis on a continuing and historical basis. This way, we will learn our own history and will not therefore, be doomed to repeat it.

Finally, the legislation for the USCPO should have a ten-year sunset clause so that the organization will either survive or be dissolved after 10 years of operations. At the ninth year, there should be full-sale USCPO-led evaluations on its effectiveness and continued viability, as well as scrutiny from the GAO, Congress and private groups. The intent of creating the USCPO is not to create bureaucracy for the sake of bureaucracy. If the structural and cultural changes now being implemented by other USG agencies are fully successful in this time period, there may not be a continuing need for the USCPO in which case, it may be dissolved by Congress. If not, then the U.S. will have a model upon which to base its future overseas contingency operations.

In conclusion, this chapter highlighted certain definitional problems and confusion in identifying failing and failed states. Further, there is no coherent overall U.S. Government (USG) response to such crises based on inherent structural, cultural and practical problems. The proposal of establishing a U.S. Center for Peace Operations addresses these problems within an interim 10-year period with an assessment of whether to disband it or to use it as a platform for a new USG approach to failing and failed states.

8

Operationalizing the Concept of the New Soldier:

A Model Case Study of the NATO Response Force and the African Union StandbyForce

This chapter will address how to operationalize the concept of the New Soldier, and the institutional framework in which to do so. The training and deployment of the New Soldier will be discussed in relation to the NATO Response Force (NRF), and the African Union Standby Force (ASF). Moreover, the synergies in terms of NATO support for the creation and training of ASF forces will be explored within the context of controlling and eradicating fundamentalist Islamic-based terrorists operating in North Africa (the Sahel), and West Africa.

Chapter Six examined NATO's International Security Assistance Force (ISAF) within the context of its operations in Afghanistan beginning in 2001. NATO has also "stood up" the NATO Response Force (NRF) consisting of about 21,000 troops.[1] The NRF is designed to be a rapid response expeditionary force that should be viewed as one that is extremely suitable for deploying the New Soldier, as explained below.

Interestingly, the idea for a NATO rapidly deployable response force was suggested by former U.S. Defense Secretary Donald Rumsfeld during a September 2002 meeting of NATO Defense Ministers.[2] The potential political reasons underlying this suggestion vary greatly from giving NATO a push toward developing a credible warfighting capacity in exigent circumstances, to better incorporating NATO into ongoing operations in Afghanistan at the time.[3] In any case, the NRF was created in 2002 "as the vehicle for the 'transformation' of NATO from a large, static force designed to fend off massive Soviet armies into an agile expeditionary outfit."[4]

One commentator notes that, "[t]o NATO's credit, its 1999 adaptation to the end of the Cold War was fundamental, monumental and appropriate; it finally and formally recognized that its traditional threat was gone; it moved from the static/active defense concepts of the prior decades toward a strategic concept that emphasized security missions outside of traditional NATO areas; and it stressed the importance of developing new capabilities to meet new threats. Furthermore, operations in the Balkans and Afghanistan have accelerated thinking that NATO's military relevancy lies, not in the ability to provide heavy land forces or tactical fighter planes in defense of NATO territory, but rather in the ability to act quickly to stabilize distant situations which, if left unattended, could break out into a larger conflict. Political, social and economic chaos is the new perceived enemy of The Western State. This changed environment requires new tools: better intelligence, quicker force generation, greater power projection, and more precise weaponry."[5]

Stepping back one step, the NRF should be viewed within the context of the Defense Capability Initiative (DCI) launched in September 1999 during NATO's Washington summit. By the 2002 Prague summit, it was clear that DCI was failing to merge European and U.S. military technology and warfghting capabilities. It was at this time that the U.S. proposed creating the NRF, and the DCI was "quietly retired and replaced by the Prague capability Commitment (PCC)."[6]

Thus, by creating a highly mobile and responsive expeditionary force, the NRF could be very useful in meeting future military challenges by deploying, for example, unmanned aerial vehicles, missile defense, nuclear-biological-chemical detection and decontamination units.[7] Additionally, NRF's air, land and maritime components could give greater inter-operability as part of a joint or combined force with either the European Union's European Rapid Reaction Force or with U.S. forces.

The NRF was designed to include about 25,000 troops at full operational capability capable of deploying after five days' notice for military operations lasting 30 days or longer, if re-supplied. "At full operational capability, the NRF would consist of a brigade-sized land component with a forced-entry capability, a naval task force comprised of one carrier battle group, an amphibious task group and a surface action group, an air component capable of generating 200 sorties a day, and a special forces component."[8]

At the Istanbul Summit, NATO delineated the NRF's possible missions as:

> ➤ a stand-alone force for Article 5 [of NATO's articles of association] collective defense or non-Article 5 crisis response operations, such as evacuations, disaster relief and consequence management, humanitarian or counterterrorism operations;

> ➤ an initial entry force facilitating the arrival of larger follow-on forces; and,

> ➤ deterrence of crises by demonstrating NATO determination and solidarity.[9]

Further, after a six-month training program, the NRF would be put "on call" for six months. After each NRF rotation, these force components will be replaced every six months by a fresh set of units that have completed the six-month training cycle.

Full operating capability was declared for the NRF at the NATO Riga Summit in November 2006. The NRF has a total force structure of approximately 25,000 personnel, and is under the operational command of the Allied Joint Fore Command Headquarters Brunssum (JFC HQ Brunssum).[10] The NRF may be deployed wherever the North Atlantic Council, the policy and decision-making body of NATO, feels that it should be utilized, and those operations may take place well beyond the borders of actual NATO members.

In fact, two deployments have already been made, first, during the NATO Katrina Support Operation in the United States and second, in the NATO Disaster Relief Operation in Pakistan (October 2005-February 2006) after the October 8, 2005 earthquake hit Pakistan.[11] In addition, the NATO Response Force was used during the 2004 Olympic Games, the 2004 Iraqi Elections, and for providing humanitarian relief to Afghanistan.[12]

Of course, naysayers believe that the "NRF has failed to fill its roster, and has been informally cut back," and further, that "the NRF is a force that should be on steroids, and instead it's on life support,"[13] but it may be too soon to make such definitive pronouncements. Indeed, the NRF shows great promise to be an effective military tool.

Indeed, General James Jones, the former NATO Supreme Allied Commander (SACEUR), was quick to point out that, "I think that NATO's best days are very possibly in its future. But we must do a better job of understanding what that future is, of explaining it to our nations on both sides of the Atlantic, and understanding that the future of NATO is not to be a reactive, defensive static alliance, but it is to be more flexible, more proactive."[14]

The NRF duly takes note of that counsel, and is designed to be NATO's first permanent expeditionary force to respond quickly to crises (whether military or humanitarian in nature). The NRF provides a "technologically advanced, flexible, deployable, interoperable and sustainable force including land, sea, and air elements ready to move quickly to wherever needed, as decided by the [Atlantic] Council.' The NRF concept was a far cry from the static fight-in-place force that has been the foundation for NATO throughout the Cold War. The expeditionary nature of the unit would give NATO the ability to pursue the full spectrum of options with regards to addressing security issues at the sources."[15] Indeed, General Jones noted that the creation of the NRF was "an important recognition on the part of the Alliance that the international security environment has changed dramatically."[16]

NRF's troops (and their commanders) must make quick, informed judgments on how to best resolve conflicts and stabilize the situation at hand. These are precisely the sort of circumstances that require the exercise of judgment informed by intuition, cultural intelligence and empathy. For example, of the five past deployments of the NRF, three were relief and humanitarian missions. The other two (namely, the Iraqi elections and the Olympic Games both of which took place in 2004) involved discrete events that were very short in duration.

Thus, with regard to humanitarian and relief operations of the NRF, using the New Soldier profile could be a very useful starting point. For example, the NRF soldiers could be trained to excise "active" listening skills to ascertain the problems as perceived by the affected civilian populations.

Demonstrating "empathy" or an understanding of the losses felt by affected civilians and the ensuring panic they are feeling over losing loved ones, homes and businesses does not mean the individual soldier is losing himself or herself in the emotions of others. It simply means demonstrating a calm outward demeanor while expressing some human understanding of the difficulties and the painful emotions that the civilians are experiencing. Rather than adding to the tensions implicit in any crisis situation, the emotionally receptive demeanor of the New Soldier may help dampen the underlying sources of conflict and calm the affected civilian populations.

Moreover, being aware of the cultural setting and the context that the specific crisis is unfolding in is also key in terms of understanding and resolving the conflict as expeditiously as possible. Cultural sensitivity and language skills may be very important factors in bringing the crisis to a close.

The reason that the NRF (or NATO in general) may be an optimal choice with respect to the first deployment of the New Soldier. The choice is two-fold: first, NATO is already a multinational, multilingual, multicultural military force where the profile of the New Solider is already a natural "fit," and second, by engaging in expeditionary, rapid response, humanitarian and related missions, NATO troops will need to navigate quickly and assuredly through many difficult and challenging physical, cultural and emotional terrains.

Indeed, NATO training may already require that different linguistic and cultural (both nationally and in terms of military cultures) be integrated in order to ensure the smooth operation of its troops in the field. The qualities of the New Soldier could be added to the NATO's six-month long training for its NRF troops which may help bring a human face to its humanitarian mission. This will mean that the command structure, training, doctrine may need to be adjusted accordingly. In sum, the mission scope of the NRF lends itself to using the New Soldier profile, especially for the reasons described below.

NATO in Africa

While there have not been any NRF-specific interventions in Africa to date, there has been a substantive NATO presence in Africa from 2005 onward. Beginning in 2005, NATO began its collaboration with the African Union Mission in Sudan (AMIS). This was NATO's first Africa-based mission and the African Union (AU) viewed it as a "very positive and promising level of cooperation"[17] between the two institutions.

In providing assistance to AMIS, NATO made its airlift capacity available to over 37,500 AU peacekeepers in and out of Darfur, Sudan. This support reflects NATO's commitment to strengthen the AU's capability to expand its presence in Darfur to attempt to contain the growing violence. Apart from providing logistical support in terms of strategic airlift and other operations, NATO transported approximately 3,800 AU troops, including 49 members of the civilian police force.[18]

In addition, NATO provided Staff Capacity Building workshops for the AU's officers within the Deployed Integrated Task Force (DITF) Headquarters in Ethiopia. For example, one training session was held from August 1-22, 2005, and addressed command and control issues, intelligence collection and analysis, situational awareness and standard operating procedures development and refinement.[19]

NATO assistance to AMIS terminated on December 31, 2007, after the actual termination of AMIS in December 2007. NATO was then involved in the UN-AU Mission in Darfur (UNAMID), a hybrid mission that succeeded AMIS. UNAMID commenced its operations on January 1, 2008.[20] In fact, the AU has already requested further NATO assistance in Darfur.[21]

Further, in June 2007, NATO accepted the request to assist the African Union Mission in Somalia (AMISOM), and mainly provided airlift support for personnel and supplies contributed by AU member states. The assistance was extended to June 17, 2009, and further extensions are expected.[22]

Additionally, in relation to Somalia, NATO defense ministers responded to a request from the United Nations by authorizing a "fleet of naval vessels to help protect U.N. World Food Program ships carrying relief supplies to Somalia."[23] In 2009 alone, Somali piracy demands for ransom amounted to over US$30 million. As of Spring 2009, NATO replaced the flotilla conducting anti-piracy patrols off Somalia with a new force that will continue the operation "indefinitely."[24]

In May 2009, NATO defense ministers met in Brussels to consider ways to combat piracy in one of the world's busiest shipping lanes, and ordered the long-term deployment of a naval squadron—known as Standing Naval Maritime Group 2—to the region. The new force will continue to operate in the Gulf of Aden and the Indian Ocean, where international patrols involving warships from NATO, the European Union and other nations have been working to reduce attacks on merchant ships by Somali pirates.[25]

In fact, the AU has actively sought long-term cooperation with NATO in terms of meeting Africa's security needs. The African Union Commissioner for Peace and Security, former Ambassador Said Djinnit, visited NATO's headquarters in Brussels, Belgium on March 2, 2007, and met with former NATO Secretary General Jaap de Hoop Scheffer. He addressed the North Atlantic Council, NATO's principal decision-making body, and discussed avenues of cooperation between NATO and the African Union, particularly in terms of NATO's support for AU efforts to bring peace to the strife-torn Darfur region.[26]

On September 5, 2007, the North Atlantic Council agreed to provide assistance to the AU by providing a study on the operational readiness of the AU's Standby Force (ASF) brigades. NATO received a Note Verbale from the AU on December 13, 2007 to continue NATO's support to the newly formed ASF.[27] The relevance of NATO's support for the AU Standby Force will be explored below.

Fundamentalist Islamic-based terrorists in Africa

The relevance of NATO's intervention in Africa and its support for the ASF should be viewed in the broader context of fundamentalist Islamic-based terrorists in Africa. In attempting to understand the nature of this terrorist threat in Africa, it is important to note that "there are distinct regional variations to the presence and extent of Islamist terrorist networks across Africa. The threat in Southern and Central Africa is almost non-existent, and for a clear reason: there are relatively few Muslims in Central and Southern Africa (see Figure One, below). In these areas, Islamists are attempting to convert Christians to Islam, rather than proliferating radical Islamist networks.[28]

Islam is much more prevalent in Northern, Eastern and Western Africa, and accordingly there are more Islamist groups, both radical and non-radical, in these areas than farther south."[29] It is also important to bear in mind that "Africa has more Muslims than the Middle East or Southeast Asia."[30] Therefore, it is important to begin with certain distinctions in mind both in terms of geography, and in terms of religion.

Figure 1: Islam in Africa

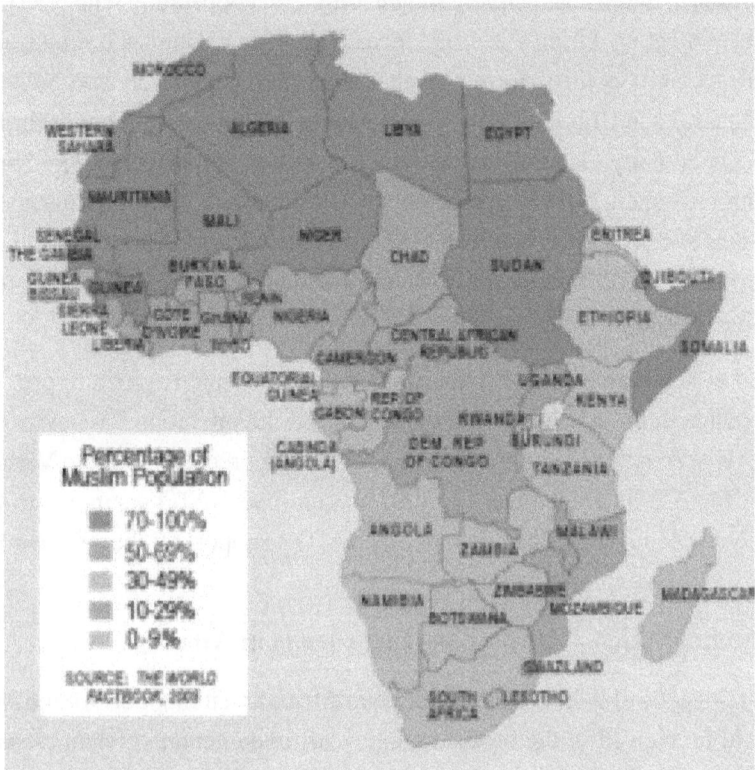

Source: United States Institute of Peace (2009).

East Africa, of course, has been a long-time concern for the international community because of its early links to transnational Islamic terrorism. In 1998, United States Embassies in Dar es Salaam, Tanzania, and Nairobi, Kenya, were bombed, killing a handful of U.S. citizens and hundreds of Kenyans and Tanzanians. In fact, terrorists who attacked the U.S. embassies in Kenya and Tanzania were closely linked to cells in Sudan and Somalia, both of which have served as training grounds and as transit routes for Al Qaeda.

Most importantly, East Africa has also been home to both al-Qaeda and Osama Bin Laden. "In 1991 the leader of Sudan's National Islamic Front (NIF) government, Hassan al Turabi, invited Osama bin Laden to live in Sudan. During this time, bin Laden established multiple businesses in Sudan, and established al-Qaeda training camps in the more remote areas."[31]

Indeed, the "Horn of Africa—an area that includes Sudan, Eritrea, Ethiopia, Djibouti, Somalia, Kenya, Uganda, and Tanzania—has been seen as ripe for terrorist activity, given the region's weak and often corrupt governments, ongoing violent conflicts, porous borders, ungoverned spaces, and grinding poverty. Osama bin Laden also based his operations in Khartoum, Sudan from 1991 through early 1996."[32]

However, West Africa and the Sahel (i.e., Mauritania, Mali, Niger and Chad) are also highly problematic since, "[f]ailed or failing states in central and West Africa have already provided opportunity for al Qaeda and criminal networks possibly affiliated with it for profit from the marketing of diamonds and other precious gems. Wars in the Democratic Republic of the Congo, Sierra Leone and Liberia opened this door and local warlords like Charles Taylor, [the former president of Liberia], readily collaborated."[33]

One commentator notes that "[w]hile examples of state failure can be found in almost every region of the world, the problem has been especially prevalent in economically depressed and politically unstable areas of sub-Saharan Africa. Within that region, Liberia, Sierra Leone, and Somalia provide concrete examples of state failure."[34] In fact, "the weaknesses of many of the regimes in this area, their inability to monitor events in remote regions, and the vulnerability of impoverished populations to proselytizing and recruitment by radical Muslim elements affiliated with or drawing inspiration from Al Qaeda."[35]

In setting forth a case study methodology based on terrorism and counterterrorism efforts in Sierra Leone, Liberia and Somalia, there is a differentiation to be made of terrorist network components between "hubs" and "nodes." Marc Sageman in a 2004 analysis of Al Qaeda distinguishes "hubs" which provide "centralized direction and communication linkages" to the nodes. The "nodes" are decentralized, independent cells.[36]

While the linkages between hubs and nodes may be weak, the following perspective may be useful.

Two very different kinds of terrorist threats in a failed state context. Nodes represent the threat of direct terrorist attack, either in the country in which they are operating, or in other countries to which the nodes have access. The threat posed by hubs is different and indirect. It is reflected in the ability of the hub to facilitate the operations of preexisting nodes and to enable attacks by those nodes on whatever targets the nodes determine are appropriate.[37]

And further,

The case of Somalia suggests that failed states do, in fact, offer an effective venue for operations by evolved terrorist hubs. The environment in such states can provide what may be the greatest level of protection available to terrorist organizations from counterterrorism operations by military forces or law enforcement agencies. The case of Somalia also suggests that the violent and chaotic conditions within failed states may reduce dramatically the impact of local attacks by terrorist nodes, but will not preclude terrorist hubs from operating in their new, evolved mode to inspire ideologically or assist financially or materially the operations of geographically distributed nodes.[38]

Thus, the new focus on Africa is being driven by fundamentalist Islamic-based terrorists finding new safe havens in the Horn of Africa, the Sahel, and now West Africa where the increased production of oil in Nigeria and Angola, and the discovery of oil in Cameroon, Congo, Gabon and Equatorial Guinea are complicating matters.[39] West Africa is continually plagued with instability, corruption, and separatist movements.

Further, the lack of operational maritime fleets and real maritime security in the Gulf of Guinea has led the U.S. Navy to donate patrol boats to Nigeria to help secure its ports and to engage in anti-piracy activities. In addition, it is trying to shore up maritime security in the Gulf of Guinea by launching a 10-year effort to develop and improve maritime security in countries such as Angola, Benin, Cameroon, Equatorial Guinea, Gabon, Ghana, Nigeria, the Democratic Republic of Congo, Sao Tome and Principe and Togo.[40] Moreover, fears of al-Shabab in Somalia fanning out through East Africa has also attracted the attention of the U.S. military.

In February 2012, the AU announced its plans to expand the African Union Mission in Somalia (AMISOM) established in January 2007, from 12,000 to 18,000 troops.[41] It is preparing to deploy these troops to southern and central Somalia for the first time.

The force consists primarily of soldiers from Uganda, Burundi, Djibouti and Sierra Leone. The boot camp, known as the Singo Training School, is located in Uganda. However, the instruction is being provided by MPRI, a U.S. State Department contractor, is a subsidiary of L-3 Communications based in Washington, D.C.[42] Former U.S. Army and Marines with experience in Iraq and Afghanistan lead the 10-week training camps. To date, the United States has spent about $550 million to train, equip and subsidize the AMISOM mission.[43] Other donors include the UN and the European Union.

Not only has the U.S. military taken note of Africa's need to strengthen its security architecture in light of multiplying terrorist threats, but so has NATO. As early as 2004, NATO officials were negotiating with Mauritania on ways to secure its borders against infiltration by potential terrorists.[44] However, despite preventive measures to protect against terrorist infiltration, the situation has actually worsened over time.

Al Qaeda's affiliate, Al Qaeda in the Maghreb (AQIM), operates in North Africa and has launched a string of deadly attacks against Westerners and African security forces spurring fears that foreign fighters from the Iraq and Afghanistan conflicts are establishing a base in the area.[45] Retaliation by AQIM for France's policies banning the burqua and directed against the European countries who sent troops to Iraq and Afghanistan are very much feared. The unpoliced, vast expanses of space in Mauritania, Niger, Mali and southern Algeria may have created hospitable grounds to harbor terrorists or an insurgency movement.[46] Thus, NATO members are now more committed to assisting Africa's efforts to stem the tide of extremist violence and terrorist infiltration in Africa's Muslim-dominated countries.

Indeed, the question has been posed: "can Europe build a NATO for Africa?"[47] While the answer is uncertain, it is clear that NATO is taking a strong interest in assisting Africa develop a stronger and more robust security architecture. One commentator notes that the NRF is one model for the African Union Standby Force (ASF) to use in developing an indigenous expeditionary capability to meet exigent security threats in the African continent. The NRF is described as a "coherent, high readiness, joint, multinational force package" that allows the NRF to power project a 25,000 troop force worldwide. High tempo combat conditions may be sustained for 30 days, and longer if replenished.[48] The relevance of the NRF to the ASF is important, but let us step back for a moment and trace the institutional development of the ASF.

Creation of the African Standby Force (ASF): An Historical Overview

Beginning in the 1990s, African leaders began to discuss the need for a revamped security architecture that would address the continent's needs. The deteriorating security framework, the end of the Cold War, and the need for collective action in light of previous failed attempts at changing the security grid led to a seminal conference held in Kampala, Uganda in 1991.

Over 500 African leaders met at the all-African Conference on Security, Stability, Development and Cooperation in Kampala to discuss security-related problems. The Kampala Document was issued at the end of the conference and later adopted by the Organization of African Unity (OAU) Assembly of Heads of State and Governments.[49] The Kampala Document called for the establishment of a Conference on Security, Stability, Development and Cooperation in Africa (CSSDCA) designed to promote and strengthen the cooperation of all African nations in ensuring the security of Africa as a whole. The 36th session of the OAU Assembly of Heads of State and Governments in Lomé, Togo in July 2000, adopted the CSSDCA Solemn Declaration.[50]

Meanwhile, in 1992, the OAU Secretary-General issued a report entitled, "Proposals for an OAU Mechanism for Conflict Prevention, Management and Resolution," which advocated for an overall institutionalized rather than an *ad hoc* approach to security issues in Africa. A year later, in 1993, the OAU members formally established the Mechanism for Conflict Prevention, Management and Resolution at a meeting in Cairo, Egypt.[51] In 2002, the OAU was replaced by the African Union (AU) modeled on the European Union.

In May 2003, the African Chiefs of Defence and Security (ACDS) adopted a document entitled, "The policy framework document on the establishment of the African Standby Force (ASF) and of the Military Staff Committee (MSC)."[52] Within a few days following the issuance of this document, African ministers of foreign affairs recommended that regulator consultations be held to consolidate the proposals contained in the document. The AU Heads of States and Government endorsed this recommendation, and adopted an amended framework document in July 2004.[53]

At the first session of the AU, the AU assembly created the Peace and Security Council (PSC), a standing decision-making organ, to be supported by the AU Standby Force, among other supporting architecture.[54] The protocol establishing the PSC and the ASF entered into force in December 2003, a rapid accession that evidenced the seriousness of the AU members in their political commitment to establish the ASF, among other things. The ASF supplanted earlier attempts to create a viable security architecture continent-wide for Africa. It is a part of a larger, institutionalized security framework that has several supporting components.

"The incorporation of the New Partnership for Africa's Development (NEPAD) as well as the formulation of a Common African Defense and Security Policy which delineates the member states' collective responses to both internal and external security threats in February 2004 completed this institutional architecture,"[55] as set forth in the figure below.

Figure 2: The African Peace and Security Architecture

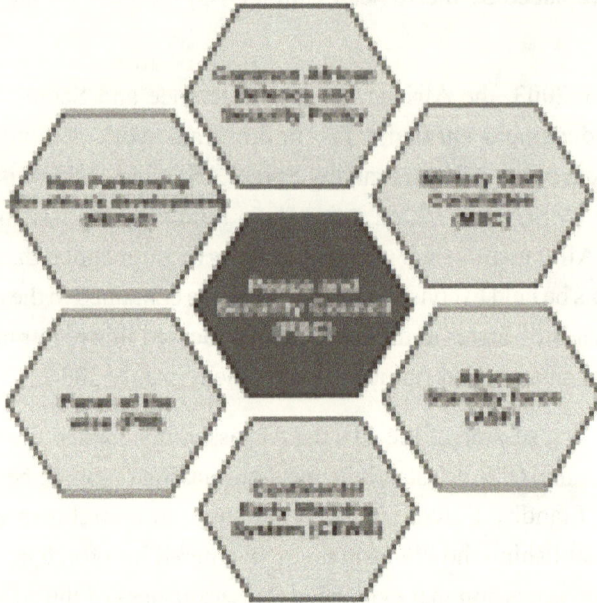

Source: Benedikt Franke, "Enabling a Continent to Help Itself: U.S. Military Capacity Building ad Africa's Emerging Security Architecture," 6 *Strategic Insights* (January 2007), available at http://doc.operationspaix.net/serv1/frankeJan07.pdf (last visited on July 16, 2009).

"The purpose of the ASF is to provide the African Union with capabilities to respond to conflicts through the deployment of peacekeeping forces and to undertake interventions pursuant to article 4(h) and (i) of the Constitutive Act in terms of which the AU was established. The ASF is intended for rapid deployment for a multiplicity of peace support operations that may include, *inter alia*, preventive deployment, peacekeeping, peace building, post conflict disarmament, demobilisation, re-integration and humanitarian assistance."[56]

The final concept for the ASF was to create five brigade level forces, one in each of Africa's five regions, supported by civilian police forces and other force augmentation. The roll-out of the ASF force structure would require an Africa-wide integrated, interoperable command, control and communication and information systems (C3IS) infrastructure that will link deployed units with ASF Headquarters and the regional bases.

The brigade level consists of 5,000 troops per brigade and are ready for rapid deployment. Sub-regional ASF leadership would exercise command and control over each of the five standby brigades as control the C3IS infrastructure. The AU's Peace and Security Council and the AU Commission will establish command and control over the five brigades (25,000 troops) along with the civilian components, including the underlying intelligence and communications operations.[57]

Figure 3: The African Peace and Security Architecture

PEACE AND SECURITY COUNCIL (PSC): Individual Components
➤   Common African Defence and Security Policy
➤   Military Staff Committee (MSC)
➤   African Standby Force (ASF)
➤   Continental Early Warning System (CEWS)
➤   Panel of the Wise (PW)
➤   New Partnership for Africa's Development (NEPAD)

Source: Adapted from Benedikt Franke, "Enabling a Continent to Help Itself: U.S. Military Capacity Building and Africa's Emerging Security Architecture," 6 *Strategic Insights* (January 2007), available at http://doc.operationspaix.net/serv1/frankeJan07.pdf (last visited on July 16, 2009).

The operationalization of the ASF was painstakingly detailed in the "Roadmap for Operationalization of the African Standby Force," adopted by a group of experts' meeting held in Addis Ababa, Ethiopia between March 22-23, 2005.[58]

"The ASF structure–with its associated deployment timelines–is informed by six missions and scenarios:

> **Scenario 1:** AU/regional military advice to a political mission. Deployment required within 30 days of an AU mandate provided by the PSC.

> **Scenario 2:** AU/regional observer mission co-deployed with a UN mission. Deployment required within 30 days of an AU mandate.

> **Scenario 3:** Stand-alone AU/regional observer mission. Deployment required within 30 days of an AU mandate.

> **Scenario 4:** AU/regional peacekeeping force for UN Chapter VI and preventive deployment missions (and peace building). Deployment required within 30 days of an AU mandate.

> **Scenario 5:** AU peacekeeping force for complex multidimensional peacekeeping missions, including those involving low-level spoilers. ASF completed deployment required within 90 days of an AU mandate, with the military component being able to deploy in 30 days.

> **Scenario 6:** AU intervention, for example in genocide situations where the international community does not act promptly. Here it is envisaged that the AU would have the capability to deploy a robust military force within 14 days."[59]

The ASF was designed to be phased into being in two stages. The first phase (up to June 2005) was designed to establish a strategic management capacity of Scenarios 1 and 2-related missions. In addition, Regional Economic Communities (RECs), discussed below, were intended to complement the efforts of the ASF by establishing regionally-based standby forces up to a brigade size capable of handling Scenario 4 missions (see above). In other words, the ASF uses the existing military and institutional structures of RECs rather than trying to duplicate them. The second phase of operationalizing the ASF (July 2005-June 30, 2010) projected that the ASF would be able to handle complex peacekeeping operations that incorporate full Scenario 5 and 6-related missions.

In other words, by 2010, the ASF was expected to meet the challenges posed by all six scenarios which include: Scenario 4 (AU peacekeeping and preventive deployment within 30 days of a mandate); Scenario 5 (a multidimensional peacekeeping operation, including the possibility of enforcement, with the military component deploying in 30 days and the entire mission in 90 days); and Scenario 6 (deployment of a robust military presence in 14 days to stop a genocide.) For AU's leadership, the most important (and challenging) scenario was the sixth scenario–to be able to stop another genocide like the one that occurred in Rwanda in 1994.[60] Additionally, RECs would be required to continue to develop their capacity to deploy forces capable of handling Scenario 4 cases.

Next, it is important to understand the linkage of the ASF to RECs. The five regions in Africa to host regional ASF standby forces are eastern, western, southern, central and northern.

East Africa

The Eastern ASF brigade coordinates with the Eastern Africa Community (EAC) to form the Eastern African Standby Brigade (EASBRIG). The Eastern Africa Chiefs of Defense Staff (EACDS) met in Junja, Uganda, from February 13-14, 2004, and adopted a Policy Framework and a Legal Framework to operationalize EASBRIG. The framework was approved by the meeting of Ministers of Defense held on July 16-17, 2004, in Addis Ababa, Ethiopia, with an approved US$2.5 million budget. EASBRIG now has three components: the brigade HQs to be located in Addis Ababa, the Planning Element to be based in Nairobi and the Logistic base to be co-located with the Brigade HQs in Addis Ababa.[61]

The members of the Eastern Africa Standby Force now include Comoros, Djibouti, Eritrea, Ethiopia, Kenya, Rwanda, Seychelles, Somalia, Sudan and Uganda. Burundi has asked to join Eastern Africa and is therefore no longer considered to be a member of the central area. Tanzania, Madagascar and Mauritius, who had previously been members, are active in Southern Africa.[62]

EASBRIG does have its share of difficulties in standing up since international donors financially sustain much of EASBRIG along with supplying it with military advisers and contractors. Cooperation between Ethiopia and Kenya, EASBRIG's two anchor states, continues to be slow thus impeding the progress made in establishing the brigade and creating the command and control structures. Also, two of the most conflict-ridden countries in Africa, Sudan and Somalia, are located in Eastern African and pose daunting challenges to the sub-region.[63]

West Africa

The ECOWAS brigade (ECOBRIG) appears to be the farthest along since it has designated 5,000 troops on "standby" status, and has established command and control mechanism with international donor assistance. A high readiness component, the ESF task force, consisting of about 3,000 soldiers has also been established which is able to deploy within 30 days under Nigerian leadership. The task force headquarters is located in Abuja, Nigeria, and ECOBRIG has already completed its concept of operations, doctrine, and standard operating procedures.[64]

Training needs have been identified, and several centers for excellence have been established to provide strategic, operational and tactical levels of education and training. Specifically, there are three centers of training excellence, namely, the National Defence College in Abuja for strategic level, the Kofi Annan International Peacekeeping Training Centre in Accra for operational level, and the École de Maintien de la Paix Alioune Blondin Beye in Bamako, Mali, for tactical level training.[65] In addition, a logistics center has been established.[66]

Southern Africa

The Southern African Development Community (SADC) chiefs of defense staff and police chiefs approved the formation of a SADC Standby Brigade (SADCBRIG) in July 2004, in Maseru, Lesotho. SADCBRIG was officially launched in August 2007, and has made steady progress with respect to its operationalization, but has only met part of its commitment to have 5,000 troops on standby.[67] A Planning Element (PLANELM) and a center of excellence have been established. Further, South Africa and Botswana are able to provide airlift, and South Africa is capable of providing sea-lift within the region.[68]

Issues still faced by SADCBRIG include funding (now mainly sourced form international donors), logistical support and deciding where to locate the military depot. Additionally, interoperability, effective communication and capacity building still remain as challenges.[69]

Central Africa

The Economic Community of Central African States (ECCAS) is composed of 11 member states, namely Angola, Burundi, Cameroon, Central African Republic, Chad, Congo (Brazzaville), Democratic Republic of Congo, Equatorial Guinea, Gabon, Rwanda and São Tomé et Príncipe. ECCAS has now approved a structure for the regional headquarters and the ECCAS PLANELM. By 2008, the regional PLANELM in Libreville, Gabon had about 20 staff members as well as equipment for the ECCAS standby brigade. The brigade currently has a troop force of about 3,000.[70]

"The proposed centers of excellence for ECCAS are CSID (Cours Supérieur Inter-Armées de Defense, created in 2005 and funded by France) in Youndé, Cameroon, for the strategic level, EEML (École d'État-Major de Libreville, created in 2003 and also funded by France) in Libreville, Gabon, for operational training and EFOFAA in Luanda, Angola, for tactical level training. There are also plans to develop a school in Cameroon into an international police training centre of excellence. In addition, the region has a number of smaller national centers, including one for medical training (Libreville) and one for engineers (Congo), that could play a regional role in due course. The region has also agreed to locate the logistic base for the ECCAS Standby Force in Doula, Cameroon."[71]

French bilateral support for ECCAS is critical, and without its direction, it is unclear whether Central African support for ERCCAS would have continued into the future. Underfunding ECCAS's operations nevertheless continues to be a major problem. Moreover, the persisting conflicts in Chad, Central African Republic and the Democratic Republic of the Congo remain problematic.[72] Other problems include ECCAS' weak harmonization with the AU decision-making structure, weak managerial capacity and the inadequate skills of many officers attached to the PLANELM.[73]

North Africa

The Arab Maghreb Union (AMU) was originally nominated to be the coordinator for the northern region for the ASF, but as Egypt was not a member of the AMU, this posed difficulties. Libya later became the coordinator, and the region established the North Africa Regional Capability (NARC) which includes Egypt. NARC has the mandate to establish the North Africa Standby Force, and accordingly, a memorandum of understanding has been signed at the ministerial level by a number of heads of states and government. The brigade headquarters is located in Libya, and the PLANELM is located in Egypt. Moreover, Egypt has offered to designate the Cairo peacekeeping training school of a regional center of excellence.[74] In addition, the UN has also offered the use of its Brindisi logistic facilities in Italy–either as a continental logistic base or for use by the North Africa Standby Force.[75]

In assessing the ASF at this stage, it is clear that the ASF has not met its goal of becoming fully operational by 2010. While the regionally-based brigades should be able to meet the needs of Scenarios 1-4 which primarily require observation, meeting the needs of Scenario 5 of multidimensional peacekeeping mission with deployments of 30 days is unlikely.

Indeed, the results of the African-led operations in Darfur (AMIS) and in Somalia (AMISOM) are not encouraging. AMIS was consistently undermanned with a few thousands peacekeepers, and lacked sufficient mobility capability or equipment. While the UN instituted a hybrid mission thereby expanding the number of troops up to 26,000, this was a UN-led rather than an ASF-led measure. AMISOM only deployed 1,500 troops and was generally considered to be a failure. Indeed, right now, the Somali government is fighting against renewed insurgencies with little support, and the Ethiopians have refused its request to intervene militarily.

With regard to meeting the needs of Scenario 6, stopping genocide, one commentator discouragingly notes that, "there is no way in which the ASF will have the capacity in 2010 or even in 2020."[76] He further notes that, "The will and capabilities to stop genocide will require an outside power, such as the United States, Britain or France and perhaps a regional hegemon, such as Nigeria or South Africa, to decide to intervene and to take on most of the burden. A multinational force will be unable to achieve the unity of effort to deploy and stop genocide. African militaries lack enforcement and counterinsurgency capabilities to stop genocide."[77]

Thus, "[g]iven the scarcity of resources and dependence on donors and the likelihood of more internal conflict in weak African states, the ASF and the sub-regional commands are not sustainable and will not be for a very considerable period of time to come. Donor fatigue will eventually pose problems for the ASF."[78] This is certainly a disappointing conclusion, but one that indicates that the ASF has nevertheless made uneven, sporadic progress over the past several years. The largest impediment is financial support for "standing up" the ASF standby forces. However, the lack of capacity, staffing and training has also been problematic, and one commentator notes that this failing ultimately translates into "an absence of leadership."[79]

In light of the fact that there is only a slim likelihood that the UN will stage major interventions or robust peacekeeping operations under Chapter VII of the UN Charter in the future, there is an expanded role for the ASF to play. Moreover, there is also a general agreement that the ASF should deploy in advance of the UN to meet peacekeeping needs in Africa.[80]

Thus, if the ASF deploys first with the UN following with a multidimensional peace support operation, there are two problems that may arise in this context. First, the deployment of the ASF first could lead to a severe and early depletion of ASF forces in its regional capacity. This may mean that a supplementation by Pakistani, Bangladeshi and Indian troops may be necessary. Secondly, there is anecdotal evidence that African troops prefer being deployed in a UN mission over an ASF one.[81]

So, rather than relying in principle on future supportive UN peacekeeping operations, one approach that may be worthy of future exploration is to partner the NATO Response Force (NRF) with the ASF. There are already important strategic European-based interests that support military intervention in order to assist Africa to meet its regional peacekeeping requirements.

Further, the organization and command structure of the NRF may be well-suited in terms of providing back-up support for ASF-led missions. Fuller integration and rapid force deployment in coordination between the two rapid response forces may be a interesting avenue to explore, if it is not being done already. This partnership will help the ASF to meet its Scenario 4 needs of deploying within 30 days to engage in peacekeeping operations and preventive deployments.

An integration between the NRF and the ASF to permit interoperability with respect to advance warning systems, rapid deployments, and joint training may be worthwhile options to explore. In addition, the NRF may be able to provide tactical airlift and sealift to the ASF in some instances. This sentiment is echoed by another commentator who states unequivocally that the, "North Atlantic Council should be prepared to deploy the NATO Response Force and other key assets to support AU or UN peace operations, or stand-alone interventions in Africa if necessary."[82] Indeed, as mentioned earlier in the text, the AU has already sent a Note Verbale to NATO requesting further assistance.

More generally, NATO's involvement in the overall strengthening of Africa's peace and security architecture from the perspective of improved command structure, interoperability, communications and information sharing, training, logistics, and other related issues may be a very constructive future dialogue. In fact, it is clear that NATO is committing itself more to addressing the terrorist and related threats emanating from Africa, and has strategic interests in Africa's continued stability. Most of its members are only separated by Africa by a body of water, the Mediterranean Sea. Thus, in terms of a sustained military relationship between the NRF and the ASF, there are many avenues worth exploring.

Further, as explored earlier in this chapter, there is a platform for applying the concept of the New Soldier to the NRF. If this approach is accepted, then the same training may be applied to the ASF forces whether in partnership with the NRF or as a stand-alone training exercise. Moreover, as discussed earlier, there may be a need to train not just the leadership level but the non-commissioned officer level as well. The importance of the "boots on the ground" aspect of countervailing the Fearful Symmetry should not be underestimated. The "lessons learned" from these training exercises for the New Soldier may be especially relevant in quelling insurgencies, inter-ethnic and other types of intrastate conflict. Indeed, former U.S. Defense Secretary, Robert Gates, has encouraged, "more cooperative military training and exercise participation to promote interoperability among participating countries' armed forces."[83] Interoperability between the NRF and the ASF would be an excellent goal to strive toward.

NATO in Libya

As a footnote to this discussion, let us consider NATO's recent involvement in Libya. There may be lessons learned from this involvement, and it may also shed some light on future NATO engagements in Africa, and beyond.

In February 2011, a peaceful protest in Benghazi, Libya against the 42-year rule of Colonel Mummar Qadhafi was met with violent force causing the deaths of dozens of protesters in several days.[84] This began a number of protests throughout the country prompting the UN Security Council (UNSC) to adopt Resolution 1970 on February 26, 2011, which expressed "grave concern" over the escalating violence in Libya and imposing an arms embargo against it. NATO began increasing its surveillance operations in the Mediterranean by deploying its Airborne Warning and Control Systems (AWACS) aircraft in order to keep an eye on the volatile situation in Libya.

In response to the further deterioration of the security situation in Libya, the UNSC issued Resolution 1973 on March 17, 2011, condemning the "gross and systematic violations of human rights, including arbitrary detentions, enforced disappearances, torture and summary executions."[85] The resolution called for a no-fly zone and authorized member states acting through appropriate regional organizations to use "all necessary measures" to protect civilian Libyans from further violence and repression.

Pursuant to UNSC Resolution 1973, Operation Odyssey Dawn was launched on March 19, 2011, by a multilateral coalition consisting of the United States, France, the United Kingdom, Italy and Canada (but not NATO).[86] French airstrikes were followed by 124 Tomahawk Land Attack Cruise Missiles launched from U.S. ships and submarines.[87] On March 20, 2011, U.S. Africa Command (AFRICOM) announced that three B-2 stealth bombers originating from Whiteman Air Force Base in Missouri had attacked Libyan airfields.[88] AFRICOM led Operation Odyssey Dawn and by March 24, 2011, its mission was limited to protecting civilians. The arms embargo and no-fly zone enforcement duties had been turned over to NATO and on March 31, 2011, AFRICOM ended Operation Odyssey Dawn.[89]

Also pursuant to UNSC Resolution 1973, on March 22, 2011, NATO launched an operation to enforce the UN's arms embargo against Libya, and NATO ships began interdicting weapons and mercenaries to Libya by sea.[90] On March 22, 2011, NATO began formally enforcing the no-fly zone over Libya by preventing all air flights into Libyan airspace with the exception of humanitarian aid flights. By March 31, 2011, and in consultation with the Arab League and other partners, NATO took sole command and control of the international military effort to protect Libyan civilians from further violence under the NATO-led Operation Unified Protector (OUP).[91]

Subsequent international meetings were held in Berlin on April 14, 2011, and in Paris on September 1, 2011, reaffirming the international community's commitment to support the Libyan people and put pressure on the Qadhafi regime to step down from power.[92] The UNSC adopted Resolution 2009 on September 16, 2011, which unanimously reasserted NATO's mandate to protect Libyan civilians, and establishing a United Nations Support Mission in Libya (UNSMIL).[93]

Although discussions to end the OUP began in October 2011, it was not until the stronghold of Sirte, Libya fell and the death of Colonel Qadhafi on October 20, 2011, that the North Atlantic Council agreed to end OUP by the end of the month. On October 31, 2011, NATO concluded its last AWACS sortie and the following day, NATO maritime assets began heading toward their home ports, thus ending NATO's formal engagement in Libya.[94]

The Aftermath

The aftermath of the Libyan engagement had downstream consequences for both the United States and NATO. In response to a letter to him from Speaker of the House, John Boehner, President Obama transmitted a letter dated June 15, 2011, describing how his Administration's actions in Libya did *not* violate the War Powers Resolution. Specifically, the President concluded that:

> The initial phase of U.S. military involvement in Libya was conducted under the command of the U.S. Africa Command. By April 4,

however, the United States had transferred responsibility for the military operations in Libya to NATO and the U.S. involvement has assumed a supporting role in the coalition's efforts. Since April 4, U.S. participation has consisted of: (1) non kinetic support to the NATO led operation, including intelligence, logistical support, and search and rescue assistance; (2) aircraft that have assisted in the suppression and destruction of air defenses in support of the no fly zone; and (3) since April 23, precision strikes by unmanned aerial vehicles against a limited set of clearly defined targets in support of the NATO led coalition's efforts. Although we are no longer in the lead, U.S. support for the NATO based coalition remains crucial to assuring the success of international efforts to protect civilians and civilian populated areas from the actions of the Qadhafi regime, and to address the threat to international peace and security posed by the crisis in Libya. With the exception of operations to rescue the crew of a U.S. aircraft on March 21, 2011, the United States has deployed no ground forces to Libya.[95]

Despite this argument in favor of a lawful Libyan engagement, President Obama was sued by ten U.S. lawmakers alleging that the military action taken in Libya was taken without war authorization by Congress, and that the president used multilateral and international organizations to circumvent this requirements of the act.[96] The lawsuit was dismissed by a federal district court judge on October, 20, 2011.[97]

The Libyan engagement also gave rise to certain negative assessments of NATO's performance. Rather than being a showcase for European military leadership, NATO's performance was criticized as faltering, underequipped and overly dependent on U.S. strategic, logistical and tactical support.[98] Europe's most sophisticated militaries were unable to sustain the Libyan operation on their own, even in their own neighborhood, since they lacked specialized aircraft and trained personnel needed to intercept Libyan government communications in order to verify targets.

Further, NATO did not have sufficient precision-guided missiles. NATO had to rely on U.S. reconnaissance and refueling aircraft capacities, a critical component in this type of operation. "The operational failures in Libya grow directly out of Europe's chronic military underinvestment and out-of-date strategic priorities."[99] Indeed, the United States spends about

4.8 percent of its GDP on military spending while European members of NATO average about 1.6 percent.[100] Too little was spent by NATO European countries on military modernization and combating terrorism over the past several decades.

This dismal assessment was reflected in a 37-page NATO report dated February 28, 2012, to be endorsed by NATO Ministers at a Brussels meeting in April 2012.[101] The report finds that European and Canadian plans carried out the majority of the nearly 8,000 combat sorties, while the United States provided the military support critical to accomplishing the mission. The U.S. became the "default" specialist in assisting NATO in precision-guided munitions. The NATO report identified 15 "lessons learned" including shortcomings in the political, organizational and equipment-based Libyan engagement.[102]

Another downside to the NATO operation in Libya was the civilian toll, and the allegations that NATO naval vessels did not assist boats in distress carrying migrants who later perished at sea.[103] The Libyan engagement may be ending on a sour note since the Chief Prosecutor for the International Criminal Court, Luis Moreno-Ocampo, announced on April 25, 2012, that he intends to investigate Libyan war crimes that may have been committed by NATO as well as National Transitional Council (NTC) forces.[104] The NTC estimates that civilian death tolls may be around 25,000 (in contrast to the U.S. estimate of 8,000)—this toll may have been lower if the United States had added its firepower thus ending the Libyan conflict sooner.[105]

The Libyan engagement may be the first real sign that it is time for European nations in NATO to reorganize their priorities in terms of their mutual defense since the United States is no longer in position to provide them with a "free ride."[106] The Libyan conflict was the first time that NATO engaged in combat operations with the United States playing a support role. While it may have been reasonable to assume that NATO forces could engage in such combat without a commitment of ground troops so near to their own territories, but these expectations were disappointed overall.[107]

The lack of specialized aircraft, targeting specialists, battlefield management and communications left gaps that had to be filled by the U.S. military. It was an illustration of the real cost of decades of underinvestment in military strategy, technology, equipment and training by NATO member countries. In the end, this may have led to severely undercutting their ability to engage in extended foreign military operations. If radical changes are not made soon, NATO may risk becoming irrelevant over time, and that would be a disappointment indeed.

From the U.S. perspective, the Obama Administration has been criticized for "leading from behind," in the Libyan context. This phrase was used in a *New Yorker* article, and has been appropriated for all sorts of politically-driven purposes,[108] but it nevertheless, is a shrewd policy that may create the real possibility of a full future partnership with other NATO countries. Ironically, it does so by exposing the weaknesses of both the United States (economically, not militarily) and the European members of NATO (both militarily and economically). The two sides of the Atlantic may finally be coming together in unexpected ways—the challenge is to strengthen and not weaken this powerful alliance in the end.

In sum, this chapter explored the possibility of using the New Soldier concept in the context of NATO partnering with the AU Standby Forces. There is a more diffuse and complex application of the concept, however, and it serves as a final ending note to this discussion. I have been reading Jeffrey Gettleman, a reporter for the *New York Times,* for years and his insight on warfare in Africa is very powerfully moving. In a recent book review he authored, he states simply that:

> This is the story of conflict in Africa these days. What we are seeing is the decline of the classic wars by freedom fighters and the proliferation of something else—something wilder, messier, more predatory, and harder to define. The style of warfare has shifted dramatically since the liberation wars of the 1960s and 1970s (Zimbabwe, Guinea-Bissau), the cold-war wars of the 1980s (Angola, Mozambique), and the large-scale killings of the 1990s (Somalia, Congo, Rwanda, Liberia). Today the continent is plagued by countless nasty little wars, which in many ways aren't really wars at all. There are no front lines, no battlefields, no clear conflict zones, and no distinctions between combatants and civilians, which is why the kind of massacre that happened near Niangara [Congo] is sadly common.[109]

Wars are identified as civil wars (in-country, and not cross border conflicts) that differ dramatically from former African wars of liberation. Gettleman writes in addition that:

> Today, we see dozens of small-scale, dirty wars in Congo, Somalia, the Central African Republic, Burundi, Sudan, South Sudan, Chad, Niger, and Nigeria, from east to west, from some of Africa's mightiest nations to its smallest and least significant. The specific situation in each of Africa's fifty-five different countries varies widely. But it is safe to say that many of the rebels are simply thugs.

> A few decades ago, Africa produced some very cunning and ultimately successful rebel leaders, committed to fighting colonialism, tyranny, and apartheid. Some were skillful enough to run countries, among them Ethiopia's Meles Zenawi, Rwanda's Paul Kagame, Uganda's Yoweri Museveni, and Eritrea's Isaias Afewerki. None was committed to democracy. All are still clinging to power by means of brute force, but each was well educated and each had a vision of how he and his country might survive.[110]

The lack of ideological indoctrination for adult converts is a significant part of the problem. These internecine wars have no real purpose other than to terrorize local populations. The sheer brutality of these incessant attacks on civilians may not have an actual political purpose, and may result in an uncertain political outcome. What is clear is that what follows is a raw accumulation of power for the sake of power, terror for the sake of terror. This alone is not sufficient for adults to join these rebels without a cause.

Even more chillingly, Gettleman explains further:

> There's often very little effort by rebel leaders to develop a persuasive ideology and win converts and new recruits. About the only people, then, who these types of rebels can get to fight for them are children, whom they kidnap and turn into four-foot-tall killing machines. Children are the perfect weapon—tough, easily manipulated, intensely loyal, fearless, and, most important—especially in Africa—in endless supply. A reliance on child soldiers often means a reliance on magic and superstition. Children are told to rub themselves with palm kernel oil as a shield against bullets.[111]

This sad but hidden reality exacerbates an already dire situation. Moreover, the complexity of the factors involved simply make the inaction of the international community even more intractable.

The end of Cold War politics also meant an end to (largely covert) superpower involvement in the African continent. The political landscape has changed vastly, the description and explanation for which lies outside the scope of this discussion. However, if there is to be constructive engagement to end Africa's "dirty wars,' the New Soldier concept is a means to change the nature of the dialogue with a view to creating a different ending to this never-ending story.

EPILOGUE

A Way Forward

In conclusion, the above discussion gives a detailed analysis using the dialectical method leading to the Fearful Symmetry. The rationale for using this methodology has been described above. Further, a broad distinction has been drawn in terms of distinguishing Islamic-based separatists' movements from global jihadists. In addition, the rationale for using the "failure of the state" as the basis for the rise of Islamic-based separatists' movements was contrasted with the "failure of ideology" giving rise to global jihadists.

With respect to allocating the respective roles of international actors, four filters of analysis were used: military, diplomatic/political, economic and cultural. These filters were applied to both separatists and jihadists to yield different courses of actions to be pursued by different parties. With regard to Islamic-based separatists, for example, a cohesive and well-integrated diplomatic front along with a detailed, tranched political process needs to be created and actively pursued.

Additionally, economic measures aimed at empowerment and poverty alleviation need to be put in place along with cultural initiatives that are designed to win over young, impressionable would-be and actual terrorists. With respect to global jihadists, however, economic, diplomatic and political measures are largely irrelevant. Military action in terms of traditional law enforcement activities along with creating a new soldier to fight the Fearful Symmetry needs to strategized and acted on militarily. Finally, a cultural war also needs to be waged, and this poses a grave challenge to the Muslim world and to the international community since the promise of a future has been betrayed to Islamic-based terrorists and needs desperately to be restored.

In conclusion, however, in order to resolve the Fearful Symmetry, a new soldier will need to be created. This soldier needs to demonstrate the highly subjective qualities of empathy and intuition along with a heightened perception of his surroundings enabling him or her to move fearlessly in different cultural, linguistic and emotional domains. Such a soldier needs to be both intuitive and wise–thus, different cultural values (within the military and more broadly in Western-based societies) will need to be cultivated in order to create this new kind of soldier.

Several chapters are devoted to a detailed examination of the application of the concept of the New Soldier in the context of U.S. military operations unfolding in Afghanistan. The concept is further broadened in terms of its potential application to the multilateral forces of both NATO and the African Union Standby Forces, both hopefully acting in concert with each other. The usefulness of the concept of the New Soldier depends on its deployment not only among leadership ranks but also among non-commissioned officers as well or the so-called "boots on the ground." Thus, the concept requires a 360° application in terms of its use in unilateral and multilateral forces. The concept should also be applied to the military leadership along with the so-called "strategic corporal." This is indeed, a wide prescription for change, but I feel that it is a necessary step in the way forward from this point.

In the final analysis, however, despite any efforts to create and deploy a New Soldier, the Fearful Symmetry will only be resolved when and if the global terrorists themselves learn to love–not us, but themselves. Only by giving up their destructive and self-destructive nihilism and replacing it with a sense of self-respect, and the respect for others, will the Fearful Symmetry truly end. This is the complex challenge that is posed by the Fearful Symmetry, and it is my sincere hope that we may all work together to revive hope and restore the faith in the future. The true leaders in the Fearful Symmetry are those who can inspire hope, faith, trust and finally, love. Only when we are able to live peaceably together will the promise of the future be restored to us. At that point, we may move past the Fearful Symmetry and welcome a new era of history that will begin when this one ends.

NOTES

PREFACE

[1] Michael Mazarr, "The Folly of 'Asymmetric War,'" *31 Wash*. Q.33-53 (2008). Professor Mazarr is a professor of national security strategy at the U.S. National War College.

[2] Id. at 35-36.

[3] Id. at 39-41.

[4] Jeffrey Record, "Why the Strong Lose," *Parameters* 16, 20-22 (Winter 2005-06).

[5] Id. at 25.

[6] Id. at 26.

[7] Carl von Clausewitz, ON WAR, ed. and trans. Michael Howard and Peter Paret. (Princeton University Press, 1976) at 87, 89.

[8] Michael Mazarr, "The Folly of 'Asymmetric War,'" *31 Wash. Q., supra,* at 38.

[9] Id. at 50. Professor Mazarr further argues that, "The United States should powerfully enhance its efforts to reduce instability, conflict and radicalism in key areas of the world and to shore up institutionalization and governance in critical states. It should do so, however, by relying on an expanded and deepened set of nonmilitary tools and do so largely in an anticipatory and collaborative manner rather than an ex post facto and interventionist one." Id. at 35.

[10] Robert Gates, "Beyond Guns and Steel: Reviving the Nonmilitary Instruments of American Power," Remarks delivered by the Defense Secretary at Manhattan, Kansas (26 November 2007), available at http://www.defenselink.mil/speeches/ speech.aspx?speechid=1199 (last visited on August 22, 2008).

[11] Thom Shanker, "G.I.'s to Fill Civilian Gap to Rebuild Afghanistan," *NY Times* (April 23, 2009), available at http://www.nytimes.com/2009/04/23/world/ asia/23military.html?_r=1 (last visited on July 12, 2009).

[12] Id.

[13] Id.

[14] Id.

[15] "Counterinsurgency," U.S. Army Field Manual FM 3-24 (MCWP 3-33.5) (December 2006) at 1-4. General Patraeus further points that that, "Recently, ideologies based on extremist forms of religious or ethnic identities have replaced ideologies based on secular revolutionary ideals. These new forms of old, strongly held beliefs define the identities of the most dangerous combatants in these new internal wars. These conflicts resemble the wars of religion in Europe before and after the Reformation of the 16th century. People have replaced nonfunctioning national identities with traditional sources of unity and identity. When countering an insurgency during the Cold War, the United States normally focused on increasing a threatened but friendly government's ability to defend itself and on encouraging political and economic reforms to undercut support for the insurgency. Today, when countering an insurgency growing from state collapse or failure, counterinsurgents often face a more daunting task: helping friendly forces reestablish political order and legitimacy where these conditions may no longer exist." Id.

[16] RAND, AMERICA'S ROLE IN NATION-BUILDING: FROM GERMANY TO IRAQ (RAND 2003) (James Dobbins, *et al*,eds.) at 69.

[17] Department of Defense Directive 3000.05 (26 November 2005), ¶ 4.2, available at http://www.dtic.mil/whs/directives/corres/pdf/300005p.pdf.

[18] Id. at ¶ 4.3. *See also* Counterinsurgency, FM 3-24 (MCWP 3-33.5) (December 2006), a U.S. Army field manual devoted to conducting a counterinsurgency campaign coauthored by General David Patraeus. The manual states clearly that, "[Counterinsurgency] involves the application of national power in the political, military, economic, social, information, and infrastructure fields and disciplines. Political and military leaders and planners should never underestimate its scale and complexity; moreover, they should recognize that the Armed Forces cannot succeed in [Counterinsurgency Operations] alone. Id. at 1-1.

[19] Sean McFate, "U.S. Africa Command: a New Strategic Paradigm?" *Mil. Rev.* (January-February 2008), available at http://findarticles.com/p/articles/mi_m0PBZ/is_1_88/ai_n25410262 (last visited on August 22, 2008).

[20] Id.

[21] RAND, AMERICA'S ROLE IN NATION-BUILDING: FROM GERMANY TO IRAQ, *supra*, note 16 at xxv, xxxvi, xxxvii-xxxviii.

[22] *See* Robert Gates, "Beyond Guns and Steel: Reviving the Nonmilitary Instruments of American Power," Remarks delivered by the Defense Secretary at Manhattan, Kansas (26 November 2007), available at http://www.defenselink.mil/speeches/speech.aspx?speechid=1199, *supra*, endnote 10.

INTRODUCTION

[1] Immanuel Kant, CRITIQUE OF PURE REASON (Paul Gruyer & Allen W. Wood (eds.) Cambridge University Press 1998). The first edition of the volume was

published in 1781.

2 Georg Hegel, THE PHENOMENOLOGY OF THE MIND, VOL. 1 (1st ed. 1910), republished by Routledge (2002).

3 *See the* U.S. Army website available at http://www.awg.army.mil/ (last visited on July 25, 2007).

4 William Blake, SONGS OF INNOCENCE AND OF EXPERIENCE (R. Brimley Johnson, 1901).

5 Clinton J. Ancker & III, Michael D. Burke "Doctrine for Asymmetric Warfare," *Mil. Rev.* (July-August 2003) at 19, available at http://findarticles.com/p/articles/mi_m0PBZ/is_4_83/ai_109268858/ (last visited on July 2, 2009).

6 William Olson, "War Without a Center of Gravity: Reflections on Terrorism and Post-Modern War," Small Wars and Insurgencies, Vol. 18, No. 4, 559, 559 (December 2007).

7 Id. at 560.

8 Id. at 571.

9 Id. at 561.

10 Rosa Brooks, "Failed Sates, or the State as Failure?" 72 *Chi. L. Rev. 1159* (2005).

11 John Hamre & Gordon Sullivan, "Toward Postconflict Reconstruction," 25 *Wash. Q* 85, 85 (2002), available at http://muse.jhu.edu/journals/washington_quarterly/v025/25.4hamre.html (last visited on July 3, 2009).

12 Jochen Hippler, "Low intensity warfare and its implications for NATO, (December 1988), available at http://www.jochen-hippler.de/Aufsatze/low-intensity_conflict/low-intensity_conflict.html (last visited on July 2, 2009).

13 *See* DOD Dictionary of Military and Associated Terms, available at http://www.js.pentagon.mil/doctrine/jel/doddict/ (last visited on July 2, 2009).

14 *See* Marine Corps Warfighting Laboratory Wargaming Division, Small Wars Center of Excellence, available at http://www.smallwars.quantico.usmc.mil/ (last visited on July 2, 2009.)

15 Janine Davidson, "Principles of Modern American Counterinsurgency: Evolution and Debate," (June 8, 2009), available at http://www.brookings.edu/~/media/Files/rc/papers/2009/0608_counterinsurgency_davidson/0608_counterinsurgency_davidson.pdf. (last visited on July 2, 2009.)

16 Id.

17 Fareed Zacharia, "The Rise of the Rest," *Newsweek* (May 12, 2008), available at http://www.fareedzakaria.com/ARTICLES/newsweek/051208.html (last visited on July 2, 2009).

18 Id.

[19] Fareed Zacharia, "The Future of American Power: How America Can Survive the Rise of the Rest," *For. Aff.* (May/June 2008), available at http://www.foreignaffairs.com/articles/63394/fareed-zakaria/the-future-of-american-power (last visited on July 4, 2009).

[20] Id.

[21] Richard Haas, "The Age of Nonpolarity: What Will Follow U.S. Dominance," *For. Aff.* (May/June 2008), available at http://www.foreignaffairs.com/articles/63397/richard-n-haass/the-age-of-nonpolarity (last visited on July 4, 2009).

[22] Id.

CHAPTER 1

[1] *See* U.S. Department Fact Sheet dated Oct. 11, 2005 available at http://www.state.gov/s/ct/rls/fs/37191.htm (last visited on July 25, 2007).

[2] *See* Council of Foreign Relations Backgrounder on Hamas available at http://www.cfr.org/publication/8968/ updated on June 8, 2007 (last visited on July 25, 2007).

[3] *See* Council of Foreign Relations, http://www.cfr.org/publication/9365/#12007 (last visited on July 25, 2007).

[4] For an in depth discussion of the radical Islam and the Abu Sayyaf in the Philippines, *see* Graham Turbiville, Jr., "Bearers of the Sword Radical Islam, Philippines Insurgency, and Regional Stability," *Mil. Rev.* (March-April 2002), available at http://www.smallwars.quantico.usmc.mil/search/LessonsLearned/philippines/bearers.asp (last visited on July 2, 2009).

[5] "Making Peace in the Philippines: JAM to Moros," *The Economist*, October 13, 2012 at 17-18.

[6] Terrorism Focus, Jamestown Foundation (Vol. 4, Issue 3, February 27, 2007) available at http://jamestown.org/terrorism/news/article.php?articleid=2370262 (last visited on July 25, 2007).

[7] *See e.g.,* James Risen & Judith Miller, "Pakistani Intelligence Had Links to Al Qaeda, US Officials Say," *NY Times* (October 29, 2001), extract available at http://select.nytimes.com/gst/abstract.html?res= F40912F73D540C7A8EDDA 90994D9404482 (last visited on August 6, 2007), full article available at http://tiger.berkeley.edu/sohrab/politics/isi_problems.html. *See also* Suba Chandran, "Terrorism and Organized Crime in India," (February 28, 2003) available at http://www.ipcs.org/Kashmir_articles2.jsp?action=showView&kValue= 925&issue=1 012&status=article&mod=a (last visited on August 6, 2007).

[8] Bruce Riedel, Al Qaeda Strikes Back, *For. Aff.* (May/June 2007), available at http://www.foreignaffairs.org/20070501faessay86304/bruce-riedel/al-qaeda-strikes-back.html?mode=print (last visited on July 25, 2007).

9 Gardiner Harris, "In Kashmir, Killing Ebbs, but Killers Roam Free," *NY Times* (June 25, 2012), available at http://www.nytimes.com/2012/06/26/world/asia/ kashmiris-await-justice-for-realtives-killed-in-warfare.html?pagewanted= all&_moc. semityn.www (last visited on September 27, 2012).

10 For a discussion generally of the role of Hezbollah in Lebanon, *see* William Mooney, Jr., "Stabilizing Lebanon: Peacekeeping or Nation-Building," Parameters (Autumn 2007), 26-41, available at http://www.carlisle.army.mil/usawc/ Parameters/07autumn/mooney.htm (last visited on July 2, 2009).

11 *See* generally F. Gregory Gause III, "Can Democracy Stop Terrorism?" *For.att.* (September/October 2005) available at http://www.foreignaffairs. org/20050901faessay84506/f-gregory-gause-iii/can-democracy-stop-terrorism. html (last visited on August 15, 2007).

12 Tamara Makarenko, "The Crime"Terror Continuum: Tracing the Interplay between Transnational Organised Crime and Terrorism," 6 *Global Crime* 129, 136-137 (February 2004).

13 Id. at 141.

14 Ethan Bronner, "Hamas Shifts From Rockets to Culture War," *NY Times* (July 23, 2009), available at http://www.nytimes.com/2009/07/24/world/ middleeast/24gaza.html (last visited on August 17, 2009).

15 Reuven Paz, Between Ideology and Strategy, Edition 31, Vol. 3 (August 18, 2005) available at http://www.bitterlemons-international.org/previous.php?opt= 1&id=98#397 (last visited on July 25, 2007).

16 *See* the Failed States Index 2009, available at http://www.fundforpeace.org/ global/?q=fsi (last visited on May 11, 2012).

17 Manan Ahmed, "Legends of the Fail," *National* (May 7, 2009), available at http:// www.thenational.ae/article/20090508/REVIEW/705079996/1008 (last visited on July 3, 2009). *See also* op-ed of President Asif Ali Zardari, "Talk to, not at, Pakistan," Wash. Post (October 2, 2011) at A17, where he states, "It is not as if Pakistanis will not stop reclaiming our terrain, inch by inch, from the extremists, even without the help of the United States. We are a tenacious people. We will not allow religion to become the trigger for terrorism or persecution."

18 Ismail Khan & Declan Walsh, "Taliban Free 384 Inmates in Pakistan," *NY Times* (April 15, 2012), available at http://www.nytimes.com/2012/04/16/world/asia/ pakistani-taliban-assault-prison-freeing-almost-400.html (last visited on April 16, 2012).

19 Id.

20 Id.

21 Mark Landler & Thom Shanker, "U.S. May Label Pakistan Militants as Terrorists," *NY Times* (July 13, 2010, available at http://www.nytimes.com/2010/07/14/world/ asia/14diplo.html (last visited on April 16, 2012).

[22] Eric Schmitt, "U.S. Seems Set to Brand Militant Group as 'Terrorist,'" *NY Times* (August 31, 2012), available at http://www.nytimes.com/2012/09/01/world/asia/us-seems-set-to-designate-haqqani-network-as-terror-group.html?pagewanted=all (last visited on September 27, 2012).

[23] Id.

[24] Qasim Nauman, "Pakistan spy chief denied his country aids militant group," *Wash. Post* (September 30, 2011) at A11.

[25] *See* http://www.treasury.gov/resource-center/sanctions/OFAC-Enforcement/Documents/taliban_notice_06212011.pdf (last visited on April 16, 2012).

[26] Id. For a fuller discussion of the history of ISI leadership and its impact on assisting, aiding and abetting militants in Afghanistan, the Pakistan Taliban and the Haqqani network, *see* Mark Mazzetti, *et al*, "Pakistan Aids Insurgency in Afghanistan, Reports Assert," *NY Times* (July 25, 2010), available at http://www.nytimes.com/2010/07/26/world/asia/26isi.html?pagewanted=all (last visited on April 16, 2012).

[27] Declan Walsh & Eric Schmitt, "New Boldness from Militants Poses Risk to U.S.-Pakistan Relations," *NY Times* (July 30, 2012), available at http://www.nytimes.com/2012/07/31/world/asia/haqqani-network-threatens-us-pakistani-ties.html?pagewanted=all (last visited on September 27, 2012).

[28] Editorial," 60 Miles from Islamabad," *NY Times* (April 26, 2009), available at http://www.nytimes.com/2009/04/27/opinion/27mon1.html (last visited on May 11, 2012).

[29] Bill Roggio, "Pakistan Peace Agreement Cedes Ground to the Taliban," *Long War J.* (February 18, 2009), available at http://www.longwarjournal.org/archives/2009/02/analysis_pakistan_pe.php (last visited on July 3, 2009).

[30] Id.

[31] Zakaria: "'Spiraling chaos' possible in Pakistan," *CNN News*, available at http://www.cnn.com/2009/WORLD/asiapcf/04/22/zakaria.pakistan/index.html (last visited on July 3, 2009).

[32] Id.

[33] Richard Rotberg, The New Nature of Nation-State Failure," *Wash. Q* (Summer 2002), at 86, available at http://www.twq.com/02summer/rotberg.pdf (last visited on July 3, 2009).

[34] David Sanger, "Strife in Pakistan Raises U.S. Doubts on Nuclear Arms, *NY Times* (May 3, 2009), available at http://www.nytimes.com/2009/05/04/world/asia/04nuke.html (last visited on July 3, 2009). Carlotta Gall & Eric Schmitt, "U.S. Questions Pakistan's Will to Stop Taliban," *NY Times* (April 24, 2009), available at http://www.nytimes.com/2009/04/24/world/asia/24pstan.html (last visited on July 3, 2009).

[35] *See e.g.*, the demolition of the house where Osama bin Laden lived in Abbotabad, Pakistan for ten years and where he was killed by U.S. Navy SEALS in May 2011. The house had acquired "a painful symbolism for Pakistan's powerful military, which was badly embarrassed by the raid." Declan Walsh, "Pakistan Razing House Where Bin Laden Lived," *NY Times* (February 25, 2012), available at http://query.nytimes.com/gst/fullpage.html?res=9C06E2D71231F935A15751C0A9649D8B63 (last visited on April 17, 2012).

[36] Declan Walsh, *et al*, "United States Talks Fail as Pakistanis Seek Apology," *NY Times* (April 27, 2012), available at http://www.nytimes.com/2012/04/28/world/asia/talks-between-us-and-pakistan-fail-over-airstrike-apology.html (last visited on April 30, 21012).

[37] Id.

[38] Eric Schmitt & David Sanger, "Some in Qaeda Leave Pakistan for Somalia and Yemen," *NY Times* (June 12, 2009), available at http://www.nytimes.com/2009/06/12/world/12terror.html (last visited on July 3, 2009). *See also* Jeffrey Gettleman, "No Winner Seen in Somalia's Battle with Chaos," *NY Times* (June 1, 2009), available at http://www.nytimes.com/2009/06/02/world/africa/02somalia.html (last visited on July 3, 2009).

[39] "Al Qaeda in Yemen and Somalia: A Ticking Time Bomb," Report to the U.S. Senate Committee on Foreign Relations (January 21, 2010), available at http://www.gpoaccess.gov/congress/index.html (last visited on April 16, 2012).

[40] Eric Schmitt, "As Al Qaeda Loses a Leader, Its Power Shifts From Pakistan," *NY Times* (June 7, 2012), available at http://www.nytimes.com/2012/06/08/world/asia/al-qaeda-power-shifting-away-from-pakistan.html (last visited on September 27, 2012).

[41] *See generally* Mark Bowden, Black Hawk Down: the Story of a Modern War (Grove Press 2010).

[42] Id.

[43] "Ethiopia rejects Somali request," *BBC News* (June 21, 2009), available at http://news.bbc.co.uk/2/hi/africa/8111312.stm (last visited on July 14, 2009); *see also* Mohammed Ibrahim, "Somali Rebels Pledge to Send Fighters to Aid Yemen Jihad," *NY Times* (January 2, 2010), available at http://www.nytimes.com/2010/01/02/world/africa/02somalia.html (last visited on April 16, 2012).

[44] Mohammed Ibrahim, "Somalia Selects an Activist as Leader," *NY Times* (September 10, 2012), available at http://www.nytimes.com/2012/09/11/world/africa/parliament-selects-mohamud-as-somalias-president.html (last visited on September 27, 2012).

[45] Kevin Peraino, "Somalia Strikes Out," *Newsweek* (July 26, 2010) at 42, 43.

[46] Mohammed Ibrahim, "Somali Rebels Pledge to Send Fighters to Aid Yemen Jihad," *NY Times* (January 2, 2010), available at http://www.nytimes.com/2010/01/02/

world/africa/02somalia.html (last visited on April 16, 2012).

[47] Id.

[48] "No arts; no letters; no society; and which is worst of all, continual fear and danger of violent death; and the life of man, solitary, poor, nasty, brutish, and short."Thomas Hobbes (1588-1679), British philosopher. Leviathan, part 1, ch. 13 (1651).

[49] Al Qaeda in Yemen and Somalia: A Ticking Time Bomb," Report to the U.S. Senate Committee on Foreign Relations (January 21, 2010), available at http://www.gpoaccess.gov/congress/index.html (last visited on April 16, 2012).

[50] Id.

[51] Eric Schmitt & David Sanger, "Some in Qaeda Leave Pakistan for Somalia and Yemen," *NY Times* (June 12, 2009), available at http://www.nytimes.com/2009/06/12/world/12terror.html (last visited on July 3, 2009).

[52] Mohammed Ibrahim, "Somalia Selects an Activist as Leader," *NY Times* (September 10, 2012), available at http://www.nytimes.com/2012/09/11/world/africa/parliament-selects-mohamud-as-somalias-president.html (last visited on September 27, 2012). Also, the reports of Somali piracy are decreasing, but political turmoil in Somali may again encourage piracy which caused over $5 billion per year in insurance and security expenses for shipping vessels. *See* Thom Shanker, "U.S. Reports That Piracy Off Africa Has Plunged," *NY Times* (August 28, 2012), available at http://www.nytimes.com/2012/08/29/world/africa/piracy-around-horn-of-africa-has-plunged-us-says.html (last visited on September 27, 2012).

[53] Jeffrey Gettleman, "Last Somali Militant Bastion Falls, Kenya Claims," *NY Times* (September 28, 2012), available at http://www.nytimes.com/2012/09/29/world/africa/kenya-says-it-captures-last-islamist-bastion-in-somalia.html (last visited on October 1, 2012).

[54] Chris Welch, "Minnesota Men Charged in Somali Recruiting," *CNN News* (July 13, 2009), available at http://www.cnn.com/2009/CRIME/07/13/somalia.americans.killed/index.html (last visited on July 14, 2009).

[55] Id.

[56] "Ethiopia rejects Somali request," *BBC News* (June 21, 2009), available at http://news.bbc.co.uk/2/hi/africa/8111312.stm (last visited on July 14, 2009).

[57] Andrea Elliott, "A Call to Jihad From Somalia, Answered in America" *NY Times* (July 12, 2009), available at http://www.nytimes.com/2009/07/12/us/12somalis.html?pagewanted=all (last visited on April 16, 2012).

[58] Al Qaeda in Yemen and Somalia: A Ticking Time Bomb," Report to the U.S. Senate Committee on Foreign Relations (January 21, 2010), available at http://www.gpoaccess.gov/congress/index.html (last visited on April 16, 2012).

[59] "Al-Shabaab and Somali pirates strengthen links," *Radio Netherlands Worldwide* (October 21, 2011), available at http://www.rnw.nl/africa/article/al-shabaab-and-somali-pirates-strengthen-links (last visited on April 16, 2012); *see also* Jonathan Saul & Camila Reed, "Shabaab-Somali pirate links growing: UN Adviser," *Reuters* Africa (October 21, 2011), available at http://af.reuters.com/article/topNews/idAFJOE79J0G620111020 (last visited on April 16, 2012).

[60] AMISOM Background available at http://amisom-au.org/about/amisom-background/ (last visited on April 16, 2012).

[61] "Somalia's Crisis: Unexpected Gain," *The Economist* (August 13, 2011) at 45.

[62] Id.

[63] Sudarsan Raghavan, "Islamic Militant group Al Shabab claims Uganda bombing attacks," *Wash. Post* (July 12, 2010), available at http://www.washingtonpost.com/wp-dyn/content/article/2010/07/12/AR2010071200476.html (last visited on April 16, 2012).

[64] The accessibility of Uganda as a safe haven for Somalis fleeing the violence in their country may be affected. *See* Josh Kron, "Somali Refugees Fear Loss of Ugandan Haven," *NY Times* (July 21, 2010), available at http://www.nytimes.com/2010/07/22/world/africa/22uganda.html (last visited on April 16, 2012).

[65] Id.

[66] Ross Douthat, "Libya's Unintended Consequences," *NY Times* (July 7, 2012), available at http://www.nytimes.com/2012/07/08/opinion/sunday/libyas-unintended-consequences.html?_r=0 (last visited on September 27, 2012).

[67] "Secession in Mali, An Unholy Alliance," *The Economist* (June 2, 2012) at 61.

[68] Ross Douthat, "Libya's Unintended Consequences," *NY Times* (July 7, 2012), available at http://www.nytimes.com/2012/07/08/opinion/sunday/libyas-unintended-consequences.html?_r=0 (last visited on September 27, 2012). *See* also Adam Nossiter, "Jihadists' Fierce Justice Drives Thousands to Flee Mali," *NY Times* (July 17, 2012), available at http://www.nytimes.com/2012/07/18/world/africa/jidhadists-fierce-justice-drives-thousands-to-flee-mali.html?pagewanted=all (last visited on September 27, 2012).

[69] Adam Nossiter, "Saying Mali 'Is Our Country', Militias Train to Oust Islamists," *NY Times* (August 5, 2012), available at http://www.nytimes.com/2012/08/06/world/africa/mali-militias-poorly-armed-but-zealous-to-oust-islamists.html?pagewanted=all&gwh=3A85F9A00BF71 B71324222B2C1EB4895 (last visited on September 27, 2012).

[70] Adam Nossiter, "Summer of Siege for West Africa as Discontent Boils Into Street," *NY Times* (September 8, 2012), available at http://www.nytimes.com/2012/09/09/world/africa/summer-of-siege-for-west-africa-as-discontent-shakes-streets.html? pagewanted=all&gwh=47A024A623B3163721CA1735A C843B20 (last visited on September 27, 2012).

71 "ECOWAS, Mali Settle Disagreement over Standby Force," *Voice of America* (September 6, 2012), available at http://www.voanews.com/content/ecowas-mali-settele-disagreement-over-standby-force/1503343.html (last visited on September 27, 2012).

72 Kareem Fahim, "Militants and Politics Bedevil Yemen's New Leaders," *NY Times* (April 23, 2012), available at http://www.nytimes.com/2012/04/23/world/middleeast/militants-and-politics-bedevil-yemens-new-president.html (last visited on April 23, 2012).

73 Laura Kasinof, "Protesters Set a New Goal: Fixing Yemen's Military," *NY Times* (February 27, 2012), available at http://www.nytimes.com/2012/02/28/world/middleeast/yemeni-protesters-set-new-goal-fixing-the-military.html (last visited on April 16, 2012).

74 Laura Kasinof, "In Yemen, New Leader Faces Threats in the South," *NY Times* (March 17, 2012), available at http://www.nytimes.com/2012/03/18/world/middleeast/yemens-new-president-is-facing-unrest-in-the-south.html?pagewanted=all (last visited on April 17, 2012).

75 Id.

76 Id.

77 Scott Shane, *et al*, "Secret Assault on Terrorism Widens on Two Continents," *NY Times* (August 14, 2011), available at http://www.nytimes.com/2010/08/15/world/15shadowwar.html?pagewanted=all (last visited on April 17, 2012).

78 J. David Goodman, "Qaeda Media Arm Steps Up Local Coverage in Yemen," *NY Times* (March 9, 2012), available at http://thelede.blogs.nytimes.com/2012/03/09/qaeda-media-arm-steps-up-local-coverage-in-yemen/ (last visited on April 17, 2012). *See also*, Robbie Brown & Kim Severson, "2nd American in Strike Wages Qaeda Media War," *NY Times* (September 30, 2011), available at http://www.nytimes.com/2011/10/01/world/middleeast/samir-khan-killed-by-drone-spun-out-of-the-american-middle-class.html (last visited on April 16, 2012).

79 "US Preparing to Restart Military Aid to Yemen,"

(March 10, 2012) available at http://www.usatoday.com/news/world/story/2012-03-10/us-yemen-aid/53452878/1 (last visited on April 16, 2012).

80 Eric Schmitt & Scott Shane, "Aid to Fight Qaeda in Yemen Divides U.S. Officials," *NY Times* (September 15, 2010), available at http://www.nytimes.com/2010/09/16/world/middleeast/16yemen.html (last visited on April 16, 2012).

81 Scott Shane *et al*, "Secret Assault on Terrorism Widens on Two Continents," *NY Times* (August 14, 2011), available at http://www.nytimes.com/2010/08/15/world/15shadowwar.html?pagewanted=all (last visited on April 17, 2012), *supra*, note 55.

82 Id.

[83] US CONST., Art. I, sec. 8.

[84] US CONST., Art. II, sec. 2.

[85] War Powers Act ("Resolution") of 1973, 50 U.S.C.§§ 1541-1548.

[86] Ibid. at Section 3.

[87] Charlie Savage, "Secret U.S. Memo Made Legal Case to Kill a Citizen," *NY Times* (October, 8, 2011), available at http://www.nytimes.com/2011/10/09/world/middleeast/secret-us-memo-made-legal-case-to-kill-a-citizen.html?pagewanted=all (last visited on April 17, 2012); *see also* Anna Persky, "Lethal Force," *Wash. Lawyer* (March 2012) at 25.

[88] War Powers Resolution of 1973, Section 5(b), *supra*, note 84.

[89] Executive Order 11905 (February 18, 1976), Sec. 5(g) was signed by President Gerald Ford; Executive Order 12333 (December 4, 1981) was signed by President Ronal Reagan, and was subsequently amended by President Bush on July 31, 2008, but the ban on political assassinations was kept in place (*see* http://www.techlawjournal.com/topstories/2008/20080731.asp (last visited on April 17, 2012).

[90] *See* Anna Persky, "Lethal Force," *Wash. Lawyer,supra*, at 25.

[91] 18 U.S.C. § 1119 (2000).

[92] Authorization for Use of Military Force (Public Law 3 107–40; 50 U.S.C. 1541 note).

[93] *See* Nasser Al-Aulaqi v. Barack Obama, Civ. No. 10-1469, slip op. dismissing the case available at http://www.investigativeproject.org/documents/case_docs/1436.pdf (last visited on April 17, 2012).

[94] Id. at 80.

[95] Indeed, the Court itself identifies several perplexing legal questions at the outset of its opinion citing, for example, "Can a U.S. citizen—himself or through another—use the U.S. judicial system to vindicate his constitutional rights while simultaneously evading U.S. law enforcement authorities, calling for 'jihad against the West,' and engaging in operational planning for an organization that has already carried out numerous terrorist attacks against the United States? Can the Executive order the assassination of a U.S. citizen without first affording him any form of judicial process whatsoever, based on the mere assertion that he is a dangerous member of a terrorist organization? . . . And how does the evolving AQAP relate to the core Al Qaeda for purposes of assessing the legality of targeting AQAP (or its principals) under the September 18, 2001 Authorization for the Use of Military Force?" Id. at 2-3.

[96] "Eric Holder gives legal defense for al-Awlaki killing," *wjla.com*, available at http://www.wjla.com/articles/2012/03/eric-holder-gives-legal-defense-for-al-awlaki-killing-73459.html (last visited on April 23, 2012).

[97] Id.

[98] For a fuller discussion of the constitutional implications of classifying enemy combatants by the Executive Branch, *see* Michelle Maslowski, "Classification of Enemy Combatants and the Usurpation of Judicial Power by the Executive Branch," 40 *Ind. L. Rev.* 177 (2007). The article argues that the September 18, 2001 Authorization for the Use of Military Force does not grant the president the authority to classify individuals captured outside the battlefield, and that doing so may violate the separation of powers doctrine by usurping judicial power by the executive branch.

[99] Eric Schmitt & Souad Mekhennet, "Qaeda Branch Steps Up Raids in North Africa, *NY Times* (July 10, 2009), available at http://www.timesdaily.com/article/20090710/ZNYT03/907103016?Title=Qaeda-Branch-Steps-Up-Raids-in-North-Africa (last visited on July 10, 2009).

[100] Nicholas Schmidle, "The Sahara Conundrum," *NY Times* (February 13, 2009), available at http://www.nytimes.com/2009/02/15/magazine/15Africa-t.html (last visited on July 3, 2009).

[101] *See e.g.*,http://global-security.suite101.com/article.cfm/what_is_a_failed_state (last visited on July 3, 2009).

[102] Richard Rotberg, The New Nature of Nation-State Failure," *Wash.Q supra,* at 87.

[103] Id. at 90.

[104] *See e.g.,* Hussein Adam, "Somalia: A Terrible Beauty Being Born?" at 69, 70-76, in COLLAPSED STATES: THE DISINTEGRATION AND RESTORATION OF LEGITIMATE AUTHORITY (ed., I. William Zartman) (Lynne Rienner pub., 1995), for a discussion on the collapse of Somalia.

[105] In the interest of full disclosure, the author was formerly an attorney with the Office of the General Counsel, USAID, Washington, DC.

[106] USAID, "Fragile States Strategy," at 1, available at http://www.usaid.gov/policy/2005_fragile_states_strategy.pdf (last visited on July 3, 2009).

[107] John Hamre & Gordon Sullivan, "Toward Post-conflict Reconstruction," 25 *Wash.Q*, 85 (2002), available at http://muse.jhu.edu/journals/washington_quarterly/v025/25.4hamre.html (last visited on July 3, 2009).

[108] Id. at 86-88.

[109] John Hamre & Gordon Sullivan, "Toward Post-conflict Reconstruction," 25 *Wash. Q, supra.* at 91-93.

[110] Nina Serafino & Martin Weiss, "Peacekeeping and Post-Conflict Capabilities: The State Department's Office for Reconstruction and Stabilization," CRS Report for Congress (RS22031)(January 19, 2005), footnote 1, available at http://opencrs.com/document/RS22031/ (last visited on July 11, 2009).

[111] *See* Post-Conflict Reconstruction Essential Tasks (U.S. Department of State (April 2005), available at http://www.crs.state.gov/index.cfm?fuseaction= public.

display&id=845541F4-EA4A-49BC-BDFC-53D8B8DE4865 (last visited on July 3, 2009), at Preface.

[112] *See* Post-Conflict Reconstruction Essential Tasks (U.S. Department of State (April 2005), *supra*, Preface, available at http://www.crs.state.gov/index.cfm?fuseaction=public.display&id=845541F4-EA4A-49BC-BDFC-53D8B8DE4865.

[113] Richard Rotberg, The New Nature of Nation-State Failure," *Wash.Q supra,* at 95, 96.

[114] Ben N. Dunlop, "State Failure and the Use of Force in the Age of Terror," available at http://www.bc.edu/schools/law/lawreviews/meta-elements/journals/bciclr/27_2/09_TXT.htm (last visited on August 16, 2007).

[115] Id. at 87-89.

[116] Id.

[117] Ashraf Ghani, "A Ten-Year Framework for Afghanistan: Executing the Obama Plan … and Beyond," *Atlantic Council* (April 2009) at 1, available at http://vls571760.qcp.hosting.com/files/publication_pdfs/65/AfghanistanReport-200904.pdf (last visited on July 11, 2009).

[118] Michael Slackman, "Iran Protesters Take to Street Despite Threats," *NY Times* (July 10, 2009), available at http://www.nytimes.com/2009/07/10/world/middleeast/10iran.html (last visited on July 10, 2009).

[119] *See e.g.,* "Israel, Palestine, and America: Both States Must be Real," *The Economist* (June 18, 2009), available at http://www.economist.com/displayStory.cfm? story_id=13862529 (last visited on July 4, 2009).

[120] Susan Willette, "The Economics of Security in the Developing World," Disarmament Forum (1999) at 19, available at http://www.unidir.org/pdf/articles/pdf-art261.pdf (last visited on August 20, 2007).

[121] Id. at 22.

[122] Id. at 27.

[123] *See e.g.,* Rumu Sarkar, INTERNATIONAL DEVELOPMENT LAW: THE RULE OF LAW, HUMAN RIGHTS AND GLOBAL FINANCE (Oxford University Press, 2009).

[124] F. Gregory Gause III, "Can Democracy Stop Terrorism?" *For. Aff.* (September/October 2005) available at http://www.foreignaffairs.org/20050901faessay84506/f-gregory-gause-iii/can-democracy-stop-terrorism.html (last visited on August 15, 2007).

[125] James Dobbins, *et al.,* AMERICA'S ROLE IN NATION-BUILDING: FROM GERMANY TO IRAQ (RAND, 2003), available at http://www.rand.org/pubs/monograph_reports/MR1753.html (last visited on May 14, 2012).The study examines the last 60 years of post-war stabilization and reconstruction efforts

beginning with the military occupations of Germany and Japan, later examining peacekeeping operations in Somalia, Haiti, Bosnia, Kosovo, Afghanistan and Iraq led by the United States. The second volume examines UN-led missions in the former Belgian Congo, Namibia, Cambodia, El Salvador, Mozambique, Eastern Slovenia, East Timor and Sierra Leone.

[126] A RAND study defines nation-building as "the use of armed force in the aftermath of a conflict to underpin an enduring transition to democracy." *See* James Dobbins, "Nation-Building: The Inescapable Responsibility of the World's Only Superpower," *RAND Review*, available at http://www.rand.org/publications/ randreview/issues/summer2003/nation.html (last visited on August 1, 2007.)

[127] James Dobbins, *et al.,* AMERICA'S ROLE IN NATION-BUILDING: FROM GERMANY TO IRAQ (RAND, 2003), at xix, 161 *see* endnote 124, *supra.* Further, a multilateral effort that dismantled institutions wholesale from within as in the case of Germany was less successful in the medium-term than in Japan where a unilateral U.S. effort to reform existing institutions from within was more successful in the short-term.

CHAPTER 2

[1] Dominique Moïsi, *The Geopolitics of Emotion: How Cultures of Fear, Humiliation, and Hope Are Reshaping the World* (Anchor Books, 2009), at 83.

[2] *See e.g., Counterterrorism*, Osen, LLC, available at http://www.osen.us/index. php? id=57 (last visited on May 16, 2012).

[3] Fareed Zacharia, "The Politics of Rage: Why Do They Hate Us?" available at http://www.fareedzakaria.com/ARTICLES/newsweek/101501_why.html (last visited on July 25, 2007).

[4] Id.

[5] Eric Chaney, "Democratic Change in the Arab World, Past and Present," (2012), available at http://www.brookings.edu/~/media/Files/Programs/ES/BPEA/2012_ spring_bpea_papers/2012_spring_BPEA_chaney.pdf; *see also* "Arab Democratic Deficit not Due to Islam, New Brookings Paper Finds," March 22, 2012, available at http://www.brookings.edu/economics/bpea/Latest-Conference/chaney.aspx (last visited on April 23, 2012).

[6] Fareed Zakaria, "A Region at War with Its History, *TIME* (April 16, 2012), available at http://www.fareedzakaria.com/home/Articles/Entries/2012/4/6_A_ Region_at_War_with_Its_History.html (last visited on April 23, 2012).

[7] Dominique Moïsi, *The Geopolitics of Emotion: How Cultures of Fear, Humiliation, and Hope Are Reshaping the World, supra,* note 1 at 5.

[8] Id. at 5-6.

[9] Id. at 61.

[10] Id. at 78.

[11] Khaled Abou El Fadl, "The Place of Tolerance in Islam," *Boston Review* (December 2001/January 2002) available at http://bostonreview.net/BR26.6/elfadl.html (last visited on August 15, 2007). The author, a distinguished Fellow in Islamic Law at UCLA, alleges that the theological premises of global terrorism derived from "the intolerant Puritanism of the Wahabi and Salafi creeds." Salafism was founded in the early 20th century, and argued, according to the author, that the demands of modernity should be responded to by "a return to the original sources of the Qur'an and Sunnah (tradition of the Prophet)." While "Wahabism narrowly defined orthodoxy, and was extremely intolerant of any creed that contradicted its own," the author argues that it "does not bear the primary responsibility for the existence of terrorist groups in Islam today." He argues that "Wahabism is distinctively inward-looking"although focused on power, it primarily asserts power over other Muslims. . . . Militant puritan groups, however, are both introverted and extroverted"they attempt to assert power against Muslims and non-Muslims. As populist movements, they are a reaction to the disempowerment most Muslims have suffered in the modern age at the hands of harshly despotic governments, and at the hands of interventionist foreign powers. These groups compensate for extreme feelings of disempowerment by extreme and vulgar claims to power. Fueled by supremacist and puritan ideological creeds, their symbolic acts of power become uncompromisingly fanatic and violent."

[12] Ekaterina Stepanova, TERRORISM IN ASYMMETRICAL CONFLICT: IDEOLOGICAL AND STRUCTURAL ASPECTS (Oxford University Press, 2008), at 85.

[13] Id. at 86.

[14] President George W. Bush, "President Discusses Global War on Terror," White House Press Release dated September 5, 2006, available at http://www.whitehouse.gov/news/releases/2006/09/20060905-4.html (last visited on August 15, 2007).

[15] *See e.g.,* Rohan Gunaratna, *Inside Al Qaeda: Global Network of Terror* (Cambridge University Press, New York)(2002) at 55, 89; *see also* F. Gregory Gause III, "Can Democracy Stop Terrorism?" *For. Aff.* (September/October 2005) available at http://www.foreignaffairs.org/20050901faessay84506/f-gregory-gause-iii/can-democracy-stop-terrorism.html (last visited on August 15, 2007).

[16] "Interestingly, Islamic tradition does not have a notion of holy war. 'Jihad' simply means to strive hard or struggle in pursuit of a just cause, and according to the Prophet of Islam, the highest form of jihad is the struggle waged to cleanse oneself from the vices of the heart." Andrea Elliott, "A Call to Jihad From Somalia, Answered in America" *NY Times* (July 12, 2009), available at http://www.nytimes.com/2009/07/12/us/12somalis.html?pagewanted=all (last visited on April 16, 2012).

[17] Sebastian Gorka, "The Age of Irregular Warfare: So What?" 58 *JFQ* 33 (2010),

available at http://www.ndu.edu/press/irregular-warfare.html (last visited on April 18, 2012).

[18] *See e.g.*, Kirsten Aiken, "Spain Withdraws Iraq War Support Following Madrid Bombings," March 16, 2004, available at http://www.abc.net.au/worldtoday/content/2004/s1066920.htm (last visited on August 6, 2007). *See also* Georgina Blakeley, *'It's politics, stupid!': the Spanish General Election of 2004.* 59 *Parliamentary Affairs* at 331-349 (2006), which states in part, "While the terrorist bombings undoubtedly influenced the general election, this article argues that a more detailed reading of the last four years of the Spanish political context shows that the change of government was not simply a result of the 'four days that changed Spain'. The Madrid bombings acted as a catalyst for change, but the desire for change had built up gradually."

[19] Reuven Paz, *Between Ideology and Strategy*, Edition 31, Vol. 3 (August 18, 2005) available at http://www.bitterlemons-international.org/previous.php?opt=1&id=98#397 (last visited on July 25, 2007).

[20] Khaled Abou El Fadl writes eloquently that, "The [Muslim] puritans construct their exclusionary and intolerant theology by reading Qur'anic verses in isolation as if the meaning of the verses were transparent–as if moral ideas and historical context were irrelevant to their interpretation. In fact, however, it is impossible to analyze these and other verses except in the overall moral thrust of the Qur'anic message." And further, "[t]he Qur'an itself refers to general moral imperatives such as mercy, justice, kindness, or goodness . . . . . [it also] recognizes the legitimate multiplicity of religious convictions and laws." Khaled Abou El Fadl, "The Place of Tolerance in Islam," *Boston Review* (December 2001/January 2002) available at http://bostonreview.net/BR26.6/elfadl.html (last visited on August 15, 2007).

[21] World Development Report "Conflict, Security and Development," (2011), available at http://wdr2011.worldbank.org/sites/default/files/pdfs/WDR2011_Full_Text.pdf (last visited on April 23, 2012).

[22] "Conflict and poverty: The economics of violence," *The Economist* (April 16, 2011) at 65.

[23] Id.

[24] Id. at 66.

[25] Guilain Denoeux & Lynn Carter, "Draft Guide to the Drivers of Violent Extremism," prepared for USAID (February 2009) at 53.

[26] Id. at 54.

[27] Id. at 56-57.

[28] Alan Kruegar, WHAT MAKES A TERRORIST (Princeton, 2004) at 3.

[29] Jane Perlez & Pirzubai Shah, "Taliban Exploit Class Rifts In Pakistan," *NY Times* (April 17, 2009), available at http://www.nytimes.com/2009/04/17/world/

asia/17pstan.html (last visited on July 4, 2009).

30 Id.

31 Sabrina Tavernise, "Pakistan's Islamic Schools Fill Void, but Fuel Militancy," *NY Times* (May 4, 2009), available at http://www.nytimes.com/2009/05/04/world/asia/04schools.html (last visited on July 4, 2009).

32 Jane Perlez & Pirzubair Shah, "Landowners Still in Exile from Unstable Pakistan Area," *NY Times* (July 28, 2009), available at http://www.nytimes.com/2009/07/28/world/asia/28swat.html (last visited on July 30, 2009).

33 Sabrina Tavernise, "Taliban Stir Rising Anger of Pakistanis," *NY Times* (June 5, 2009), available at http://www.nytimes.com/2009/06/05/world/asia/05refugees.html (last visited on July 4, 2009).

34 Id.

35 David Kilcullen, THE ACCIDENTAL GUERRILLA: FIGHTING SMALL WARS IN THE MIDST OF A BIG ONE (Oxford University Press, 2009) at 262.

36 Id. at 35.

37 Id. at 36-37.

38 Id. at 37-38.

39 Id. at 38.

40 Selig Harrison, "Pakistan's Ethnic Fault Line," *Wash. Post* (May 11, 2009, available at http://www.washingtonpost.com/wp-dyn/content/article/2009/05/10/AR2009051001959_pf.html (last visited on July 6, 2009)

41 Id.

42 Id.

43 Maleeha Lodhi, "The Future of Pakistan-U.S. Relations: Opportunities and Challenges," (INSS Special Report, April 2009) at 2.

44 Selig Harrison, "Pakistan's Ethnic Fault Line," *Wash. Post, supra,* note 40.

45 Id.

46 Maleeha Lodhi, "The Future of Pakistan-U.S. Relations: Opportunities and Challenges", *supra,* note 43 at 5.

47 Joseph Collins, "Afghanistan: Winning a Three Block War," XXIV *J. Conflict Stud.*, No. 2 (2004), available at http://www.lib.unb.ca/Texts/JCS/contents/winter04.html (last visited on July 8, 2009). The author goes on to state in no uncertain terms that, "[Afghanistan's] rulers, the Taliban-an illegitimate offspring of Pakistani intelligence services-were among the most ignorant, cruel, sadistic, misogynistic, and inefficient tyrants on all of history."

48 *See e.g.,* "The Taliban Opium Connection," (September 11, 2008), available at

http://www.terroristplanet.com/opium.htm (last visited on July 8, 2009). The articles states that, "In 2007, five provinces which are under Taliban influence and control: Helmand, Kandahar, Uruzgan, Nimroz and Farah were responsible for 77.7% of the country's opium cultivation. Helmand province alone produced 53% of the nation's total crop.

Opium is fuelling the war in Afghanistan and without this crop it would be very difficult for the group to raise the capital needed to finance their war in Afghanistan and to conduct terrorist attacks in Pakistan as well as the Kashmir region. Opium is a big part of what is allowing the Taliban to become a formidable enemy once again after a lengthy rebuilding period following the U.S. and Coalition invasion following 9/11 that removed the Taliban from control over the country."

[49] Sean Alfano, "Taliban Violence Surges in Afghanistan: Dozens Killed; NATO Declines 2,500 Extra Troops as Insurgency Grows," *CBS News*, available at http://www.cbsnews.com/stories/2006/09/13/terror/main2007059.shtml; Animesh Raol, "Enduring Taliban Violence Push Pakistan to the Brink," *Asia Security Initiative* (MacArthur Foundation), available at http://asiasecurity.macfound.org/blog/entry/enduring_taliban_violence_push_pakistan_to_the_brink/ (last visited on July 8, 2009).

[50] Carlotta Gall, "Another Insurgency Gains in Pakistan," *NY Times* (July 12, 2009), available at http://www.nytimes.com/2009/07/12/world/asia/12baluchistan.html (last visited on July 12, 2009).

[51] Huma Imtiaz, "US Cogressman tables bill for Baloch right to independence," *Express Tribune* (February 18, 212), available at http://tribune.com.pk/story/338079/us-congressman-tables-resolution-calling-for-independence-of-baloch/ (last visited on April 18, 2012).

[52] Id.

[53] *See* Chidanand Rajghatta, "Balochistan resolution drives Pakistan crazy," *Times of India* (February 18, 2012), available at http://articles.timesofindia.indiatimes.com/2012-02-18/pakistan/31074736_1_balochistan-baluchistan-province-kalat (last visited on April 18, 2012), where Pakistanis were questioning the U.S. commitment to Pakistan's sovereignty. *See also*, Dana Rohrabacher, "Why I won't apologize to Pakistan," *Wash. Post* (April 8, 2012) at A17.

[54] F. Gregory Gause III, "Can Democracy Stop Terrorism?" *For. Aff.* (September/October 2005), available at http://www.foreignaffairs.org/20050901faessay84506/f-gregory-gause-iii/can-democracy-stop-terrorism.html (last visited on August 15, 2007).

[55] Guilain Denoeux & Lynn Carter, "Draft Guide to the Drivers of Violent Extremism," endnote25, *supra*, at 51.

[56] Id. at vii-ix.

[57] David Kilcullen, THE ACCIDENTAL GUERRILLA, endnote 35, *supra*, at 258.

[58] Id. at 14.

[59] Id. 15-16.

[60] Franz Fanon, THE WRETCHED OF THE EARTH (Grove Press, 2004).

[61] "Lashkar-e-Taiba," *NY Times* (April 3, 2012), available at http://topics.nytimes. com/top/reference/timestopics/organizations/l/lashkaretaiba/index.html (last visited on May 22, 2012).

[62] *See e.g.,* A.K. Roy, "Afghanistan Factor in Central and South Asian Politics," *Kashmir Information Network,* available at http://www.kashmir-information. com/afghanistan/akray.html (last visited on May 22, 2012).

[63] Id. at 21.

[64] Id. 14-15.

[65] *See e.g.,* James S. Robbins, "Al-Qaeda Versus Democracy," 9 *J. Int'l Security Affairs* (Fall 2005) available at http://www.securityaffairs.org/issues/2005/09/ robbins.php (last visited on August 15, 2007).

[66] "Islam's philosophical divide: Dreaming of a caliphate," *The Economist* (August 6, 2011), available at http://www.economist.com/node/21525400 (last visited on April 18, 2012).

[67] *See generally* Amartya Sen, DEVELOPMENT AS FREEDOM, (Oxford University Press, 1999).

CHAPTER 3

[1] *See e.g.,* C.J. Chivers, "Rebels Make Gains in Blunting Syrian Air Attacks," *NY Times* (September 26, 2012), available at http://www.nytimes.com/2012/09/27/ world/middleeast/rebels-make-gains-in-blunting-syrian-air-attacks.html? nl=todaysheadlines&emc=edit_th_20120927 (last visited on September 27, 2012).

[2] "Tunisia marks the 1st anniversary of the Arab Spring," *USAToday* (January 14, 2012), available at http://www.usatoday.com/news/world/story/2012-01-14/ tunisia-revolution-anniversary/52552862/1 (last visited on April 30, 2012).

[3] Id. For a masterful interactive timeline of all the salient events of the Arab Spring in countries ranging from Algeria to Yemen, *see* Garry Blight, *et al,* "Arab spring: an interactive timeline of Middle East protests," *Guardian* (January 5, 2012) available at http://www.guardian.co.uk/world/interactive/2011/mar/22/middle- east-protest-interactive-timeline (last visited on April 30, 2012).

[4] Seth Sherwood, "Tunisia After the Revolution," *NY Times* (April 5, 2012), available at http://travel.nytimes.com/2012/04/08/travel/tunisia-after-the-revolution.html? pagewanted=all (last visited on May 2, 2012).

[5] "Post-revolutionary Tunisia: moving ahead," *The Economist* (July 16, 2011),

available at http://www.economist.com/node/18958251 (last visited on May 2, 2012).

[6] Nazali Fathi & Michael Slackman, "Iran Stepping Up Efforts to Quell Election Protest," *NY Times* (June 24, 2009), available at http://www.nytimes.com/2009/06/25/world/middleeast/25iran.html (last visited on May 1, 2012).

[7] "Pro-democracy protests in Iran: Still Defiant in Iran," *The Economist* (June 17, 2009), available at http://www.economist.com/node/13854486 (last visited on May 1, 2012).

[8] Lev Grossman, "Iran's Protests: Twitter: the Medium of the Moment," *Time* (June 17, 2009), available at http://www.time.com/time/world/article/0,8599, 1905125,00. html (last visited on May 1, 2012).

[9] Id.

[10] "Coverage of the protests: but the real winner was an unusual hybrid of old and new media," *The Economist* (June 17, 200(0, available at http://www.economist.com/node/13856224 (last visited on May 1, 2012).

[11] "Egypt court to deliver Mubarak trial verdict on 2 June," *BBCNews* (February 22, 2012), available at http://www.bbc.co.uk/news/world-middle-east-17120915 (last visited on May 3, 2012).

[12] David Kirkpatrick, "New Turmoil in Egypt Greets Mixed Verdict for Mubarak," *NY Times* (June 2, 2012), available at http://www.nytimes.com/2012/06/03/world/middleeast/egypt-hosni-mubarak-life-sentence-prison.html?pagewanted=all& pagewanted=print (last visited on September 26, 2012).

[13] Id.

[14] Jeremy Sharp, "Egypt in Transition," *Cong. Research Service* (November 18, 2011), RL 33003, available at http://pomed.org/wordpress/wp-content/uploads/2011/11/Egypt-in-Transition-CRS-Report.pdf (last visited on May 2, 2012).

[15] Id. at 10.

[16] Id. at 6.

[17] David Kirkpatrick, "Egyptians Gather on First Anniversary of Revolt," *NY Times* (January 25, 2012), available at http://www.nytimes.com/2012/01/26/world/middleeast/egyptians-mark-anniversary-of-revolt-in-tahrir-square.html? pagewanted=all (last visited on May 2, 2012).

[18] "Egypt News—Presidential Elections, May 2012," *NY Times (World),* May 2, 2012, available at http://topics.nytimes.com/top/news/international/countriesandterritories/egypt/index.html (last visited on May 3, 2012).

[19] David Kirkpatrick, "Egyptians Gather on First Anniversary of Revolt," *NY Times* (January 25, 2012), available at http://www.nytimes.com/2012/01/26/world/middleeast/egyptians-mark-anniversary-of-revolt-in-tahrir-square.

html?pagewanted=all (last visited on May 2, 2012).

[20] David Kirkpatrick, "Authorities Bar 3 Leading candidates in Egypt Race," *NY Times* (April 14, 2012), available at http://www.nytimes.com/2012/04/15/world/middleeast/ten-candidates-barred-from-egyptian-election.html?pagewanted=all

[21] Id.

[22] Kareem Fahim & Mayy el Sheikh, "Fierce Clashes Erupt in Egypt Ahead of Presidential Vote, *NY Times* (May 2, 2012), available at http://www.nytimes.com/2012/05/03/world/middleeast/deadly-clashes-erupt-in-egypt-ahead-of-vote.html (last visited on May 3, 2012).

[23] "Egypt News—Presidential Elections, May 2012," *NY Times (World)*, May 2, 2012, available at http://topics.nytimes.com/top/news/international/countriesandterritories/egypt/index.html (last visited on May 3, 2012).

[24] "Celebration in Egypt as Morsi Declared Winner," *Aljazeera.com* available at http://www.aljazeera.com/news/middleeast/2012/06/201262412445190400.html (last visited on September 26, 2012).

[25] Kareem Fahim, "Egypt's Military and President Escalate their Power Struggle," *NY Times* (July 9, 2012), available at http://www.nytimes.com/2012/07/10/world/middleeast/egypt-tension-after-order-to-reconvene-parliament.html?ref=world &_r=0 (last visited on September 26, 2012).

[26] Kareem Fahim, "In Upheaval for Egypt, Morsi Forces Out Military Chiefs," *NY Times* (August 12, 2012), available at http://www.nytimes.com/2012/08/13/world/middleeast/egyptian-leader-ousts-military-chiefs.html?pagewanted=all (last visited on September 26, 2012).

[27] David Kirkpatrick, "Mass March by Cairo Women in Protest Over Abuse by Soldiers," *NY Times* (December 25, 2011), available at http://www.nytimes.com/2011/12/21/world/middleeast/violence-enters-5th-day-as-egyptian-general-blames-protesters.html?pagewanted=all (last visited on May 2, 2012).

[28] David Kirkpatrick, "Islamist Victors in Egypt Seeking Shift by Hamas," *NY Times* (March 24, 2012), available at http://www.nytimes.com/2012/03/24/world/middleeast/egypts-election-victors-seek-shift-by-hamas-to-press-israel.html?pagewanted=all (last visited on May 3, 2012).

[29] Id.

[30] Id. *See also* Mark Landler & Steven, "Obama Sees '67 Borders as Starting Point for Peace Deal," *NY Times* (May 19, 2011), available at http://www.nytimes.com/2011/05/20/world/middleeast/20speech.html?pagewanted=all (last visited on May 3, 2012).

[31] Id.

[32] Nicholas Kristof, "Repressing Democracy, With American Arms," *NY Times* (December 17, 2011), available at http://www.nytimes.com/2011/12/18/opinion/

sunday/kristof-repressing-democracy-with-american-arms.html (last visited on May 3, 2012). It should also be noted that in mid-march 2012, the Saudi Government sent a convoy of tanks and heavy artillery across the 16-mile King Fahd Causeway between Saudi Arabia and Bahrain to crush democracy protests in Bahrain. *See* Helene Cooper & Robert Worth, "In Arab Spring, Obama Finds a Sharp Test," *NY Times* (September 24, 2012), available at http://www.nytimes.com/2012/09/25/us/politics/arab-spring-proves-a-harsh-test-for-obamas-diplomatic-skill.html?pagewanted=all&gwh=A12BDA9658191F1EA1676C7F B6659D13 (last visited on September 26, 2012).

[33] Rick Gladstone, "Bahrain Is Criticized for Its 'Torrent' of Tear Gas Use," *NY Times* (August 1, 2012), available at http://www.nytimes.com/2012/08/01/world/middleeast/bahrain-criticized-for-torrent-of-tear-gas-use.html?_r=0 (last visited on September 24, 2012).

[34] Id.

[35] Id.

[36] Anthony Shadid, "Bahrain is Nervously Awaiting Report on Its Forgotten Revolt," *NY Times* (November 21, 2011), available at http://www.nytimes.com/2011/11/22/world/middleeast/bahrain-nervously-awaits-revolt-reports-findings.html?pagewanted=all (last visited on May 3, 2012).

[37] Id.

[38] Nada Bahkri, "Torture used on Protesters in Bahrain, Report Finds," *NY Times* (November 23, 2011), available at http://www.nytimes.com/2011/11/24/world/middleeast/report-details-excessive-force-used-against-bahrain-protests.html?pagewanted=all (last visited on May 3, 2012).

[39] Id.

[40] Rick Gladstone, "Bahrain Is Criticized for Its 'Torrent' of Tear Gas Use," *NY Times* (August 1, 2012), available at http://www.nytimes.com/2012/08/01/world/middleeast/bahrain-criticized-for-torrent-of-tear-gas-use.html?_r=0 (last visited on September 24, 2012).

[41] Anthony Shadid, "Bahrain is Nervously Awaiting Report on Its Forgotten Revolt," *NY Times* (November 21, 2011), available at http://www.nytimes.com/2011/11/22/world/middleeast/bahrain-nervously-awaits-revolt-reports-findings.html?pagewanted=all (last visited on May 3, 2012).

[42] Id.

[43] "The Arab Spring: A Long March," *The Economist* (February 18, 2011), available at http://www.economist.com/node/21547853 (last visited on May 3, 2012). *See also* "The Arab Awakening: Revolution Spinning in the Wind," *The Economist* (July 14, 2010), available at http://www.economist.com/node/18958237 (last visited on May 3, 2012).

[44] "The Arab Awakening: Revolution Spinning in the Wind," *The Economist* (July

14, 2010), available at http://www.economist.com/node/18958237 (last visited on May 3, 2012).

45 Stephen Farrell, "Demonstrations Whisper of an Arab Spring in Jordan," *NY Times* (February 9, 2012), available at http://www.nytimes.com/2012/02/10/world/middleeast/jordan-protests-whisper-of-an-arab-spring.html (last visited on May 3, 2012).

46 "Syria," *NY Times (World)* (May 2, 2012), available at http://topics.nytimes.com/top/news/international/countriesandterritories/syria/index.html (last visited on May 3, 2012).

47 Steven Erlanger, "Push in Paris for More Pressure on Syria as Money Ebbs and Cease-Fire Wobbles," *NY Times* (April 17, 2012), available at http://www.nytimes.com/2012/04/18/world/middleeast/russia-says-outside-forces-threaten-syrian-cease-fire.html (last visited on May 3, 2012).

48 Id.

49 David Kirkpatrick, "Airstrikes Push Waves of Syrians to Jordanian Camps," *NY Times* (September 1, 20120), available at http://www.nytimes.com/2012/09/02/world/middleeast/airstrikes-push-syrians-to-refugee-camps-in-jordan.html?pagewanted=all&_moc.semityn.www (last visited on September 26, 2012).

50 Steven Erlanger & Rick Gladstone, "France Grants Its Recognition to Syria rebels," *NY Times*, November 13, 2012.

51 Mark Kennedy, "Syria issue 'more complex than Libyan' Harper tells U.S. think-tank," *Canada.com* (April 2, 2012), available at http://www.canada.com/news/Syrian+issue+more+complex+than+Libyan+Harper+tells+think+tank/6399945/story.html (last visited on May 3, 2012).

52 Tim Arango, "Syrian War's Spillover Threatens a Fragile Iraq," *NY Times* (September 24, 2012), available at http://www.nytimes.com/2012/09/25/world/middleeast/iraq-faces-new-perils-from-syrias-civil-war.html?pagewanted=all (last visited on September 26, 2012).

53 Rod Nordland, "Al Qaeda Taking Deadly New Role in Syria Conflict," *NY Times* (July 24, 2012), available at http://www.nytimes.com/2012/07/25/world/middleeast/al-qaeda-insinuating-its-way-into-syrias-conflict.html?pagewanted=all (last visited on September 26, 2012).

54 Michael Schmidt, "From a Few Iraqis, a Word to Libyans on Liberation," *NY Times* (August 29, 2011), available at http://www.nytimes.com/2011/08/30/world/middleeast/30baghdad.html (last visited on May 3, 2012).

55 Rick Gladstone, "Iran Concerned West Will Benefit From Arab Uprisings," *NY Times* (August 31, 2011), available at http://www.nytimes.com/2011/09/01/world/middleeast/01tehran.html (last visited on May 8, 2012).

56 Saeed Dehghan, "Tehran supports the Arab Spring . . . but not in Syria," *Guardian* (April 18, 2011), available at http://www.guardian.co.uk/commentisfree/2011/

apr/18/iran-arab-spring-syria-uprisings (last visited on May 8, 2012).

[57] Rick Gladstone, "Iran Concerned West Will Benefit From Arab Uprisings," *NY Times* (August 31, 2011), available at http://www.nytimes.com/2011/09/01/world/middleeast/01tehran.html (last visited on May 8, 2012).

[58] David Herszenhorn, "Putin Winds, but Opposition Keeps Pressing," *NY Times* (March 4, 2012), available at http://www.nytimes.com/2012/03/05/world/europe/russia-votes-in-presidential-election.html?pagewanted=all (last visited on May 8, 2012).

[59] Thomas Friedman, "Politics of Dignity," *NY Times* (January 31, 2012), available at http://www.nytimes.com/2012/02/01/opinion/friedman-the-politics-of-dignity.html (last visited on May 8, 2012).

[60] *See* David Herszhenhorn & Ellen Barry, "Large Anti-Putin Protest Signals Growing Resolve," *NY Times* (June 12, 2012), available at http://www.nytimes.com/2012/06/13/world/europe/anti-putin-demonstrators-gather-in-moscow.html?pagewanted=all (last visited on September 24, 2012).

[61] David Herszhenhorn & Ellen Barry, "Russia Demands U.S. End Support of Democracy Groups," *NY Times* (September 18, 2012), available at http://www.nytimes.com/2012/09/19/world/europe/russia-demands-us-end-pro-democracy-work.html?pagewanted=all (last visited on September 24, 2012).

[62] Jeffrey Gettleman, "Somalia's Insurgents Embrace Twitter as a Weapon," *NY Times* (December 14, 2011), available at http://www.nytimes.com/2011/12/15/world/africa/somalias-rebels-embrace-twitter-as-a-weapon.html (last visited on May 8, 2012).

[63] Jeffrey Gettleman, "U.S. Considering Combating Somali Militants' Twitter Use," *NY Times* (December 10, 2011), available at http://www.nytimes.com/2011/12/20/world/africa/us-considers-combating-shabab-militants-twitter-use.html (last visited on May 8, 2012).

[64] Robert Worth & Eric Schmitt, "Qaeda Link Seen in Deadly Blast in Yemen Capital," *NY Times* (May 21, 2012), available at http://www.nytimes.com/2012/05/22/world/middleeast/suicide-attack-in-yemen.html (last visited on May 22, 2012).

[65] Id.

[66] Alissa Rubin, "Taliban Using Modern Means to Add Sway," *NY Times* (October 4, 2011), available at http://www.nytimes.com/2011/10/05/world/asia/taliban-using-modern-means-to-add-to-sway.html?pagewanted=all (last visited on May 8, 2012).

[67] "Riots in Britain: Anarchy in the UK," *The Economist* (August 13, 2011) at 14. *See also* "Riots in England: The first this time," *The Economist* (August 13, 2011) at 51.

[68] "Riotous Behavior," *The Economist* (June 30, 2012) at 14.

[69] Rick Gladstone, "Anti-American Protests Flare Beyond the Mideast," *NY Times* (September 14, 2012), available at http://www.nytimes.com/2012/09/15/world/middleeast/anti-american-protests-over-film-enter-4th-day.html?pagewanted=all&gwh=CAEC01A82AC94B5B20159A13244D8F9A (last visited on September 26, 2012).

[70] David Kirkpatrick, "Cultural Clash Fuels Muslims Angry at Online Video," *NY Times* (September 16, 2102), available at http://www.nytimes.com/2012/09/17/world/middleeast/muslims-rage-over-film-fueled-by-culture-divide.html?pagewanted=all&gwh=77F43B76F5225976B018995EC5BA8E86 (last visited on September 26, 2012).

[71] Id.

[72] Suliman Alizway & Kareem Fahim, "Angry Libyans Target Militias, Forcing Flight," *NY Times* (September 21, 212), available at http://www.nytimes.com/2012/09/22/world/africa/pro-american-libyans-besiege-militant-group-in-benghazi.html? pagewanted=all&_moc.semityn.www (last visited on September 26, 2012).

[73] Steven Lee Myers, "Clinton Suggests Link to Qaeda Offshoot in Deadly Libya Attack," *NY Times* (September 26, 2012), available at http://www.nytimes.com/2012/09/27/world/africa/clinton-cites-clear-link-between-al-qaeda-and-attack-in-libya.html?nl=todaysheadlines&emc=edit_th_20120927 (last visited on September 27, 2012).

[74] Id. *See also*, Eric Schmitt & David Kirkpatrick, "U.S. Is Tracking Killers in Attack on Libyan Mission," *NY Times* (October 2, 2012), available at http://www.nytimes.com/2012/10/03/world/africa/us-said-to-be-preparing-potential-targets-tied-to-libya-attack.html?pagewanted=all (last visited on October 6, 2012).

[75] David Kirkpatrick, Helene Cooper & Mark Landler, "Egypt, Hearing from Obama, Moves to Heal Rift From Protests, *NY Times* (September 13, 2012), available at http://www.nytimes.com/2012/09/14/world/middleeast/egypt-hearing-from-obama-moves-to-heal-rift-from-protests.html?pagewanted=all&gwh=AE9D3AA1C2D3CDE8F426B727DFD91E9D (last visited on September 26, 2012).

[76] *See* Steven Lee Myers, "To Back Democracy, U.S. Prepares to Cut $1 Billion From Egypt's Debt," *NY Times* (September 3, 2012), available at http://www.nytimes.com/2012/09/04/world/middleeast/us-prepares-economic-aid-to-bolster-democracy-in-egypt.html?pagewanted=all (last visited on September 26, 2012). The United States is supporting a $4.8 billion IMF loan being extended to Egypt along with $375 million in financing and loan guarantees from U.S. investors, plus the United States is establishing a $60 million investment fund for Egyptian businesses. Moreover, $1 billion in Egyptian debt owed to the U.S. under the Food for Peace program may be relieved out of a total $3 billion owed by Egypt to the United States. Additionally, debt swaps to relieve other Egyptian debt are being considered by the Obama Administration.

[77] Mary Beth Sheridan, "Zawahiri Named New Al Qaeda Leader," *Wash. Post* (June 16, 2011).

[78] Declan Walsh & Eric Schmitt, "Drone Strike Killed No. 2 in Al Qaeda, U.S. Officials Say," *NY Times* (June 5, 2012), available at http://www.nytimes.com/2012/06/06/world/asia/qaeda-deputy-killed-in-drone-strike-in-pakistan.html (last visited on June 7, 2012).

[79] David Kirkpatrick, "New Turmoil in Egypt Greets Mixed Verdict for Mubarak," *NY Times* (June 2, 2012), available at http://www.nytimes.com/2012/06/03/world/middleeast/egypt-hosni-mubarak-life-sentence-prison.html?hp (last visited June 7, 2012).

[80] Declan Walsh, "My mother said democracy is best revenge–Bhutto's son," *Guardian* (December 30, 2007, available at http://www.guardian.co.uk/world/2007/dec/31/pakistan.topstories35 (last visited on October 6, 2012).

CHAPTER 4

[1] Alan Beyerchen, *Clausewitz, Non-Linearity and the Unpredictability of War*, available at http://www.clausewitz.com/CWZHOME/Beyerchen/CWZandNonlinearity.htm#1 (last visited on August 2, 2007).

[2] Robert Scales, *Clausewitz and WW IV, Armed Forces J.* (July 2006) available at http://www.armedforcesjournal.com/2006/07/1866019 49 (last visited on August 2, 2007).

[3] Janine Davidson, "Principles of Modern American Counterinsurgency: Evolution and Debate," (June 8, 2009), available at http://www.brookings.edu/~/media/Files/rc/papers/2009/0608_counterinsurgency_davidson/0608_counterinsurgency_davidson.pdf. (last visited on July 2, 2009.) Apparently. Clausewitz's non-linear view of war and historical events in general were commented on favorably in relation to the theory of dialectical materialism by Engels and Lenin.

[4] Id. at 18-19.

[5] Id.

[6] Id.

[7] Id.

[8] Thomas Hammes, "Insurgency: Modern Warfare Evolves into a Fourth Generation," *Strategic Forum*, INSS (January 2004) at 1, 2, available at http://www.au.af.mil/au/awc/awcgate/ndu/sf214.pdf (last visited on July 6, 2009).

[9] Id. at 2.

[10] Id. at 3.

[11] Id. at 6.

[12] Id. at 2.

[13] General Charles C. Krulak, 'Three Block War', *Vital Speeches of the Day*, Vol. 64, Issue 5 (December 15, 1997).

[14] "The Marines' Three-Block War in Iraq," *Center for Defense Info.*, (October 28, 2003), available at http://www.cdi.org/friendlyversion/printversion.cfm? documentID=1834 (last visited on July 8, 2009).

[15] Id.

[16] Id.

[17] Joseph Collins, "Afghanistan: Winning a Three Block War," XXIV *J. Conflict Stud.*, No. 2 (2004), available at http://www.lib.unb.ca/Texts/JCS/contents/ winter04.html (last visited on July 8, 2009).

[18] "The Marines' Three-Block War in Iraq," *supra*.

[19] Joseph Collins, "Afghanistan: Winning a Three Block War," *supra*.

[20] Id.

[21] Charles Krulak," The Strategic Corporal: Leadership in the Three Block War," *Marines Mag.*, (January 1999), available at http://www.au.af.mil/au/awc/awcgate/ usmc/strategic_corporal.htm (last visited on July 8, 2009).

[22] Charles Krulak, "'Cultivating Intuitive Decision Making," *Marine Corps Gazette* (May 1999), available at http://www.au.af.mil/au/awc/awcgate/usmc/ cultivating_intuitive_d-m.htm (last visited on July 8, 2009).

[23] Id.

[24] Id.

[25] Id.

[26] Id.

[27] Id.

[28] Id.

[29] Id.

[30] "Counterinsurgency," Introduction, available at http://www.usgcoin.org/library/ doctrine/COIN-FM3-24.pdf (last visited on July 8, 2009).

[31] Id., Section 7-20 at 7-4.

[32] Benedict Carey, "In Battle, Hunches Prove to be Invaluable," *NY Times* (July 28, 2009), available at http://www.nytimes.com/2009/07/28/health/research/28brain. html (last visited on July 30, 2009).

[33] Richard Haas, "The Age of Nonpolarity: What Will Follow U.S. Dominance," *For. Aff.* (May/June 2008), available at http://www.foreignaffairs.com/articles/63397/

richard-n-haass/the-age-of-nonpolarity (last visited on July 4, 2009). See footnote 66.

[34] Martin Buber, *I AND THOU* (Touchstone, 1970).

[35] *See* "Martin Buber's *I and Thou,*" available at http://www.angelfire.com/md2/timewarp/buber.html (last visited on July 8, 2009).

[36] Id.

[37] *See* Kate Clark, "Handing over Night Raids," September 4, 2012, *Afghan Analysts Network*, available at http://aan-afghanistan.com/index.asp?id=2647 (last visited on April 12, 2012).

[38] David Zucchino & Laura King, "U.S. to limit airstrikes in Afghanistan to help reduce civilian deaths," *LA Times* (June 23, 2009), available at http://articles.latimes.com/2009/jun/23/world/fg-afghan-air23 (last visited on May 16, 2012).

[39] Ashraf Ghani, "A Ten-Year Framework for Afghanistan: Executing the Obama Plan . . . and Beyond," *Atlantic Council* (April 2009), available at http://www.acus.org/files/publication_pdfs/65/AfghanistanReport-200904.pdf, at 26.

[40] Rajiv Chandrasekaran, "A Fight for Ordinary Peace," *Wash. Post* (July 12, 2009), available at http://www.washingtonpost.com/wp-dyn/content/article/2009/07/11/AR2009071102815.html (last visited on July 13, 2009).

[41] Id.

[42] Lecture presentation by General Patraeus at the National Defense University on April 29, 2009, *see e.g.,* http://www.ndu.edu/info/WhatsNew/pastevents.cfm (last visited on July 11, 2009).

[43] Notes on FM 3-24 Counterinsurgency (January 28, 2008), available at http://www.2ndbn5thmar.com/coinman/Notes%20on%20FM%203-24%20Counterinsurgency.pdf at 1 (last visited on July 8, 2009).

[44] John Burns, "Britain Urges Afghan Political Effort," *NY Times* (July 28, 2009), available at http://www.nytimes.com/2009/07/28/world/asia/28afghan.html?_r=1 (last visited on July 30, 2009).

[45] Id.

[46] Notes on FM 3-24 Counterinsurgency (January 28, 2008), available at http://www.2ndbn5thmar.com/coinman/Notes%20on%20FM%203-24%20Counterinsurgency.pdf at 1, *supra*.

[47] Rudyard Kipling, "The White Man's Burden," (1899), available at http://www.fordham.edu/halsall/mod/Kipling.html (last visited on July 9, 2009).

[48] Frank Hoffman, "Principles for the Savage Wars of Peace," at 1, available at http://www.smallwars.quantico.usmc.mil/search/Articles/SavageWarsofPeace.pdf (last visited on July 9, 2009).

[49] Montgomery McFate, "Anthropology and Counterinsurgency: The Strange Story

of Their Curious Relationship," *Mil. Rev.* (March-April 2005) at 24, available at http://www.au.af.mil/au/awc/awcgate/milreview/mcfate.pdf (last visited on July 9, 2009).

[50] Robert Scales, "Culture-Centric Warfare," *Naval Institute Proceedings* (October 2004), available at http://www.military.com/NewContent/0,13190,NI_1004_Culture-P1,00.html (last visited on July 9, 2009).

[51] Frank Hoffman, "Principles for the Savage Wars of Peace," at 7-8, *supra.*

[52] Id. at 8.

[53] William Wunderle, "Through the Lens of Cultural Awareness: A Primer for US Armed Forces Deploying to Arab and Middle Eastern Countries," (Combat Studies Institute Press, 2006) at 9, available at http://www-cgsc.army.mil/carl/download/csipubs/wunderle.pdf (last visited on July 9, 2009).

[54] Robert Scales, "Culture-Centric Warfare," *supra,* note 50.

[55] Id.

[56] Frank Hoffman, "Principles for the Savage Wars of Peace," at 9, *supra.*

[57] Montgomery McFate, "Anthropology and Counterinsurgency: The Strange Story of Their Curious Relationship," *supra,* at 24.

[58] David Kilcullen, THE ACCIDENTAL GUERRILLA: FIGHTING SMALL WARS IN THE MIDST OF A BIG ONE (Oxford University Press, 2009) at 27.

[59] Robert Scales, "Culture-Centric Warfare," *supra,* note 50..

[60] Counterinsurgency (FM 3-24), *supra,* Section 7-16 at 7-3. *See also* Chaitra Hardison, *et al,* "Cross-Cultural Skills for Deployed Air Force Personnel," RAND 2009, available at http://www.rand.org/pubs/monographs/2009/RAND_MG811.pdf (last visited on July 8, 2009).

[61] Robert Scales, "Culture-Centric Warfare," *supra,* note 50..

[62] Sarah Sewall, "Ethics on the Battlefield," *SFGate* (July 1, 2007), available at http://www.sfgate.com/cgi-bin/article.cgi?file=/c/a/2007/07/01/EDG3IQ8J6F1.DTL (last visited on July 9, 2009).

[63] Id.

[64] *See* Stanford Encyclopedia of Philosophy, "War," available at http://plato.stanford.edu/entries/war/ (last visited on July 9, 2009). Cf. *jus ad bellum* which means that a state may launch a war only for the right reason. The just causes most frequently mentioned include: self-defense from external attack; the defense of others from such; the protection of innocents from brutal, aggressive regimes; and punishment for a grievous wrongdoing which remains uncorrected.

[65] Neta Crawford, "A New Soldier: Non-Violent Conflict Transformation Disciplines for Winning Hearts and Minds," (May 2009), at 8-9, draft made available to the author by the National Defense University, Institute for National Security Ethics

and Leadership.

[66] Id. at 9.

[67] Id. at 14.

[68] Paul Lederach. THE MORAL IMAGINATION: THE ART AND SOUL OF PEACEBUILDING (Oxford University Press, 2005) at 39.

[69] "Stability Operations," U.S. Army Field Manual (FM) 3-07 (October 6, 2008), available at http://usacac.army.mil/cac2/repository/FM307/FM3-07.pdf (last visited on July 10, 2009), Sec. 1-23 at 1-6.

[70] Id. at Sec. 1-25 at 1-6.

[71] Greg Jaffe, "Pakistan fertilizer gets U.S. interest," *Wash. Post* (November 26, 2011), at A1, available at http://www.washingtonpost.com/world/national-security/to-stop-afghan-bombs-a-focus-on-pakistani-fertilizer/2011/11/23/gIQAg6j0wN_ story.html (last visited on April 12, 2012).

CHAPTER 5

[1] Carl von Clausewitz, ON WAR ed. and trans. Michael Howard and Peter Paret. (Princeton University Press, 1976) at 87, 89.

[2] Antonio Munera IV, "Bridging the Gap Between Instability and Order: Establishing a Constabulary Capacity in the Department of Defense for 21st Century Stability and Reconstruction Operations," available at http://www.dtic.mil/cgi-bin/GetT RDoc?AD=ADA450713&Location=U2&doc=GetTRDoc.pdf (last visited on July 3, 2009).

[3] *See* RAND, AMERICA'S ROLE IN NATION-BUILDING: FROM GERMANY TO IRAQ (RAND 2003) (James Dobbins, *et al*, eds.) at xxv-xxvi, 165-66.

[4] Id. at Table S.3 at xxxi.

[5] Id. at xxxvii.

[6] *See generally*, Jose E. Alvarez, "Crimes of State/Crimes of Hate: Lessons from Rwanda," 24 *Yale J. Int'l L.* 365 (1999).

[7] RAND, AMERICA'S ROLE IN NATION-BUILDING: FROM GERMANY TO IRAQ (RAND 2003), *supra*, at 21.

[8] Id. at xxv-xxvi.

[9] F. Gregory Gause III, "Can Democracy Stop Terrorism?" *For. Aff.* (September/October 2005) available at http://www.foreignaffairs.org/20050901faessay84506/f-gregory-gause-iii/can-democracy-stop-terrorism.html (last visited on August 15, 2007).

[10] Ben N. Dunlop, "State Failure and the Use of Force in the Age of Terror,"

available at http://www.bc.edu/schools/law/lawreviews/meta-elements/journals/
bciclr/27_2/09_TXT.htm (last visited on August 16, 2007).

[11] *See* Kimberly Marten, ENFORCING THE PEACE: LEARNING FROM THE
IMPERIAL PAST (Columbia University Press, 2004) at 4, see generally, Chapter
3.

[12] Id. at 147.

[13] Id. at 146-47.

[14] Id. at 155.

[15] Id. at 165.

[16] Kenneth Clark, THE ROMANTIC REBELLION: ROMANTIC VERSUS
CLASSIC ART (Harper & Row 1973). "During the second half of the eighteenth
century, when the spirit of revolution was rising through Europe, a division
appeared in all the arts, deeper and more radical than any that had preceded it.
Rivalry arose between the two schools of painting, the Romantic and the Classic.
The doctrine of Classic art aspired to the ideal found in Graco-[sic] Roman
antiquities; subjects were drawn from episodes in antique history or poetry that
pointed to a moral — acts of self-sacrifice or patriotism. Romantic art appealed to
the emotions, in particular, the fear and exhilaration aroused by storm, bloodshed
and ferocity, so prevalent at the time. The emotional effect of a picture was
heightened by color, violent light and shade and exaggerated movement, made
shockingly natural — far removed from the tranquility and sculptural forms of
classicism. In practice, however, the two schools overlapped. Both attached
importance to subject matter and looked to the past for it. "Every great classical
artist was a romantic at heart and vice versa; the distinction between them is
more conventional than real," writes Kenneth Clark; the "Romantic Rebellion"
in painting emerged from the spirit of the times." (Excerpt from the front book
jacket.)

[17] *See* Liberal Studies class discussion on October 11, 1994, by Ian Johnston of
Malaspina University-College, Nanaimo. The text was later revised for a lecture
delivered on October 2, 1996, and available at *http://www.mala.bc.ca/~johnstoi/
introser/romantic.htm* (last visited on August 6, 2007).

[18] *See* http://www.msnbc.msn.com/id/19745684/ (last visited on August 28, 2007).

[19] Ambassador Chan Heng Chee, "Singapore's Treatment of Terrorists," *Wash. Post*
(June 11, 2009), available at http://www.washingtonpost.com/wp-dyn/content/
article/2009/06/10/AR2009061003697.html (last visited on July 10, 2009).

[20] *See* Angel Rabasa, Cheryl Benard, Peter Chalk, C. Christine Fair, Theodore W.
Karasik, Rollie Lal, Ian O. Lesser, David E. Thaler, "U.S. Strategy in the Muslim
World After 9/11," available at http://www.rand.org/pubs/research_briefs/2005/
RAND_RB151.pdf (last visited on August 16, 2007), which proposes, *inter alia*,
that the curricula of madrassas (Islamic-based religious schools) be reformed,

that moderate or "civil Islam" be supported to foster moderation and modernity, and that closer military-to-military ties to key Muslim countries be fostered. *See also*, Angel Rabasa, Cheryl Benard, Lowell H. Schwartz, Peter Sickle, "Building Moderate Muslim Networks," *RAND.org.*, (2007), available at http://www.rand.org/pubs/monographs/2007/RAND_MG574.pdf (last visited on October 6, 2012).

[21] Marla Haims, *et al*, "Breaking the Failed-State Cycle," RAND Occasional Paper (2008) at 9, available at http://www.rand.org/pubs/occasional_papers/2008/RAND_OP204.pdf (last visited on July 14, 2009).

[22] Id. at 10-12.

CHAPTER 6

[1] Nina Serafino, "Peacekeeping and Related Stability Operations: Issues of US. Military Involvement," *CRS Issue Brief for Congress* (May 18, 2006), available at http://www.fas.org/sgp/crs/natsec/IB94040.pdf (last visited on July 10, 2009).

[2] Id. at CRS-3.

[3] Id.

[4] Department of Defense Directive 3000.05, "Military Support for Stability, Security, Transition and Reconstruction (SSTR) Operations." (November 28, 2005), available at http://www.dtic.mil/whs/directives/corres/pdf/300005p.pdf (last visited on July 10, 2009).

[5] Id. at 2.

[6] FM 3-07 (October 6, 2008), available at http://usacac.army.mil/cac2/repository/FM307/FM3-07.pdf (last visited on July 10, 2009).

[7] Id. at vii.

[8] Id. at 1-3.

[9] Id., Sec. 1-49 at 1-10.

[10] Id. Sec. 1-65, 1-66 at 1-13 to 1-14.

[11] Id., Sec. 1-66 at 1-14.

[12] Id., Sec. 1-67, 1-68 at 1-14.

[13] John Bass, "The State Department Office of Reconstruction and Stabilization and its Interaction with the Department of Defense," *CSL Issue Paper* (Vol. 09-05)(July 2005), available at http://www.js.pentagon.mil/doctrine/training/csl_crs_paper.pdf (last visited on July 10, 2009). For fuller descriptions of the organization chart and functions of S/CRS, *see* the Office of Reconstruction and Stabilization PowerPoint (October, 27, 2004), available at http://www.au.af.mil/au/awc/awcgate/state/37564.pdf; *see also,* "A Whole of Government Approach to Stability," available at http://blogs.state.gov/index.php/entries/government_

approach_stability/ (last visited on July 11, 2009).

[14] *See generally*, "Security for a New Century: A Local Worldviews Series," *Stimson Research*, available at http://www.stimson.org/newcentury/?SN=NC2001112949 / (last visited on July 11, 2009).

[15] "The Principles of War," U.S. Army, Field Manual 100-5, (1994), available at http://www.pvv.ntnu.no/~madsb/home/war/fm1005/principles.php (last visited on July 11, 2009).

[16] Id., *see also* http://militaryhistorypodcast.blogspot.com/2007/02/clausewitzs-principles-of-war.html (last visited on July 11, 2009).

[17] Andrew Natsios, "The Nine Principles of Reconstruction and Development," *Parameters* (Autumn 2005) at 7, available at http://www.dtic.mil/cgi-bin/GetT RDoc?AD=ADA486423&Location=U2&doc=GetTRDoc.pdf (last visited on July 11, 2009).

[18] Id. at 7-17.

[19] Nina Serafino, "Peacekeeping and Related Stability Operations: Issues of US. Military Involvement," *CRS Issue Brief for Congress, supra,* at CRS-3.

[20] *See generally*, RAND, AMERICA'S ROLE IN NATION-BUILDING: FROM GERMANY TO IRAQ (RAND 2003) (James Dobbins, *et al*, eds.).

[21] *See* UN Sec. Council Res. 1386 (December 20, 2001), available at http://daccessdds.un.org/doc/UNDOC/GEN/N01/708/55/PDF/N0170855.pdf? OpenElement (last visited on July 11, 2009).

[22] Nina Serafino, "Peacekeeping and Related Stability Operations: Issues of US. Military Involvement," *CRS Issue Brief for Congress, supra,* at CRS-4.

[23] Thom Shanker & Steven Erlanger, "NATO Meeting to Highlight Strains on Afghanistan," *NY Times* (April 3, 2009), available at http://www.nytimes. com/2009/04/03/world/europe/03nato.html (last visited on July 14, 2009).

[24] Vincent Morelli & Paul Belkin, "NATO in Afghanistan: A Test of the Transatlantic Alliance," *CRS* (7-5700)(April 17, 2009) at 1, available at http://www.fas.org/ sgp/crs/row/RL33627.pdf (last visited on July 14, 2009).

[25] Id. at 1.

[26] Id. at 8.

[27] Nina Serafino, "Peacekeeping and Related Stability Operations: Issues of US. Military Involvement," *CRS Issue Brief for Congress, supra,* at CRS-5-6.

[28] Vincent Morelli & Paul Belkin, "NATO in Afghanistan: A Test of the Transatlantic Alliance," *CRS, supra,* at 8-9.

[29] Peter Jakobsen, "PRTs in Afghanistan: Successful but not Sufficient," DIIS Report 2005:6), (2005), at 15, available at http://www.diis.dk/graphics/Publications/ Reports2005/pvj_prts_afghanistan.pdf (last visited on July 13, 2009).

[30] Michael Dziedzic & Michael Seidl, "Provincial Reconstruction Teams and Military Relations with International and Nongovernmental Organizations in Afghanistan," *U.S. Institute of Peace* (September 2005), at 3, available at http://www.usip.org/files/resources/sr147.pdf (last visited on July 11, 2009).

[31] Michael McNerney, "Stabilization and Reconstruction in Afghanistan: Are PRTs a Model or a Muddle?" *Parameters* (Winter 2005-06), at 36, available at http://www.carlisle.army.mil/usawc/Parameters/05winter/mcnerney.pdf (last visited on July 11, 2009).

[32] USAID, "Provincial Reconstruction Teams in Afghanistan: An Interagency Assessment (PN-ADG-252) (June 2006), at 8, available at http://pdf.usaid.gov/pdf_docs/PNADG252.pdf (last visited on February 21, 2012).

[33] Id.

[34] Id. at 13. Cf. U.S. Embassy in Kabul that issued, "Principles Guiding PRT Working Relations with UNAMA, NGOs and Local Government," (February 2003) which gave initial guidance for all PRT activities in Afghanistan and setting milestones for ISAF activities later. *See also* Oskari Eronen, "PRT Models in Afghanistan: Approaches to Civil-Military Integration," CMC Finland Civilian Crisis Management Studies, Vol. 1, No. 5/2008 (ISSN 1797-2140), at 14, available at http://www.intermin.fi/pelastus/cmc/images.nsf/files/8442FEDCC134982CC225755 A0059D3D0/$file/Studies_5_Eronen.pdf (last visited on February 21, 2012).

[35] Id. at 10.

[36] Id. at 15.

[37] Id. at 6.

[38] Id. at 17.

[39] Oskari Eronen, "PRT Models in Afghanistan: Approaches to Civil-Military Integration," CMC Finland Civilian Crisis Management Studies, Vol. 1, No. 5/2008 (ISSN 1797-2140), *supra*, at 37.

[40] Id. at 41.

[41] Id. at 21.

[42] Id. at 41.

[43] Stewart Patrick, James Schear & Mark Wong, "Integrating 21st Century Development and Security Assistance," *CSIS* (January 2008), at 12, available at http://csis.org/files/media/csis/pubs/080118-andrews-integrating21stcentury.pdf (last visited on July 11, 2009).

[44] Id.

[45] "Provincial Reconstruction Teams," USAID/Afghanistan, available at http://afghanistan.usaid.gov/en/Page.PRT.aspx (last visited on July 13, 2009).

[46] "Civilian Surge: Key to Complex Operations," (eds. Hans Binnendijk & Patrick Cronin)(National Defense University)(December 2008) at 194, 48, available at http://www.ndu.edu/CTNSP/pubs/Civilian%20Surge%20DEC%2008.pdf (last visited on July 11, 2009).

[47] Stewart Patrick, James Schear & Mark Wong, "Integrating 21st Century Development and Security Assistance," *CSIS* (January 2008), *supra*, at 12-13.

[48] Barnett Rubin, *et al*, "Afghanistan 2005 and Beyond: Prospects for Improved Stability Reference Document," *Neth. Insti. Int'l Rels.* (April 2005), at Appendix 1, available at http://www.clingendael.nl/publications/2005/20050400_cru_paper_ barnett.pdf (last visited on July 13, 2009).

[49] "Provincial Reconstruction Teams," (GAO-09-86R) (October 1, 2008) at 8, available at http://www.gao.gov/new.items/d0986r.pdf (last visited on July 16, 2009).

[50] Peter Jakobsen, "PRTs in Afghanistan: Successful but not Sufficient," DIIS Report 2005:6), (2005), at 15-16, available at http://www.diis.dk/graphics/Publications/ Reports2005/pvj_prts_afghanistan.pdf (last visited on July 13, 2009).

[51] Id. at 16.

[52] Id.

[53] Id. at 4.

[54] Id. at 4, 32-34, and states that, "the UK PRT must be deemed a success because it had reduced the fighting between the warlords, facilitated reconstruction and helped to extend the authority of the central government. . . On the other hand, the Mazar PRT is clearly incapable of laying down the law to the warlords." Id. at 34.

[55] Michael McNerney, "Stabilization and Reconstruction in Afghanistan: Are PRTs a Model or a Muddle?" *Parameters* (Winter 2005-06), *supra*, at 43.

[56] Nima Abbaszadeh, *et al*, "Provincial Reconstruction Teams: Lessons and Recommendations," (*Woodrow Wilson School of Public and Int'l Stud.*) (January 2008) at 16, available at http://wws.princeton.edu/research/pwreports_f07/ wws591b.pdf (last visited on July 16, 2009).

[57] *See e.g.,* Goldwater Nichols DOD Reorganization Act of 1986, available at http:// www.ndu.edu/library/goldnich/goldnich.html (last visited on July 11, 2009).

[58] Nima Abbaszadeh, *et al*, "Provincial Reconstruction Teams: Lessons and Recommendations," (*Woodrow Wilson School of Public and Int'l Stud.*), *supra*, at 15.

[59] *See e.g.,* Michael Dziedzic & Michael Seidl, "Provincial Reconstruction Teams and Military Relations with International and Nongovernmental Organizations in Afghanistan," *U.S. Institute of Peace, supra,* at 6.

[60] Id. at 9.

[61] Id. at 6.

[62] Id.

[63] Id. at 7. *See also* Charlotte Watkins, "Provincial Reconstructions Teams (PRTs): an analysis of their contribution to security in Afghanistan," Chapter 2, available at http://www.institute-for-afghan-studies.org/Contributions/Projects/Watkins-PRTs/ (last visited on July 13, 2009). For a general discussion of PRTs, *see* Yuji Uesugi, "The Provincial Reconstruction Teams (PRTs) and their Contribution to the Disarmament Demobilization and Reintegration (DDR) Process in Afghanistan," HiPEC, available at http://home.hiroshima-u.ac.jp/hipec/ja/products/RP3.pdf (last visited on July 13, 2009).

[64] Marko Chiziko, "The Responsibility to Protect: Does the African Stand-By Force Need a Doctrine of Protection for Protection of Civilians?" *Council for Am. Students in Int'l Nego.* at 79 (2007), available at http://www.americanstudents.us/Preview_IJHRL_2007_Chiziko_online.pdf (last visited on July 16, 2009).

[65] Michael McNerney, "Stabilization and Reconstruction in Afghanistan: Are PRTs a Model or a Muddle?" *Parameters*, *supra*, at 44-45.

[66] Id. at 45.

[67] Vincent Morelli & Paul Belkin, "NATO in Afghanistan: A Test of the Transatlantic Alliance," *CRS, supra,* at 12.

[68] Craig Cohen, "Measuring Progress in Stabilization and Reconstruction," *U.S. Institute of Peace* (March 2006), at 1, available at http://csis.org/files/media/csis/pubs/060412_cohen_progrees.pdf (last visited on July 13, 2009). For a different matrix of 12 indicia of measuring stability in Afghanistan, and based on a stability assessment framework developed by the methodology employed by the Clingendael Conflict Research Unit (The Hague), *see* Barnett Rubin, *et al*, "Afghanistan 2005 and Beyond: Prospects for Improved Stability Reference Document," *Neth. Insti. Int'l Rels.* (April 2005), *supra*, at 7.

[69] Id.

[70] Id.

[71] Marko Chiziko, "The Responsibility to Protect: Does the African Stand-By Force Need a Doctrine of Protection for Protection of Civilians?" *Council for Am. Students in Int'l Nego., supra*, at 76.

[72] Id.

[73] Convention (IV) Relative to the Protection of Civilian Persons in Time of War, (Geneva, Switzerland) (August, 12 1949) Article 3, available at http://www.icrc.org/ihl.nsf/385ec082b509e76c41256739003e636d/6756482d86146898c125641e004aa3c5 (last visited on July 16, 2009).

[74] Marko Chiziko, "The Responsibility to Protect: Does the African Stand-By Force Need a Doctrine of Protection for Protection of Civilians?" *Council for*

Am. Students in Int'l Nego., *supra*, at 74. *See* ¶138-39 of the World Summit Outcome Document, available at http://www.responsibilitytoprotect.org/index. php? option=com_ content&view=article&id=398 (last visited on July 16, 2009). *See also* UN Security Council Res. 1674 (April 28, 2006), available at http://protection.unsudanig.org/data/sg_reports/S-Res-1674%20on%20protection%20civilians% 20in%20armed% 20conflict%20(28Apr06).pdf (last visited on July 16, 2009).

75 DOD Instruction 3000.05, "Stability Operations" (September 16, 2009), available at http://www.dtic.mil/whs/directives/corres/pdf/300005p.pdf (last visited on April 24, 2012).

76 USAID, Transition Initiatives, available at http://www.usaid.gov/our_work/cross-cutting_programs/transition_initiatives/country/afghanistan2/index.html (last visited on July 16, 2009).

77 Office of the Coordinator for Reconstruction and Stabilization (S/CRS), "A Whole-of-Government Approach to Preparing for an Responding to Conflict, (October 31, 2007), available at http://www.mofa.go.jp/POLICY/un/pko/symposium0710/US.pdf (last visited on July 15, 2009).

78 Nima Abbaszadeh, *et al*, "Provincial Reconstruction Teams: Lessons and Recommendations," (*Woodrow Wilson School of Public and Int'l Stud.*), *supra*, at 17.

79 Greg Jaffe, "U.S. weighs bigger Special Operations role in Afghanistan," *Wash. Post* (February 6, 2012), at A11.

80 Id.

81 Id.

82 Carlo Minoz, "New joint special forces ops command won't assume control of Afghan commandos," *Defcon.Hill*, available at http://thehill.com/blogs/defcon-hill/operations/244621-new-joint-special-ops-command-wont-assume-control-of-afghan-commandos (last visited on October 5, 2012).

83 Id.

84 Thom Shanker & Eric Schmitt, "U.S. Plans Shift to Elite Units as It Winds Down in Afghanistan," *NY Times* (February 4, 2012), available at http://www.nytimes.com/2012/02/05/world/asia/us-plans-a-shift-to-elite-forces-in-afghanistan.html?pagewanted=all (last visited on April 24, 2012).

85 "Obama, Karzai Sign Strategic Partnership Agreement, " *ABCNews* (May 1, 2012), available at http://abcnews.go.com/blogs/politics/2012/05/obama-karzai-sign-strategic-partnership-agreement/ (last visited on May 22, 2012).

86 The full text of the SPA may be found at http://www.whitehouse.gov/sites/default/files/2012.06.01u.s.-afghanistanspasignedtext.pdf (last visited on May 22, 2012).

87 Fareed Zakaria, "Afghan fantasy vs. reality," *Wash. Post* (March 1, 2012), at A18.

[88] Id.

[89] *See* Bhashyam Kasturi, "India's Role in Afghanistan," *Indian Defence Rev.* (February 18, 2012, available at http://www.indiandefencereview.com/geopolitics/Indias-Role-in-Afghanistan—II.html (last visited on April 24, 2012). India has made it clear that it has no "exit strategy" from Afghanistan and is moving forward with its program for training, equipping and supporting Afghan military and police forces as well as providing economic support and cooperation in the mining, transportation and related sectors.

[90] Fareed Zakaria, "Afghan fantasy vs. reality," *Wash. Post* (March 1, 2012), *supra*, at A18.

[91] Graham Bowley & Richard Oppel, Jr., "U.S. Halting Program to Train Afghan Recruits," *NY Times* (September 2, 2012), available at http://www.nytimes.com/2012/09/02/world/asia/us-halting-program-to-train-afghan-recruits.html?gwh= C97E1D132B9EF2369594456057CB7EF1 (last visited on September 27, 2012).

[92] Graham Bowley & Richard Oppel, Jr., "Afghanistan, Contradicting NATO, Blames Foreign Spies for Insider Attacks," *NY Times* (August 22, 2012), available at http://www.nytimes.com/2012/08/23/world/asia/afghanistan-blames-spies-for-insider-attacks-on-western-troops.html?gwh=1C294E6BD2BF08DFE84243E698AA6DB9 (last visited on September 27, 2012).

[93] Matthew Rosenberg & Graham Bowley, "Intractable Afghan Graft Hampering U.S. Strategy," *NY Times* (March 7, 2012), available at http://www.nytimes.com/2012/03/08/world/asia/corruption-remains-intractable-in-afghanistan-under-karzai-government.html?pagewanted=all (last visited on April 24, 2012).

[94] Id.

[95] Id.

[96] Id.

[97] Id.

[98] Graham Bowley, "Afghans Fear Downturn as Foreigners Withdraw," *NY Times* (January 21, 2012), available at http://www.nytimes.com/2012/02/01/world/asia/afghans-fear-economic-downturn-as-foreigners-leave.html?pagewanted=all (last visited on April 24, 2012).

[99] Id.

[100] James Risen, "U.S. Identified Vast Riches of Minerals in Afghanistan," *NY Times* (June 13, 20120, available at http://www.nytimes.com/2010/06/14/world/asia/14minerals.html?pagewanted=all http://www.nytimes.com/2010/06/14/world/asia/14minerals.html?pagewanted=all (last visited on April 24, 2012).

[101] Id.

[102] Id.

[103] Graham Bowley, "Potential for a Mining Boom Splits Factions in Afghanistan," *NY Times* (September 8, 20212), available at http://www.nytimes.com/2012/09/09/ world/asia/afghans-wary-as-efforts-pick-up-to-tap-mineral-riches.html? pagewanted=all&_moc.semityn.www&gwh=52790B1132F83BB038FA8 4C576248074 (last visited on September 27, 2012).

[104] Paul Collier, "In Afghanistan, a Threat of Plunder," *NY Times* (July 10, 2012), available at http://www.nytimes.com/2010/07/20/opinion/20collier.html?gwh= 4CE22ED94F6BFA24DABD07C1A3718C0C (last visited on April 24, 2012).

[105] Id.

CHAPTER 7

[1] Worth Noting, "The State-Defense Initiative: An Interagency Solution," *Inter-Agency J.* 2-2 (Summer 2011) at 68-69.

[2] Ted Stickler, "What the QDDR Says about Interagency Coordination," *Inter-Agency J.* 2-1 (Winter 2011), Worth Noting at 67-73.

[3] Portions of the following text were submitted to and awarded Third Prize by the Col. Arthur D. Simons Center for the Study of Interagency Cooperation for its 2012 Interagency Writing Competition, and has been reprinted here with the Center's kind permission. The full essay is available at http://thesimonscenter. org/iap-9w-may-2012/(last visited on October 5, 2012).

[4] Liana Wyler, "Weak and Failing States: Evolving Security Threats and U.S. Policy, *CRS* (August 28, 2008), at CRS-4, available at http://www.fas.org/sgp/crs/row/ RL34253.pdf (last visited on February 15, 2012).

[5] U.S. Department of State, *Quadrennial Diplomacy and Development Review*, 120-121.

[6] U.S. Agency for International Development, *Fragile States Strategy*, (Washington, DC: U.S. Agency for International Development, January 2005), at 1, available at http://www.usaid.gov/policy/2005_fragile_states_strategy.pdf (last visited on July 3, 2009). In the interest of full disclosure, the author was formerly an attorney with the Office of the General Counsel, USAID, Washington, DC.

[7] Id. (*See also* Table 1, the Fragility Framework, Chapter 1 of this text.)

[8] National Security Strategy (May 2010), available at http://www.whitehouse. gov/sites/default/files/rss_viewer/national_security_strategy.pdf (last visited on February 14, 2012).

[9] National Military Strategy of the United States (2011), available at http://www. jcs.mil/content/files/2011-02/020811084800_2011_NMS_-_08_FEB_2011.pdf (last visited on February 14, 2012).

[10] Id. at 4.

[11] U.S. Department of the Army, *Stability Operations*, Field Manual 3-07, (Washington, DC: U.S. Department of the Army, October 6, 2008), 1-10, ¶1-45.

[12] Id. at ¶1-46.

[13] Id. at ¶1-47.

[14] Id. at 1-3 at ¶1-14.

[15] Id. at 1-4, at ¶1-17.

[16] Id. at ¶1-19.

[17] Id. at ¶1-20.

[18] *See* the Failed States Index 2011 available at http://www.fundforpeace.org/global/?q=fsi (last visited on February 14, 2012).

[19] PUBLIC LAW 110–417—OCT. 14, 2008, as codified at 22 U.S.C. § 2151 (note) and referred to as the Reconstruction and Stabilization Civilian Management Act of 2008. "Through Title XVI of the Duncan Hunter National Defense Authorization Act for Fiscal Year 2009 (P.L. No. 110-417), Congress amended the basic foreign assistance and State Department statutes to (1) authorize the President to provide assistance for a reconstruction and stabilization crisis, (2) formally establish S/CRS and assign it specific functions, and (3) authorize a Response Readiness Corps (RRC) and a Civilian Reserve Corps (CRC). The authority to provide assistance for a reconstruction and stabilization crisis was created by amending chapter 1 of part III of the Foreign Assistance Act of 1961, as amended (FAA, 22 U.S.C. 2734 et seq.) by inserting a new section. This authority is, however, subject to a time limitation: it may be exercised only during FY2009-FY2011. The new authority for S/CRS, the RRC, and the CRC was created by amending Title I of the State Department Basic Authorities Act of 1956 (22 U.S.C. 2651a et seq.). These authorities are permanent." *See* Nina Serafina, "Peacekeeping/Stabilization and Conflict Transitions: Background and Congressional Action on the Civilian Response/Reserve Corps and other Civilian Stabilization and Reconstruction Capabilities at 11 (CRS, 7-5700) (RL32862) (February 17, 2010), available at http://www.fas.org/sgp/crs/natsec/RL32862.pdf (last visited on February 15, 2012).

[20] PUBLIC LAW 110–417—OCT. 14, 2008, as codified at 22 U.S.C. § 2151 (note), *supra*, Section 1604(a)(1).

[21] Scott Wilson & Al Kamen, "'Global War on Terror' is Given a New Name," *Wash. Post (*March 23, 2009), where a Pentagon memorandum apparently noted that "this administration prefers to avoid using the term 'Long War' or 'Global War on Terror [GWOT]. Please use 'Overseas Contingency Operation.'"

[22] Jeffrey Gettlemen, *et al*, "U.S. Swoops In to Free 2 From Pirates in Somali Raid," *NY Times*, (January 25, 2012), available at http://www.nytimes.com/2012/01/26/world/africa/us-raid-frees-2-hostages-from-somali-pirates.html?pagewanted=all (last visited on February 15, 2012).

[23] BBC News Africa, "UN report says DR Congo killings 'may be genocide'," October 1, 2010, available at http://www.bbc.co.uk/news/world-africa-11450093 (last visited on February 15, 2012); United Human Rights Council, "Genocide in Darfur," (February 15, 2012), available at http://www.unitedhumanrights.org/ genocide/genocide-in-sudan.htm (last visited on February 15, 2012).

[24] William Ferroggiaro, "The US and the Genocide in Rwanda 1994: Evidence of Inaction," *National Security Archive* (August 20, 2001), available at http://www. gwu.edu/~nsarchiv/NSAEBB/NSAEBB53/index.html (last visited on February 16, 2012).

[25] *See generally*, Asraf Ghani & Clare Lockhart, *Fixing Failed States: A Framework for Rebuilding a Fractured World* (Oxford University Press, 2008).

[26] James Traub, "Think Again: Failed States," *For. Pol'y* (July/August 2011).

[27] *See* Nina Serafina, "Peacekeeping/Stabilization and Conflict Transitions: Background and Congressional Action on the Civilian Response/Reserve Corps and other Civilian Stabilization and Reconstruction Capabilities, *supra,* at 11.

[28] The Reconstruction and Stabilization Civilian Management Act of 2008, *supra,* Section 1602(1).

[29] Id., Section 1602(3).

[30] National Security Presidential Directive 44/NSPD-44, "Management of Interagency Efforts Concerning Reconstruction and Stabilization, (December 7, 2005), available at http://www.fas.org/irp/offdocs/nspd/nspd-44.html (last visited on February 15, 2012).

[31] U.S. State Department, "Quadrennial Diplomacy and Development Review (QDDR): Leading Through Civilian Power (2010)," Executive Summary at 14, available at http://www.state.gov/documents/organization/153139.pdf (last visited on February 15, 2012).

[32] Simons Center, "State Department Announces Reorganization Changes,"(January 31, 2012), available at http://thesimonscenter.org/state-department-announces-reorganization-changes-jan-2012/ (last visited on February 16, 2012).

[33] Simons Center, "USAID Office Change Reflects Interagency Focus," (February 16, 2012), available at http://thesimonscenter.org/usaid-office-change-reflects-interagency-focus/?utm_source=feedburner&utm_medium=email& utm_campaign=Feed%3A+ADSCPublications+%28Col.+Arthur+D.+Simons+ Center+%C2%BB+Updates%29 (last visited on February 16, 2012).

[34] *See e.g.,* Col. Arthur D. Simons Center for the Study of Interagency Cooperation, "Interagency Handbook for Transitions," GCSC Foundation Press (2011); "Guiding Principles for Stabilization and Reconstruction," *U.S. Institute for Peace* (USIP Press) (November 2009), available at http://www.usip.org/files/resources/ guiding_principles_full.pdf (last visited on February 15, 2012).

[35] William "Kip" Ward, "What 'Right' Looks Like in the Interagency: A

Commander's Perspective," *Inter-Agency J.* 2-1 (Winter 2011) at 3, available at http://thesimonscenter.org/wp-content/uploads/2011/03/IAJ-2-1-pg03-10.pdf (last visited on February 16, 2012).

[36] Id.

[37] Id. at 9.

[38] Goldwater-Nichols Department of Defense Reorganization Act of 1986 P.L. 99-433, as codified at 10 U.S.C. § 162 *et seq.*

[39] William "Kip" Ward, "What 'Right' Looks Like in the Interagency: A Commander's Perspective," *Inter-Agency J.* 2-1 (Winter 2011) note 35, *supra,* at 10.

[40] Michael Miklaucic, "Learning the Hard Way: Lessons from Complex Operations," *Inter-Agency J.* 2-1 (Winter 2011) at 17, 20, available at http://thesimonscenter. org/wp-content/uploads/2011/03/IAJ-2-1-pg03-10.pdf (last visited on February 16, 2012).

[41] Id. at 19, 27.

[42] Id. at 19.

[43] Id.

[44] The Reconstruction and Stabilization Civilian Management Act of 2008, *supra,* Section 1605(b)(2).

[45] Rod Nordland, "Risks of Afghan War Shifts from Soldiers to Contractors," *NY Times* (February 11, 2012), available at http://www.nytimes.com/2012/02/12/world/asia/ afghan-war-risks-are-shifting-to-contractors.html?_r=1&ref=rodnordland (last visited on February 20. 2012).

[46] Id.

[47] Id., quoting Professor Steven Schooner, a law professor at George Washington University.

[48] Id.

[49] Id. *See also* Alissa Rubin & Taimoor Shah, "Afghanistan Faces Deadliest Day for Civilians This Year in Multiple Attacks," *NY Times* (June 6, 2012), available at http://www.nytimes.com/2012/06/07/world/asia/suicide-attack-kills-at-least-20-civilians-in-afghanistan.html (last visited on June 7, 2012).

[50] Ernesto Londoño, "Audit: Afghan guards will cost more," *Wash. Post* (March 29, 2012) at A10.

[51] Id.

[52] Id.

[53] Id.

[54] Rajiv Chandrasekaran, "Khandahar's power woes illuminate U.S. divide," *Wash. Post* (April 23, 2010) at A1.

[55] Id.

[56] Id.

[57] Id.

[58] *See* "Improving Oversight of Contingency Operations," *J. Int'l Peace Ops.*, Vol. 6, No. 6 (May-June 2011), available at http://web.peaceops.com/archives/1373 (last visited on February 21, 2012).

[59] *See generally* Fact Sheet, FY 2012—State and USAID—Overseas Contingency Operations (February 14, 2011), available at http://www.state.gov/s/d/rm/rls/fs/2011/156555.htm (last visited on February 21, 2012).

[60] A. Michael Froomkin, "Reinventing the Government Corporation, 1995 U. *Ill. L. Rev.* 543, available at http://osaka.law.miami.edu/~froomkin/articles/reinvent.htm#ENDNOTE38 (last visited on February 21, 2012).

[61] Eric Schmitt, Mark Mazzetti & Thom Shankar, "Admiral Seeks Freer Hand in Deployment of Elite Forces," *NY Times* (February 12, 2012), available at http://www.nytimes.com/2012/02/13/us/admiral-pushes-for-freer-hand-in-special-forces.html?pagewanted=all (last visited on February 21, 2012).

[62] Eric Schmitt, "Elite Military Forces Are Denied in Bid for Expansion," *NY Times* (June 4, 2012), available at http://www.nytimes.com/2012/06/05/world/special-ops-leader-seeks-new-authority-and-is-denied.html?pagewanted=all (last visited on June 7, 2012).

[63] Id.

[64] Id.

[65] Mike Mount, "Special operations rebuffed in effort to get new authority," *CNN Security Clearance* (June 5, 2012), available at http://security.blogs.cnn.com/2012/06/05/special-operations-rebuffed-in-effort-to-get-new-authority/ (last visited on June 7, 2012).

[66] Eric Schmitt, "Elite Military Forces Are Denied in Bid for Expansion," *NY Times* (June 4, 2012), *supra*, note 62, available at http://www.nytimes.com/2012/06/05/world/special-ops-leader-seeks-new-authority-and-is-denied.html? pagewanted=all (last visited on June 7, 2012).

[67] Thom Shanker, "Army Will Reshape Training, With Lessons from Special Forces," *NY Times* (May 2, 2012), available at http://www.nytimes.com/2012/05/03/us/politics/odierno-seeks-to-reshape-training-and-deployment-for-soldiers.html (last visited May 7, 2012). *See also* Ray Odierno, "The U.S. Army in a Time of Transition," *For. Aff.* (May/June 2012), comment.

[68] Id.

[69] Id.

CHAPTER 8

[1] "Transforming for Stabilization and Reconstruction Operations," eds. Hans Binnendijk & Stuart Johnson, National Defense University (November 12, 2003) at 120, available at http://www.au.af.mil/au/awc/awcgate/ndu/stab_rec_ops.pdf (last visited on July 15, 2009).

[2] Strategic Insight: NATO Response Force: Political Deftness, Economic Efficiency, Military Power," (April 1, 2003), available at http://www.ccc.nps.navy.mil/rsepResources/si/apr03/europe.asp (last visited on July 15, 2009).

[3] Id.

[4] "NATO and its future: Have combat experience, will travel," *The Economist* (March 28, 2009) at 69.

[5] Strategic Insight: NATO Response Force: Political Deftness, Economic Efficiency, Military Power," *supra*, at 2.

[6] Id.

[7] Id. at 3.

[8] Robert Bell, "Sisyphus and the NRF," *NATO Rev.* (Autumn 2006), available at http://www.nato.int/docu/review/2006/issue3/english/art4.html (last visited on July 15, 2009).

[9] Id.

[10] "The New NATO Force Structure," available at http://www.otan.nato.int/ims/docu/force-structure.htm (last visited on July 15, 2009).

[11] "NATO Response Q &As," *SHAPE [Supreme Headquarters Allied Powers Europe]*, available at http://www.nato.int/shape/issues/shape_nrf/nrf_q_a.htm (last visited on July 15, 2009). *See generally*, John Deni, "NATO's Rapid Deployment Corps: Alliance Doctrine and Force Structure," *Contemp. Sec. Pol'y* (December 1, 2004), available at http://pdfserve.informaworld.com/823447_731205536_713947077.pdf (last visited on July 15, 2009). *See also* Jeffrey Simon, "NATO Expeditionary Operations: Impacts upon New Members and Partners," *Inst. Nat'l Strategic Stud.*, Occasional Paper (March 2005), available at http://www.stormingmedia.us/38/3862/A386234.html (last visited on July 15, 2009).

[12] 'The NATO Response Force: How Did it Evolve?" available at http://www.otan.nato.int/issues/nrf/evolution.html (last visited on July 15, 2009).

[13] "NATO and its future: Have combat experience, will travel," *The Economist, supra,* (March 28, 2009) at 70.

[14] "NATO Retools for New Missions in Africa and South Asia," *America.gov* (May 26, 2006), available at http://www.globalsecurity.org/military/library/news/2006/05/mil-060526-usia01.htm (last visited on July 16, 2009).

[15] Peter Lambert, "NATO in Africa: Ready for Action?" *Air Uni.* (AU/AFF/ NNN/2006-07) (April 2007) at 9-20, available at http://74.125.93.132/ search? q=cache:TOX4xt7xkPgJ:https://www.afresearch.org/skins/rims/q_ mod_be0e99f3-fc56-4ccb-8dfe-670c0822a153/q_act_downloadpaper/q_ obj_45744244-1cae-4cfc-8f60-91581373a6ac/display.aspx%3Frs%3Dengine spage+nato+why+ africa& cd=5&hl=en&ct=clnk&gl=us (last visited on July 15, 2009).

[16] Id. at 10.

[17] "Assistance of NATO in the African Union Mission," available at http://www. imuna.nl/Research_Reports/RRs_2009/NAC1.pdf (last visited on July 15, 2009).

[18] "NATO Continues to Offer Logistical Support to African Union," *NATO* (October 6, 2005), available at http://www.nato.int/shape/news/2005/10/051006c.htm (last visited on July 15, 2009). For a fuller discussion of the evolution of NATO's assistance to AMIS and a list of key milestones, *see* "Assisting the AU in Darfur, Sudan," *NATO*, available at http://www.nato.int/issues/darfur/index.html (last visited on July 15, 2009).

[19] "NATO Continues to Offer Logistical Support to African Union," *NATO* (October 6, 2005), *supra.*

[20] 'The NATO Response Force: How Did it Evolve?" available at http://www.otan. nato.int/issues/nrf/evolution.html (last visited on July 15, 2009).

[21] NATO Update, "African Union asks further assistance for Darfur," (June 12, 2006), available at http://www.nato.int/docu/update/2006/06-june/e0607a.htm (last visited on July 15, 2009).

[22] NATO Assistance to the African Union, *NATO* (January 23, 2009), available at http://www.nato.int/issues/nato-au/index.html (last visited on July 15, 2009).

[23] Mohamed Adow, "NATO Warships Arrive to Deter Somali Pirates," *CNN News* (October 19, 2008), available at http://www.cnn.com/2008/WORLD/africa/10/19/ somalia.nato.pirates/index.html (last visited on July 15, 2009). *See also,* "NATO to Target Somali Pirates," *BBC News* (October 9, 2008), available at http://news. bbc.co.uk/2/hi/africa/7661927.stm (last visited on July 15, 2009).

[24] Slobodan Lekic, "New NATO flotilla takes over anti-piracy controls (June 29, 2009), available at http://www.sfgate.com/cgi-bin/article.cgi?f=/n/a/2009/06/28/ international/i010416D04.DTL (last visited on July 15, 2009).

[25] Id.

[26] NATO Update, "African Union looks toward long-term cooperation," (May 21, 2007), available at http://www.nato.int/docu/update/2007/03-march/e0302a.html (last visited on July 15, 2009).

[27] NATO Assistance to the African Union, *NATO* (January 23, 2009), *supra.*

[28] Jessica Piombo, "Terrorism and U.S. Counter-Terrorism Programs in Africa: An

Overview," *Strategic Insights*, Volume VI, Issue 1 (January 2007), available at http://www.ccc.nps.navy.mil/si/2007/Jan/piomboJan07.pdf (last visited on July 15, 2009).

[29] Id. at

[30] Princeton Lyman, "The Terrorist Threat in Africa," *Council on For. Rels.* (April 1, 2004), available at http://www.cfr.org/publication/6912/terrorist_threat_in_ africa.html (last visited on July 15, 2009).

[31] Jessica Piombo, "Terrorism and U.S. Counter-Terrorism Programs in Africa: An Overview," *Strategic Insights, supra.*

[32] Robert Andrews & Mark Kirk, "Integrating 21st Century Development and Security Assistance," *CSIS* (January 2008) at 4, available at http://csis.org/files/ media/csis/pubs/080118-andrews-integrating21stcentury.pdf (last visited on July 15, 2009).

[33] Princeton Lyman, "The Terrorist Threat in Africa," *Council on For. Rels., supra.* In contrast, the Maghreb generally refers to Morocco, Algeria and Tunisia. The Maghreb Union, founded in 1989, includes those nations as well as Libya and Mauritania. As of February 8, 1995, NATO announced its Mediterranean Dialogue which would include talks on terrorism, and drug trafficking with North Africa nations such as Egypt, Mauritania, Tunisia and Morocco. *See* http:// www.nato.int/med-dial/summary.htm (last visited on July 16, 2009). *See also* Jim Garamone, "NATO, European Command Working in Africa," *Am. Forces Press Serv.* (October 28, 2005), available at http://www.defenselink.mil/news/ newsarticle.aspx?id=17942 (last visited on July 16, 2009). Note that on May 2, 2012, Charles Taylor was found guilty by the International Criminal Court of war crimes and crimes against humanity for his role in inciting conflict in neighboring Sierra Leone.

[34] Thomas Dempsey, "Counterterrorism in African Failed States: Challenges and Potential Solutions," *Strategic Stud., Inst.* (April 2006), available at http://www. strategicstudiesinstitute.army.mil/pdffiles/pub649.pdf (last visited on July 15, 2009).

[35] Ricardo Laremont & Hrach Gregorian, "Political Islam on West Africa and the Sahel," *Mil. Rev.* (January-February 2006) at 35-36, available at http://usacac. army.mil/CAC/milreview/English/JanFeb06/Laremont.pdf (last visited on July 15, 2009).

[36] *See e.g.*, Marc Sageman, "Understanding Terror Networks," (Penn. Press, 2004), available at http://www.fpri.org/enotes/20041101.middleeast. sageman. understandingterrornetworks.html (last visited on July 15, 2009).

[37] Thomas Dempsey, "Counterterrorism in African Failed States: Challenges and Potential Solutions," *Strategic Stud. Inst., supra*, at 8.

[38] Id. at 16.

[39] "The Mounting Security Emphasis on West Africa," *Mil. Periscope* (October 18, 2005).

[40] Id.

[41] Craig Whitlock, "U.S. trains African troops for Somali fight," *Wash. Post* (May 14, 2012) at A1.

[42] Id.

[43] Id.

[44] "NATO aids Africa to combat terror," *BBC News* (May 11, 2004), available at http://news.bbc.co.uk/2/hi/africa/3704283.stm (last visited on July 16, 2009).

[45] Eric Schmitt & Souad Mekhennet, "Qaeda Branch Steps Up Raids in North Africa," *New York Times* (July 10, 2009), available at http://www.nytimes.com/2009/07/10/world/africa/10terror.html (last visited on July 16, 2009).

[46] Id.

[47] Richard Gowan, "Can Europe Build a NATO for Africa?" *Globalist* (January 14, 2005), available at http://www.theglobalist.com/StoryId.aspx?StoryId=4328 (last visited on July 16, 2009).

[48] Deane-Peter Baker, "The AU Standby Force and the challenge of Somalia," 16 *African Sec. Rev.* at 121-22 (2006), available at http://www.iss.co.za/dynamic/administration/file_manager/file_links/16_2BAKER.PDF?link_id=29&slink_id=4759&link_type=12&slink_type=23&tmpl_id=3 (last visited on July 16, 2009).

[49] Marko Chiziko, "The Responsibility to Protect: Does the African Stand-By Force Need a Doctrine of Protection for Protection of Civilians?" *Council for Am. Students in Int'l Nego.*, *supra*, at 75.

[50] Id.

[51] Benedikt Franke, "Enabling a Continent to Help Itself: U.S. Military Capacity Building and Africa's Emerging Security Architecture," 6 *Strategic Insights* (January 2007), available at http://doc.operationspaix.net/serv1/frankeJan07.pdf (last visited on July 16, 2009).

[52] Jackie Cilliers, "The African Standby Force: An Update on Progress, *Inst. Sec. Stud.* Occasional Paper No. 160 (March 2008) at 1, available at http://www.iss.co.za/static/templates/tmpl_html.php?node_id=3241&slink_id=5907&slink_type= 12&link_id=22 (last visited on July 17, 2009).

[53] Id.

[54] *See* Protocol Relating to the Establishment of the Peace and Security Council of the African Union (2002), Art. 2, Sec. 2, available at http://www.africa-union.org/root/AU/organs/psc/Protocol_peace%20and%20security.pdf (last visited on July 16, 2009).

[55] Benedikt Franke, "Enabling a Continent to Help Itself: U.S. Military Capacity Building ad Africa's Emerging Security Architecture," 6 *Strategic Insights, supra.*

[56] Jackie Cilliers, "The African Standby Force: An Update on Progress, *Inst. Sec. Stud., supra,* at 1.

[57] Stephen Burgess, "The African Standby Force, Sub-regional Commands, and African Militaries," *U.S. Air War College* (undated), available at http://www.au.af. mil/awc/africom/documents/BurgessSubregionalCommands.pdf (last visited on July 17, 2009).

[58] "Roadmap for Operationalization of the African Standby Force," EXP/AU-RECs/ASF/4(I)) (March 22-23, 2005), available at http://www.iss.co.za/AF/RegOrg/unity_to_union/pdfs/au/asf/roadmapmar05.pdf (last visited on July 17, 2009). This document exhaustively details the multidimensional strategic level management capability requirements, training and doctrine, logistical infrastructure requirements, harmonization among the AU and the RECs, the Regional Brigade force structure, a list of workshops to be convened between June and December 2005 that set forth the policies and procedures for establishing these components as well as defining the functions and structure of the Planning Elements (PLANELM).

[59] Jackie Cilliers, "The African Standby Force: An Update on Progress, *Inst. Sec. Stud., supra,* at 2.

[60] Stephen Burgess, "The African Standby Force, Sub-regional Commands, and African Militaries," *U.S. Air War College, supra,* at 1.

[61] "Roadmap for Operationalization of the African Standby Force," EXP/AU-RECs/ASF/4(I)), *supra,* at 2.

[62] Jackie Cilliers, "The African Standby Force: An Update on Progress, *Inst. Sec. Stud., supra.*

[63] Stephen Burgess, "The African Standby Force, Sub-regional Commands, and African Militaries," *U.S. Air War College, supra,* at 3.

[64] Id.

[65] Jackie Cilliers, "The African Standby Force: An Update on Progress, *Inst. Sec. Stud., supra.*

[66] Stephen Burgess, "The African Standby Force, Sub-regional Commands, and African Militaries," *U.S. Air War College, supra,* at 2.

[67] Id.

[68] Id.

[69] Jackie Cilliers, "The African Standby Force: An Update on Progress, *Inst. Sec. Stud., supra.*

[70] Id.

[71] Id.

[72] Stephen Burgess, "The African Standby Force, Sub-regional Commands, and African Militaries," *U.S. Air War College, supra,* at 3.

[73] Jackie Cilliers, "The African Standby Force: An Update on Progress, *Inst. Sec. Stud., supra.*

[74] Id.

[75] Id.

[76] Stephen Burgess, "The African Standby Force, Sub-regional Commands, and African Militaries," *U.S. Air War College, supra,* at 3.

[77] Id.

[78] Id. at 5.

[79] Jackie Cilliers, "The African Standby Force: An Update on Progress, *Inst. Sec. Stud., supra.*

[80] Id.

[81] Id.

[82] Marko Chiziko, "The Responsibility to Protect: Does the African Stand-By Force Need a Doctrine of Protection for Protection of Civilians?" *Council for Am. Students in Int'l Nego., supra,* at 83. While noting that NRF deployments should be made to Africa, the commentator also notes that, "while the NRF appears exceptionally well-placed to respond to fast-moving war crimes or [a] genocide-type situation like Rwanda in 1994, it is still not clear how far NATO will be prepared to deploy the NRF or other key assets to support military interventions in Africa." Id. at 84.

[83] Donna Miles, "Multilateral Cooperation Critical to Gulf Region Security, Gates Says," *Am. Forces Press Serv.* (December 8, 2007), available at http://www.defenselink.mil/news/newsarticle.aspx?id=48366 (Last visited on July 16, 2009).

[84] "NATO and Libya," *NATO,* available at http://www.nato.int/cps/en/natolive/topics_71652.htm (last visited on April 27, 2012).

[85] UN Security Council resolution (S/RES/1973) (March 17, 2011), available at http://daccess-dds-ny.un.org/doc/UNDOC/GEN/N11/268/39/PDF/N1126839.pdf? OpenElement and at http://www.guardian.co.uk/world/2011/mar/17/un-security-council-resolution (last visited on April 27, 2012).

[86] Operation Odyssey Dawn, *Global Security.com,* available at http://www.globalsecurity.org/military/ops/odyssey-dawn.htm (last visited on April 27, 2012).

[87] Id.

[88] Id.

[89] Id.

[90] "NATO and Libya," *NATO, supra*, available at http://www.nato.int/cps/en/natolive/topics_71652.htm (last visited on April 27, 2012).

[91] Id.

[92] Id.

[93] UN Security Council Resolution (S/RES/2009) (September 16, 2011), available at http://daccess-dds-ny.un.org/doc/UNDOC/GEN/N11/502/44/PDF/N1150244.pdf? OpenElement (last visited on April 27, 2012).

[94] "NATO and Libya," NATO, *supra*, available at http://www.nato.int/cps/en/natolive/topics_71652.htm (last visited on April 27, 2012).

[95] Letter from the President on the War Powers Resolution (June 15, 2011), available at http://www.whitehouse.gov/the-press-office/2011/06/15/letter-president-war-powers-resolution (last visited on April 27, 2012). *See* "United States Activities in Libya," a report submitted by the President to the U.S. Congress, available at http://info.publicintelligence.net/ObamaLibyaJustification.pdf. *See also* Charlie Savage & Mark Landler, "White House Defends Continuing U.S. Role in Libya Operation," *NY Times* (June 15, 2011), available at http://www.nytimes.com/2011/06/16/us/politics/16powers.html?pagewanted=all (last visited on April 27, 2012).

[96] *See* "10 U.S. lawmakers sue Obama over Libya strikes," *CBS News* (June 15, 2011), available at http://www.cbsnews.com/2100-250_162-20071286.html (last visited on April 27, 2012). The plaintiffs were Democratic Representatives Dennis Kucinich of Ohio, John Conyers of Michigan, and Michael Capuano of Massachusetts, and Republican Representatives Walter Jones and Howard Coble of North Carolina, Tim Johnson and Dan Burton of Indiana, Jimmy Duncan of Tennessee, Roscoe Bartlett of Maryland and Ron Paul of Texas.

[97] The lawsuit was later dismissed on October 20, 2011, *see* slip op. available at https://ecf.dcd.uscourts.gov/cgi-bin/show_public_doc?2011cv1096-14 (last visited on April 27, 2012).

[98] "NATO After Libya," *NY Times* (April 18, 2012), available at http://www.nytimes.com/2012/04/19/opinion/nato-after-libya.html (last visited on April 27, 2012).

[99] Id.

[100] Id.

[101] In examining the declaration issued by NATO at the April 2012 Chicago summit, it is a bit difficult to ascertain whether the report was formally adopted. *See* Chicago Summit Declaration (May 20, 2012), available at http://www.nato.int/cps/en/natolive/official_texts_87593.htm?mode=pressrelease (last visited on October 5, 2012).

[102] Eric Schmitt, "NATO Sees Flaws in Air Campaign Against Qaddafi," *NY Times* (April 14, 2012), available at http://www.nytimes.com/2012/04/15/world/africa/nato-sees-flaws-in-air-campaign-against-qaddafi.html?pagewanted=all (last

visited on April 27, 2012).

[103] Id.

[104] Matthew Pomy, "ICC to investigate Libya war crimes committed by NATO, NTC forces," *Jurist* (April 25, 2012), available at http://jurist.org/paperchase/2011/11/icc-to-investigate-libya-war-crimes-committed-by-nato-ntc-forces.php (last visited on April 27, 2012).

[105] Clara O'Donnell & Justin Vaïsse, "Is Libya NATO's Final Bow?" *Brookings Inst.* (December 2, 2011), available at http://www.brookings.edu/opinions/2011/1202_libya_odonnell_vaisse.aspx (last visited on April 27, 2012).

[106] "NATO's Teachable Moment," *NY Times* (August 29, 2011), available at http://www.nytimes.com/2011/08/30/opinion/natos-teachable-moment.html (last visited on April 27, 2012).

[107] Id.

[108] Katy Steinmetz, "10. Leading from Behind," *TIME* (December 7, 2011), available athttp://www.time.com/time/specials/packages/article/0,28804,2101344_2100571_2100582,00.html (last visited on April 30, 2012).

[109] Jeffrey Gettleman, "Africa's Dirty Wars," Book review of *Warfare in Independent Africa* by William Reno (Cambridge Uni. Press, 2012), *NY Review of Books* (Mar. 8, 2012), available at http://www.nybooks.com/articles/archives/2012/mar/08/africas-dirty-wars/?pagination=false (last visited on April 30, 2012).

[110] Id.

[111] Id.

Index

About the Author

Ms. Rumu Sarkar is currently serving as Senior Legal Advisor to Millennium Partners, an international development consulting group based in Charlottesville, VA. Immediately prior to this position, she was the former General Counsel for the 2005 Defense Base Closure and Realignment (BRAC) Commission. She also served as the General Counsel for the Overseas Basing Commission, prior to joining the BRAC Commission.

Ms. Sarkar was also the former Assistant General Counsel for Administrative Affairs for the Overseas Private Investment Corporation (OPIC), and formerly a staff attorney with the Office of the General Counsel of the U.S. Agency for International Development (USAID). She began her career as a litigation associate with two Wall Street law firms in New York.

Professor Sarkar is a Visiting Lecturer and is currently serving on the Advisory Board for Loyola University Chicago School of Law. She was also an Adjunct Law Professor and a Visiting Researcher at the Georgetown University Law Center where she taught a graduate law (LL.M.) seminar, and has extensively published law review articles on a variety of subjects. Professor Sarkar has authored two legal textbooks, *INTERNATIONAL DEVELOPMENT LAW (*Oxford University Press, 2009)*, and *TRANSNATIONAL BUSINESS LAW.* Professor Rumu Sarkar was awarded the 2007 Grand Prize by the St Cyr Foundation for her essay, "A Fearful Symmetry: A New Global Balance of Power?" The St. Cyr Foundation supports the St. Cyr military academy – in effect, France's West Point. An expanded version of the essay, *A FEARFUL SYMMETRY: THE NEW SOLDIER IN AN AGE OF ASYMMETRIC CONFLICT,* was published in April 2010 (Praeger). She was also awarded Third Prize by the Colonel Arthur D. Simons Center for the 2012 Interagency Writing Competition.

Dr. Sarkar completed her undergraduate studies at Barnard College,

Columbia University; her law degree from the Antioch School of Law; and her Masters of Law (LL.M.) degree, and her Ph.D. in Philosophy from Newnham College, Cambridge University.

www.ingramcontent.com/pod-product-compliance
Lightning Source LLC
Chambersburg PA
CBHW031359270326
41929CB00010BA/1242